HEALING WITH LOVE

HEALING WITH LOVE

**A Physician's Breakthrough
Mind/Body Medical Guide
for Healing Yourself and Others**

The Art of Holoenergetic Healing

Leonard Laskow, M.D.

HarperSanFrancisco
A Division of HarperCollinsPublishers

HEALING WITH LOVE: *The Art of Holoenergetic Healing.* Copyright © 1992 by Leonard Laskow. All rights reserved. Printed in the United States of America. No part of this book may be used or reproduced in any manner whatsoever without written permission except in the case of brief quotations embodied in critical articles and reviews. For information address HarperCollins Publishers, 10 East 53rd Street, New York, NY 10022.

FIRST EDITION

10/92

Library of Congress Cataloging-in-Publication Data

Laskow, Leonard.
   Healing with love : a physician's breakthrough mind/body medical guide for healing yourself and others : the art of holoenergetic healing / Leonard Laskow.
  —1st ed.
     p. cm.
   Includes bibliographical references and index.
   ISBN 0–06–250513–0 (alk. paper)
   1. Medicine, Psychosomatic. 2. Healing. I. Title.
RC49.L365 1992
615.8'52—dc20   91–55293
                                                CIP

92 93 94 95 96 HAD 10 9 8 7 6 5 4 3 2 1

This edition is printed on acid-free paper that meets the American National Standards Institute Z39.48 Standard.

*To that spirit in each of us that
desires to bring boundless love into physical being,
making the infinite finite and the finite infinite.*

Contents

Contents

List of Illustrations/ Diagrams

List of Exercises

Prayer for Healers*

Lord,
make me an instrument of your health:
where there is sickness,
let me bring cure;
where there is injury,
aid;
where there is sadness,
comfort;
where there is despair,
hope;
where there is death,
acceptance and peace.

Grant that I may not:
so much seek to be justified,
as to console;
to be obeyed,
as to understand;
to be honored,
as to love ...
for it is in giving ourselves
that we heal,
it is in listening
that we comfort,
and in dying
that we are born to eternal life.

*The Prayer of St. Francis, as modified by Charles C. Wise.
This prayer appears in the beginning of Elisabeth Kübler-Ross's
Death: The Final Stage of Growth (New York: Simon &
Schuster, 1986), p. v.

Acknowledgments

Many people contributed to the creation and writing of this book. I especially want to acknowledge my dear friend and colleague Hal Zina Bennett for his expertise, insightful sensitivity, and support in editing and refining the manuscript. The spirit in which we worked has been a source of great joy and inspiration to me.

My deepest appreciation to my dear friend Lazaris for the richness and vastness of his teaching and the depth of his love. I cherish his boundless friendship and his contribution to my life and this book.

Special thanks to Linda Prout for her editorial assistance, advice, and acumen in helping to unfold the form of this book.

Robert Simmons, a comrade and colleague, provided valuable insights and shared his wisdom and love when it was most needed.

I greatly appreciate those friends and colleagues who cared enough to take the time to read and comment on the manuscript: Bob and Ann Nunley, Jach Pursel, Vivian King, Phyllis Mar, Bob and Phronda Smith, Vernon Woolf, Jim Armstrong, David Berenson, Jim Beal, Jon Cowen, and Bill Moulton. Their contributions have been most valuable.

A dear friend I'm most grateful to is Poonjaji, an awakened being whose loving presence has helped me unveil my Self.

I wish to thank Karen Malik for her unconditional love and for sharing with me the gift of her spiritual grace.

It has been my good fortune to work with Tom Grady, vice president and associate publisher at Harper San Francisco. His creative insights, vision, and inspirational support and guidance are deeply appreciated.

Thanks to Kevin Bentley for facilitating the editorial process and making it flow smoothly.

Glen Rein, my colleague and author of one of the appendixes, has contributed valuable scientific support for the holoenergetic model. Our explorations and experiments have been a source of discovery and inspiration to me.

A special thanks to Barry and Gloria Blum, Ed Lewis, David Wise, and Bill Fahr for their loving support and friendship.

I am profoundly grateful to my wife Barbara for her heartfelt love, support, and devotion.

Finally I want to acknowledge, with deepest gratitude, my patients and workshop participants for sharing their lives with me. It was their experiences that eventually found expression as this book.

How to Use this Book

Healing with Love contains information and instructions for a program I call *holoenergetic healing*. It is intended for all readers interested in self-healing, as well as for professionals. Although I am a physician, I have written the instructions and text so that readers who have no medical background will find the material both entertaining and easy to understand. I have also drawn from my experience as a trainer of other physicians and health practitioners, providing them with the information they require to incorporate this program into their practices. In preparing this material I have intended to achieve a balance that will serve all readers, not just those in the health-care professions.

I strongly recommend that you read the entire book before you attempt to apply the program. It will be much easier for you to practice holoenergetic healing if you first have a clear picture of the scientific and intuitive aspects of the process. The step-by-step instructions are intended both as a self-healing guide and as a model that health-care professionals can incorporate into their work.

I have based the material in this book on scientific evidence and on my own clinical experience, but you will find that holoenergetic healing also draws extensively on the intuitive senses. Tools for accessing intuition and verifying information gathered in this way are described later in the book. I have found that one of the greatest assets for intuitive work is an inner guide or imaginary helper. Like a trusted friend native to a foreign country you are visiting for the first time, the inner guide can answer questions you have as you explore the territory. (Instructions for contacting your inner guide appear in the Resources section. If you are already in touch with your inner guide, he or she will be invaluable as you explore the holoenergetic healing process.)

If you are interested in further exploring the scientific research on which aspects of holoenergetic healing are based, please see appendix A, where you will find an article by Glen Rein, Ph.D., "The Scientific Basis for Healing with Subtle Energies." Rein, a neurochemist who has worked at Stanford University in California and at Mount Sinai Hospital in New York, describes principles that I employ and develop in my own healing model.

Please note: the material in this book is not intended to take the place of appropriate medical care. For many illnesses, the healing process is a collaborative effort, involving physicians and other health-care practitioners, the patient's family, the full participation of the patient, and, of course, Nature. The best choices for our personal health care frequently involve careful consideration of all of these resources.

HEALING WITH LOVE

Healing and Love— An Introduction to Holoenergetic Healing

As we ourselves are healed, we provide an example for others. And as we desire to help and heal others, we ourselves are also healed. The result is that relationships become a temple of healing in which healing is recognized as a collaborative venture that leads to the recognition of our underlying unity.

—FRANCES VAUGHAN AND ROGER WALSH

Healing occurs naturally, and love heals.

We can use our thoughts, our hands, our hearts, and our higher consciousness to facilitate healing. In the following chapters, we will explore how our energies can be harnessed and amplified to bring about transformation toward health and wholeness in our lives and the lives of others.

In my twenty-five years as a physician I have developed a good sense of how illness can effectively be treated medically. However, it has become clear to me that the physician only treats; it is Nature that does the actual healing.

By this I mean that the natural impulse of life is to heal itself, to become whole again. Every time I performed surgery, I depended on my patient's own healing process to carry him or her to full recovery. Without this natural healing impulse, even the most skilled physician would be powerless to restore health to the patient.

I became interested in what healers did to help people get well before the days of surgery and antibiotics. What tools were available to them, and how did they address disease and healing? The answers varied from one culture to another, but there was a constant in all

cases: the presence of someone to facilitate the natural healing processes, to focus attention on and encourage the patient toward recovery. In other words, the active ingredient was not surgery, antibiotics, or other mechanical methods. Rather, it was love: the
impulse toward unity, nonseparation, and wholeness. In primitive
societies, that love might have come in the form of dances, prayers,
or songs offered by the patient's family, friends, and community. In
our grandparents' day it might have come in the form of the well-
wishing of family and friends and the supportive bedside manner of
the kindly physician who made house calls.

Recent medical research has shown definite links between the
intangibles we call bedside manner, love, and caring and the tan-
gibles that we can measure, such as reduced infection, faster healing
of damaged tissue, and the patient's increased energy. People who
have close family and friends to support and encourage them have
better recovery rates than do people who are alone in the world.
These enhanced recovery rates suggest that the immune systems of
patients who have close family and friends function more efficiently
and effectively than do those of patients who are alone.

Intrigued with the idea that we can direct our healing capacities
to affect predictable, positive results that can be replicated, I began
my explorations into the realm of healing. Although at first I'd been
somewhat tentative and skeptical, I quickly saw results that were
medically incomprehensible yet astonishingly and undeniably effective.

In order to continue my research, I had to make a conscious
choice—to trust my own experience, despite its limitations, and
commit myself to finding what was true for me. I temporarily set
aside what I had been taught to believe. In doing so, I recalled that
some of the greatest discoveries in human history have come about
because people dared temporarily to suspend beliefs that were accepted as true and irrefutable. After all, only a few hundred years
ago people believed the world was flat.

This is what I have to share with you—the experiences, principles, methods, and processes that have worked for me. I present this

material not as a scientist insisting on hard data but as a clinician for whom results and effectiveness are measures of truth.

What I discovered and map out in this book is a new model that I call *holoenergetic healing*—*holo* meaning "whole," that is, healing with the energy of the "whole," with the synergy of the whole, which is greater than the sum of its parts. This model is based on expanded awareness, love, and the empowerment that comes from making a conscious choice for change. The guiding principles for this process are (1) *knowing,* which locates and illuminates what we want; (2) *loving,* which links us to what we want; (3) *willing,* in which we act upon what we want; and (4) *spirit,* which guides our knowing, loving, and willing.

Holoenergetic healing uses energy, intention, imagery, and insight to address the physical, emotional, mental, and spiritual dimensions of human life. This noninvasive system works effectively and elegantly, producing a maximum change with a minimum expenditure of energy. The healing model can be employed for self-healing or integrated with virtually any other helping system, be it allopathic medicine, homeopathy, acupuncture, chiropractic, psychotherapy, nursing, bodywork, dentistry, physical or occupational therapy, or any other I have encountered. All health-care professionals could have access to holoenergetic techniques and methods, which can be taught in their respective schools. Some people will be more adept at holoenergetic healing, just as there will be some who will be best suited to practice psychiatry, surgery, and so on. But all health professionals are capable of learning the material.

Many people in the health-care professions initially felt a humanistic calling to go into those professions. But the long and rigorous training, with its strong scientific orientation, may have subordinated and suppressed their original motivation to relate to others in a healing fashion. Learning how to psychoenergetically heal can bring back the original motivation, in effect rehumanizing the practice of medicine and other health professions. At least, that has been my experience, and I hope it will be so for those who read this book.

FOUNDATIONAL PRINCIPLES OF HEALING

To take the first step in holoenergetic healing, we must start with the understanding that change is possible and that we have choices. To "trans-form," we begin by recognizing or locating what is currently "in form" that we want to change. We then resonate with that form and take responsibility for it, releasing it by "unforming" it, and then "re-form" the released energy in accordance with our purpose.

Holoenergetic healing is based on the assumption that matter is energy in the form of vibration and that, as physicists tell us, matter and energy are interchangeable. The body consists of vast numbers of atoms, which are the building blocks of matter. Atoms are made up of charged particles called *protons,* which are positively charged; *electrons,* which are negatively charged; and *neutrons,* which are neutral. These particles themselves are whirling, pulsating fields of energy that interact with and interpenetrate other energy fields. This means that what we perceive as our physical bodies are actually fields of energy that have taken a particular form.

Energy, in a broad sense, means the ability of something to act upon or influence something else. Keep in mind that our ability to detect energy is determined in part by our ability to measure or perceive it. Thus, just as sixty years ago we lacked the ability to measure the presence of subatomic particles, today there are many more subtle energies that we cannot detect either with our five senses or with our most sophisticated scientific instruments. It is our intuitive sense that enables us to detect these subtle energies.

Energy can be perceived as existing in a wave form or in a particulate form, depending on how it is measured. At the subatomic level, distinctions between energy, form, and field no longer apply. These terms are used only to help us understand and visualize the ways in which energy takes form. It has been suggested that consciousness provides the matrix through which matter and energy unfold and manifest in our three-dimensional reality as a function of our perception.

In the holoenergetic healing model, the intent of the observing consciousness (that of the healer—either oneself or another person) determines the forming perception and initiates the transformation of energy. It is the *observer's intent*, whether conscious or unconscious, that converts particulate "matter" to its wave form and its wave form to "matter."

Intent is planned choice. By converting particulate matter to its wave form, conscious or unconscious intent allows us to come into resonance (or blend) with what we want to access or influence. Consciousness, in this sense, is like a fundamental field—that is, a primordial ocean that gives rise to waves of vibration from which are formed localized whirlpools of energy called "matter." Thus, the energy field creates the form, which then becomes resonantly structured as matter. Once structured, the field becomes self-organizing, moving from the infinite to the finite, now able to influence and maintain itself.

Consciousness in this model informs the subtle energies that influence the electromagnetic spectrum. When looking at electromagnetic energy, we find that all electrons are surrounded by an electrostatic field, that is, a field that affects other charged particles. When the electrons increase or decrease their rate of motion, they produce electromagnetic fields, which in turn influence the charged particles. Thus, we have the particulate form of charge affecting field as well as field affecting form. The fields surrounding our bodies (not confined to the fields of the electromagnetic spectrum) reflect and represent our emotional and mental states as well as the condition of our physical bodies.

Within the body, what seems most readily affected when we alter the field is the structure of water. Our bodies are more than 60 percent water. Water is composed of two hydrogen atoms and one oxygen atom linked by energy bonds; in unstructured water, the bond between the two hydrogen atoms forms an angle of 105 degrees. When energy resonant with the hydrogen bond is introduced, it is absorbed; the hydrogen bond is then stretched to an angle of 109 degrees. This newly introduced energy carries with it information that changes the form of water. Consequently, several of the physical characteristics of water are also changed, including its ability to absorb light, its pH value, its surface tension, and its solubility. In addition, the natural frequency of structured water is different from that of unstructured water; it vibrates and responds to different frequencies. It also more readily dissociates into charged atoms called *ions*. When we do healing work, we create a field that structures water, altering its ionization and thus changing its pH. Enzymatic processes, essential to life, then proceed differently.

Dr. Justa Smith measured the enzyme trypsin in water that had been treated by a healer and discovered changes in the activity of the enzyme relative to untreated water. Similarly, Dr. Bernard Grad used healer-treated water on seedlings and found that they grew significantly faster than control seedlings watered with unstructured water.[1]

In my research, when I treated water-based nutrient media with the intention of inhibiting the growth of cultured mast cell tumors, their growth was inhibited by 40 percent, relative to cells grown in identical conditions but not treated with healing energy. This indicates that the treated media were capable of storing and carrying the necessary information for the inhibition of tumor cell growth. It also implies that healing ability is more than a placebo effect. (See appendix A, page 303, for more information.)

Dolores Krieger reported hemoglobin changes in patients treated by therapeutic touch, in which the field interaction between the healer and the healed is the primary vehicle of exchange. This demonstrates that changes in the energy field can affect the physical form. Her work supports Rupert Sheldrake's theory that once pat-

---

1. See J. Smith, "The Influence on Enzyme Growth by the 'Laying on of Hands,'" in *The Dimensions of Healing: A Symposium* (Los Altos: The Academy of Parapsychology and Medicine, 1972), and B. Grad, "The Biological Effects of the 'Laying on of Hands' on Animals and Plants: Implications for Biology" in *Parapsychology: Its Relation to Physics, Biology, and Psychiatry*, ed. G. Schneidler (McTucken, NJ: Scarecrow Press, 1967).

terns exist in the larger universal field, and when changes occur in our field that match the changes in the larger field, a new form comes into existence.[2]

In order to maintain its highly organized structure, the body's physical form and its energetic form (field) must have resonant compatibility. In other words, there needs to be a resonant balance between body and mind. Both form and field (body and mind) contribute to the creation of holographic standing waves. These waves are the signatures (or evidence) of a resonant balance between form and field, and a signature can become a self-organizing force in its own right.

A negative thought form such as hatred can constitute part of a standing wave; the other part (physical form) might be a tumor. There can then be a resonant compatibility between the thought form and the tumor. They are in balance. Within itself that standing wave complex is in balance, but in its relationship to the rest of the person it may be out of balance and disharmonious to the overall field.

We often hear that health is a matter of balance. As we can see, there is a balance between field and form and a balance among our physical, emotional, and mental states, reflecting the relationship of self to self. There is also a balance between these states and our environment, reflecting the relationship of the self to anything other than the self. A fourth level of balance is that between our physical, emotional, and mental states and our spiritual state, reflecting the balance between the self and its higher spiritual aspects. It is at the spiritual level that we have a sense of our purpose and meaning even before it is given form or expression. If our daily actions are out of alignment with our spiritual purpose, whether we know this consciously or unconsciously, the seeds of illness are planted.

---

2. See Dolores Krieger, *Therapeutic Touch* (Englewood Cliffs, NJ: Prentice-Hall, 1979), and Rupert Sheldrake, *A New Science of Life* (Los Angeles: J. P. Tarcher, 1981).

When we ask "Why?" we begin to address the question of our purpose. Arthur Young, in his book *Which Way Out,* writes that every machine has four aspects: parts, a plan, a power source, and a purpose. Modern medicine focuses on the pathology of the "parts"—the organs, limbs, cells, molecules, and so on—that make up the physical body. Western medicine has gone a step further to look at the "plan," the conceptual and genetic blueprint of the parts. The energies of the body and energetic forms of illness are beginning to come under increasing scrutiny. However, allopathic medicine has yet to acknowledge that there is purpose behind the plan. What is our purpose for being, doing, and having? How does knowing and creating purpose affect our lives? In holoenergetic healing these are the most important elements.

As we have seen, science is recognizing that we are organized energetically as well as neurologically, hormonally, anatomically, and immunologically. We are also organized by a consciousness of function. Each cell, each organ, indeed the entire body has a consciousness of its function, its job. Although each is not necessarily aware of the larger purpose of the organism, nevertheless our varied functions are integrated in accordance with a higher purpose.

If we were to think of our physical nature as organized in terms of three-dimensional space, the consciousness of function might be thought of as a fourth dimension. Consciousness of purpose might be considered a fifth dimension, in that purpose organizes function and gives it meaning. Purpose, then, precedes order and function and gives both their value. Misalignment with purpose creates disorder and dysfunction, or illness.

Aligning our healing intent with a higher purpose is important in holoenergetic healing, because it is the intent of the observing consciousness that initiates the transformation of energy into matter. Thus, looking at the purpose of our lives is valuable. We find that purpose is something not only to be discovered but to be created; we can create our own purposes and give our lives meaning. Choosing ideals such as truth, wisdom, love, joy, and peace helps us to create our purposes and serves to guide our actions.

We need boundaries in order to function. Our principles and expansive beliefs give us boundaries that guide us in our growth, while our contracting beliefs and blockages limit our growth. Our boundaries are created by our ideals, purposes, principles, beliefs, blockages, and payoffs. We can establish our own boundaries in accordance with our ideals and purposes, or we can allow others to impose them on us. When we limit ourselves through our blockages ("I'm unlovable, unforgivable, a mistake!"), illness may result. However, by becoming aware of these blockages we can start to change; we can re-choose the ideals and create the purposes and principles by which we live.

To learn what our purposes are and how we create them, we must tap in to what we truly want. This process starts with the root of desire. To know and be known, to love and be loved, and to create and be created are root desires. From there we formulate our purposes, which may include learning to enjoy ourselves with harm to none, to heal with love, to learn to consciously create what we want, to fully experience and express love, or to be free to be who we really are.

Our deepest desire, the seed from which the roots grow, is the desire to become at one with the All, to return home. However, once we realize that desire, it disappears. The paradox is that as long as we desire something we are simultaneously separate from it and attracted to it. Only by releasing our desire to be at one with the All can we be One. Releasing desire is the last step. Until then, the desire to be at one is the key to the Kingdom of Heaven. However, to *enter* the Kingdom we must leave the key of desire and aspiration at the door.

Basic desire is the feeling that is in touch with our spirit. We clarify our desires through thoughts, and we clarify and expand our thoughts by weaving them into a vision. Then we maintain our focus on that vision, thought, and desire in accord with our purpose, while aligned with our higher Self. This is what allows us to create what we want to manifest in the physical realm.

The function of health is to maintain this dynamic, multilevel, multidimensional balance. The function of healing is to restore this balance and harmony, which are inherent in our body-mind. Such order and harmony can be stimulated by living a healthy life-style in a healthy environment, by invoking love, and by aligning all other aspects of ourselves with our spiritual essence.

APPLYING THE PRINCIPLES

Holoenergetic healing addresses root causes of disease by first identifying the location and form of unhealthy energy patterns. This system involves transforming undesirable energy patterns into ones of health and harmony, aligned with one's individual purpose and with the natural impulse toward wholeness.

After identifying and "resonating with" an unhealthy energy pattern (we'll examine this in chapter 8), be it in the form of sensation, image, thought, feeling, or belief, we change or transform that form. This transformation begins by discovering the positive intention behind the disharmonious pattern and by "unforming" or releasing the unhealthy pattern or form. After unforming the unhealthy energy pattern, we replace it with a healthy one. This is a little like remodeling a house; the existing order and structure are disrupted and must go through a period of disorder, or lack of coherent form, before the new order and structure are established.

In holoenergetic healing we explore and deal with patterns of fear, anger, guilt, self-pity, and shame. All these need to be examined with awareness as part of any movement toward health. When energy is held in these forms, it produces resistance to change, and thus is an impediment to natural healing processes. The release of these impediments is aided by addressing the secondary gains of illness, thus identifying the treasured wounds that make it so difficult for us to change. Forgiveness of self and others is then used to release us from the binding energy of blame and punishment.

We re-form energy patterns through a clearly defined process of unconditional love that allows us, perhaps for the first time, to experience and come into alignment with our higher consciousness, our essence. This alignment is a primary focus of holoenergetic healing.

BLENDING ANCIENT SECRETS WITH MODERN SCIENCE

Holoenergetic healing utilizes many ancient healing tools, such as chakra evaluation and biomechanical testing (dowsing) of energy fields to focus the healer's mind and energies to activate an affected area. However, holoenergetic healing is not dependent on any of these techniques; they are simply tools to help us. It is important to note that the techniques of holoenergetic healing can easily be incorporated, as a module, into any of the helping professions.

This, then, is a book about healing with love, about facilitating transformation from disease states to healthy states through the use of love, subtle energies, conscious awareness, and choice. In the following pages, you will

- Learn what these subtle energies are
- Begin to sense and feel these energies
- Learn to harness these energies through consciously directing your breath
- Learn to detect and measure subtle energies with your hands, your mind, and biomechanical testing
- Learn to amplify and focus energy, using your hands, breath, thought, imagery, and intention
- Learn to direct energy with "resonant energy transference" to produce change
- Learn to heal yourself and others

Please explore all the material presented in this book, then employ as much of it as you find useful. Rather than being attached to any particular technique, let your guide be what works for you. Learn by *doing*. Words and books, like fingers, can only point the way. It is up to all of us, as individuals, to make the journey for ourselves.

PART ONE

1

A Healer's Journey

The desire and pursuit of the whole is called love.
—PLATO

I became a physician because I wanted to have a beneficial effect on people's lives. My first recollection of my choice goes back to my childhood, to the tender age of five. My mother, who I believed was all-knowing and wise, regarded our family physician with great respect. I wanted to be a doctor so that she would feel the same way about me. In my child's mind, I wanted her love and respect.

Many years later, in medical school, I decided to become an obstetrician/gynecologist, because that specialty includes the practices of some elements of psychiatry and surgery, both of which I liked. At that time, it seemed to me that obstetrics was the only area of medicine that didn't inherently focus on disease. New life was joyful, a cause for celebration, filled with wonder. I was still motivated by my original childhood goal of getting my mother's love and respect, but now I was finding it through the women I treated in my medical practice.

In medical school I met many others who shared my desire to be helpful to other people. But then I saw us beginning to forget those early desires, as we took on the rigors of our education and developed the objective detachment that modern medicine seemed to demand. I found the science of medicine fascinating, and the techniques we were learning for dealing with medical emergencies were invaluable. But I also knew that there was much more to human illness and health than we were being taught. What was missing was "heart," but I didn't realize it at the time.

In medical school we were trained to suppress our feelings when we practiced medicine. We were educated to believe that there must be a separation between the objective and the subjective. The objective, in this case, consisted of medical tests, diagnostic procedures, and knowledge based on scientific research. We believed that as physicians we were to give no credence to our subjective experience; rather, we were to separate ourselves from our feelings. We also believed that we needed to suppress our intuitive processes, trusting instead only what could be verified statistically.

Of course, emotional detachment serves us well in some medical situations. For example, it can help surgeons stay cool and focused during critical moments in the operating room. But because it is also difficult to turn off and on at will, our detachment has tended to create an emotional distance between patients and medical providers. For me it became the source of alienation from myself, a split that caused me to feel that I was employing only a small portion of my capacities as a healer. I saw that medicine encouraged the scientist and technician within us but discouraged the healer within. In adopting this objectivity, by separating the objective from the subjective, we had fenced off the human aspects of our beings in favor of knowledge that could be quantified, measured, and weighed with scientific technology.

For centuries, physicians and other healers had struggled with the question of how to maintain objectivity while engaged with the patient at a level that was supportive and healing. The same question captured my attention and curiosity. Ironically, I began to find some answers in science itself rather than in medicine. Modern physics and the study of quantum mechanics had begun to reveal that there truly is no separation between the observer and the observed, that there is always a correlation between the two that cannot be nullified. In modern medicine, no matter what we do to objectify our involvement with the patient, there is still an energetic interchange that I am convinced is powerful and significant. There is an important truth in a statement the American philosopher William James made over fifty years ago: "The rigorously impersonal view of science might one day appear as having been a useful eccentricity rather than the definitely triumphant position which the sectarian scientist at present so confidently announces it to be."

OTHER PATHS ARE OFFERED

In many people's lives, major changes and life transformations are initiated by crisis, often in the form of physical illness. Since I am a physician, it was clearly fitting that such a transformation for me would take a medical form.

In 1971, I had a busy practice on the Monterey Peninsula in California, and I was chief of obstetrics and gynecology at the Community Hospital. Seemingly, I was committed to becoming a successful physician in the traditional mold. Then one day, while playing tennis, I experienced pain in my right shoulder. X rays revealed a bone lesion in my upper right arm, near the shoulder. My immediate concern was that I might have bone cancer.

A biopsy was taken and medical tests began. While I waited for the results, I reassessed my life. Since I was a physician, of course I knew the usual treatment for a bone cancer of this kind— amputation. Certainly there would be little call for a one-armed obstetrician, I reasoned, but until the cancer had metastasized to my brain, I could still work with my mind.

I had recently become interested in the work of Masters and Johnson, whose research gave the study of sexuality a credible entry into the medical community. Few doctors, at that time, felt knowledgeable enough to incorporate the new material into their practices. Here was an obvious need that a one-armed obstetrician could fill: I could teach sex therapy and do counseling. I arranged to take a fellowship in Psychosomatic Medicine at the University of California at San Francisco, and I became the liaison between the Department of OB/GYN and the Department of Psychiatry.

Then the results of my medical tests came back from the lab: benign! (It was a simple bone cyst that I had had since childhood.) Although I was much relieved, the incident had nevertheless signaled me that I needed to take a close look at my life. I could continue to be an obstetrician—with two arms, at that!—but what I really wanted to do was leave my position at Community Hospital, move up to San Francisco, take the fellowship at the university, and go into teaching. While I had enjoyed obstetrics, the hours and stresses associated with it were incompatible with my well-being. My illness was a call for change—a change that would touch every area of my life. I didn't know exactly where this change would lead me, but I had no doubt that it was the right course for me to take.

For several years I taught and conducted a small gynecology practice at the University of California Hospital in San Francisco. Later, I developed a busy private practice in San Francisco. During this period, I began to retrace the significant events of my life prior to the problem I'd had with my shoulder. It was important for me to discover the source of the pain I had experienced, and I knew the cyst had not been that source. My search led me back to the events surrounding my mother's death, a year before the onset of the shoulder pain. During my residency at Stanford, she had become deeply concerned about her health. Her worst fear was that she would die alone. Wanting to allay her fears, I brought her out from New York to California and helped her set up a home near mine. Then one night she suffered a heart attack and died before I could get to her. Her worst fears had come true.

Along with grief, I felt guilt. Beneath the guilt was anger, which I felt I should not have. As absurd as it seemed, I was angry at my mother for dying alone, but I didn't understand that at the time. I repressed my real emotion, because a part of me simply could not accept that I felt angry with her. Repressed in this way, my anger turned into guilt.

One way to express anger is to strike out at someone or something to release the feeling. Another way is to recognize and acknowledge that anger and resolve it at the source. If anger is not released or resolved, energy is blocked. In my case, the anger was blocked in my right shoulder, and it was this, not the bone cyst, that was the source of my pain.

Slowly I made my way through the labyrinth of emotion that my mother's death had created for me. My beliefs ran the gamut: I had failed her; I felt bound to her by my guilt; I believed that a loving son would never have allowed his mother to die alone, especially after she'd told him that this was her greatest fear.

The belief that I had been unloving was not in accord with the higher aspects of my being, and the pressures of this misalignment were ultimately manifest in my physical illness. It was as though I had created the pain in my shoulder as a metaphor for my dilemma about my mother's death. Like her, I had to confront the possibility of dying alone, since I had no close relatives.

By allowing my illness to be a transformational experience, and choosing to grow as a consequence of the illness, I was able to forgive myself and my mother and let go of my guilt, which then allowed me to move into harmony with my higher Self.

I also came to realize that no one dies alone in the spiritual sense.

ANSWERS FROM WITHIN

In San Francisco I became increasingly attracted to various healing approaches. I realize now that this interest was the vehicle for my spiritual awakening. I began to reconsider my definitions of illness, health, and healing.

While on a retreat, during a deep meditation an inner voice spoke to me with awesome clarity and authority. It said, "Your work is to heal with love." As soon as I heard this, I knew it to be so. "Oh, so I am worthy?" I then said. The voice replied, "You are no more or less worthy than anyone else. Your work is to heal with love."

I sat there awestruck, tears flowing down my cheeks, beyond thought, beyond understanding, feeling totally at one with that communing presence. It wasn't until years later that I could express what transpired in those ineffable moments, and even today I'm moved to tears in recounting it. I share those most sacred moments because I believe that we all have to learn, at some point in our evolution, to heal with love. Knowing this encourages its manifestation.

It became apparent to me that my decision to become a doctor and healer was a part not of my past but of an inner knowing, beyond my conscious awareness, that was motivating me. I didn't know exactly how all this would affect my life in the coming years or how I would become a healer; I was certain only that I had been deeply affected by this experience.

Several years later, I enrolled in a conference at Asilomar, a peaceful retreat center near Monterey. My roommate was a young man who had cancer, which had spread to his lungs. In the middle of the night he woke up and started coughing, obviously in a lot of pain. Acting purely on intuition, I placed my hands on the sides of his chest and visualized a radiant ball of light coming down through the center of my head to the level of my heart, then down my arms and out through my hands. The young man calmed down, started breathing more slowly, and said, "My pain is gone." He slept the rest of that night. This was my first experience with the phenomenon of healing. The next day, the young man said to me, "You know, you are really a healer."

I thought a lot about that. Something had happened that night that was real and profound, beyond the realm of medicine as it had been taught to me. Something within me had awakened to a different reality. I decided to begin exploring this work in my private practice. Once one makes a decision of this kind, opportunity often presents itself, usually in rather remarkable ways—and so it was for me.

I lost track of the young man until one day, eleven years later, at a conference I attended in Kansas, he appeared as a featured singer. He sang songs that he had composed and told the story of a "spontaneous remission" that he had experienced while listening to classical music, in conjunction with guided imagery, approximately six weeks after our interaction. Although I don't know if our work together had any effect on the course of his disease, it was obvious from his story that healing comes from the realm of the spirit, beyond our understanding. Since spirit is unbounded, all is possible, and where there is possibility, hope can abide.

THE FIRST TEST

A week after my Asilomar experience, a young woman came to my San Francisco office. She had had a pelvic abscess several years before, which had been treated with antibiotics. There was no current infection, but the previous infection had caused adhesions of tissue from the pelvic mass to her intestine. As a result, sexual intercourse was painful for her, and this was causing problems in her marriage.

The mass was large enough to warrant surgical removal. However, she did not want surgery, and since there was no infection at that point antibiotics were useless. I suggested that we do some energy work. She didn't know what I meant, but she agreed to give it a try. As I performed a pelvic exam, I visualized the same radiant ball of white light between my hands, surrounding and interpenetrating the tender mass. I held it there for three or four minutes. Later, as the woman was leaving, I asked her to come back in a week for a follow-up. She thanked me and agreed to the return visit.

However, she did not return. My first concern was that she might have thought my treatment strange; certainly it was unlike any other gynecological exam she had ever had. I assumed that she had decided to seek medical care elsewhere. Then, eight months later, she returned. I examined her and found there was no mass. When I asked her why she hadn't returned for the follow-up, she replied, "Well, after I left your office I was fine. No more pain. No more problems. So I figured there was no need to come back."

My concerns about patients' reactions had delayed my quest for eight months, but now I was encouraged. I began exploring energy healing with other, select patients as well as with my office staff. In the course of my explorations, I learned and refined many techniques that I eventually adapted for use in holoenergetic healing.

WHAT HIPPOCRATES KNEW

Over two thousand years ago, Hippocrates, the author of the professional oath physicians still take today, reflected that some patients "recover their health simply through their contentment with the goodness of the physician." When we embrace our whole self—not just the rational/objective mind as opposed to that vast ocean that is human consciousness—there is power in our presence that has the potential for healing. When that whole self is engaged in a healing relationship, it is what we euphemistically call "bedside manner." Something in the relationship between the physician and the patient brings comfort and facilitates healing.

What is the magic ingredient of bedside manner? I began to see that what seemed to be magic was the most universal force of all: love. Love can bring comfort or heal regardless of the malady, be it emotional, mental, spiritual, or physical. As these truths began making themselves known to me, I also realized that medical school training discounts and denies the part of us that makes energy healing possible—the self, the vehicle through which love is received and given.

Science has provided us with a great many tools for implementing the natural healing processes with which we are born. I would not want to turn back history's clock to the time before surgery, immunization, and antibiotics. So the challenge is not an easy one: to restore what modern medicine has lost without losing what it has gained. Thinking about this, I saw the task as twofold: first, to begin collecting empirical evidence for the effectiveness of love in healing;

second, to develop tools and techniques that others who wished to become healers could employ in ways that were systematic and predictable.

CLINICAL EXPERIENCE WITH HEALING HERPES

My most extensive medical research during this period was with people afflicted with herpes. I chose herpes because it has no known medical cure; therefore, it is a valuable disease model for this kind of research. Herpes is a viral disease and so involves impaired immune-system functioning. It tends to recur, is readily observable, and is stress-related. I worked primarily with patients who had twice-monthly recurrences, each lasting for a week or so.

Three factors determine whether a person will get an infection: (1) the potency, or virulence, of the disease-causing organism itself; (2) the number of infecting organisms to which the person is exposed; and (3) the host's (person's) own ability to resist the infection.

In my research, which addressed the issue of host resistance, I explored methods for evoking and directing healing energy both systemically and locally. When working systemically, I focused on the person's immune system, and especially the thymus gland, to enhance his or her overall resistance to disease. Working locally required my focusing on the physical area of the infection to reduce the lesion itself. In this way, we would determine whether it was possible to enhance both general immune function and the resistance of the specific area infected.

The herpes virus is unusual in that when it infects the body it goes into the nerves that serve the skin. The genital herpes virus travels up the pudendal nerve to the sacral nerve ganglion, near the spinal cord, where it may lie relatively dormant for varying periods of time.

Because nerve cells are not as permeable as most other cells in the body, they are less responsive to the body's natural immune defenses. The herpes virus takes advantage of this and uses nerve cells as a protective shield. When certain conditions occur—stress, hormonal change, heat, or friction—the virus becomes reactivated, traveling back down the nerve to erupt on the skin.

Initially, I attempted to increase host resistance by enhancing the vitality of the pudendal nerve so that it could resist the movement of the virus along its path. I experimented with a variety of sophisticated medical tools for doing this, including an electroacuscope (which produces microamps of electrical energy to accelerate the exchange of nutrients and toxins across cell membranes). I also explored the effectiveness of a specially designed crystal and the healing energy of my hands.

In addition to working locally with the nerve, I focused on the patient's thymus gland, which serves a key function in the immune system. The thymus gland is also related to the heart center in the body's energy system.

I began this work by coming into resonance with the person using the Transpersonal Alignment Process, described in chapter 3. This helped me in obtaining valuable information about the person's disease pattern, in balancing and "recharging" the person's own energy, and in sending healing energy to the person. As the healing work progressed, I learned how to tap in to the source of the unwanted patterns that sustain illness. (We'll explore this resonance in detail later in the book.)

The combination of local and general work produced dramatic reductions in the severity, frequency, and duration of recurrences. Although I did not keep statistics in this observation and discovery phase of the work, patients reported that their herpes eruptions were reduced from two to four per month to two or three per year or less.

RELIEF FROM RHEUMATOID ARTHRITIS

One of my most remarkable healing experiences of these early explorations involved a woman I'll call Marie. When she came to me, at age 62, she had severe rheumatoid arthritis. She walked with a cane, had difficulty making a fist, and could no longer hold a pen to write. Her rheumatologist had confirmed her condition with a positive blood test for this disease and was treating her with steroids.

Marie and I worked together using an early form of the healing techniques described in this book. By the time we had finished working together that first hour, the swelling around her hands, knees, and ankles had subsided. As her daughter watched in amazement, Marie picked up her cane and threw it to her, then started doing deep knee bends, exclaiming, "Look! The pain is gone. I can move my hands!"

Marie also had diabetes and high blood pressure. After the healing work, her insulin requirement dropped to one-third of its previous level, and her internist stopped her antihypertensive medication. Following another session, during which I gave her self-healing instructions, she was able to reduce her insulin level even further. Subsequent blood tests showed that the rheumatoid factor had reverted to normal.

After four years, Marie was still free of rheumatoid arthritis and required no medications for her diabetes and hypertension.

CANCER TREATMENT REPORT

I also did research with cervical dysplasia, a precancerous lesion of the cervix. The work involved seven patients who had moderate cervical dysplasia and two who had cancer of the cervix in situ. Five of the seven cervical dysplasia patients reverted to normal after two ten-minute holoenergetic treatments and continued to have normal Pap smears over the next two years. At the end of the two-year period, one of these patients reverted to a moderate dysplastic condition.

One woman with in situ cancer of the cervix had a cone biopsy performed following two sessions with me; the biopsy showed no evidence of cancer. Another patient with carcinoma in situ reverted to moderate dysplasia, which was treated with laser surgery, rather than the more invasive and expensive operation that carried more risk and would have required anesthesia.

RESEARCH WITH BACTERIA AND CANCER CELLS

As exciting as the above results were, I needed to conduct further research to differentiate the actual effect of energy healing from the placebo effect. To do so I began working with a biophysicist, Dr. Beverly Rubik, then at the University of California, who measured my interaction with bacterial cultures. There I discovered that I could send energy with the intention of inhibiting growth into bacterial cultures in test tubes and reduce their growth by 50 percent over controls.

In another experiment, we subjected two identical groups of bacteria to varying doses of antibiotics that normally would inhibit their growth. However, before introducing the antibiotics, I focused loving energy on one group of bacteria. The group protected with loving energy survived and remained motile, while the group that received no protection became increasingly immobile and perished.[1]

In further research, I found I could inhibit the growth of cultured tumor cells by as much as 40 percent, using intention and imagery along with energy transference. I also found I could stimulate growth of these tumor cells by varying the intention and imagery to induce stimulation. (See appendix A for more details.)

These experiments finally convinced me that the results obtained with energy healing could not be attributed solely to the psychologically induced placebo effect or even to psychoneuroimmunology in general.

---

1. Somewhat similar experiments were carried out by Olga Worrell at the same laboratory. See appendix B for details.

A TURNING POINT

I could no longer turn back. Once I knew that love was a real force in preserving life, and not only a placebo effect, I sold my practice and dedicated myself to the exploration of healing with love.

I have now developed a model for mobilizing healing energy. In the following pages I present this model and give step-by-step instructions for use both in self-healing and in healing in clinical settings. In chapter 3, I provide an overview of a new model of healing. This model is the foundation upon which the practical aspects of holoenergetic healing are built.

Please join me on a journey to a magical land where thoughts are as real as matter, where matter may take the form of thoughts, and where beliefs are the seeds of experience. It is a land of love and will and conscious awareness. It is a place where we create our own reality for the purpose of growing and enjoying, where truth is what is, as well as what we choose it to be, and where means and end are one and the same, where *process is the product*. This territory offers vast, unexplored regions for the adventurous.

So let us begin our journey together with love.

2

The Subtle Energies
of Healing

Let us think of life as a process of choices, one after another. At each point, there is a progression choice and a regression choice. There may be movement toward defense, toward safety, toward being afraid, but over on the other side, there is the growth choice. To make the growth choice instead of the fear choice, a dozen times a day, is to move a dozen times a day toward self-actualization.

—ABRAHAM H. MASLOW

In his book *Safe and Alive,* Terry Dobson tells a story that beautifully illustrates how love can transform and heal.[1]

Terry was in Tokyo studying the martial arts. On a drowsy spring afternoon he entered a train near the suburbs. At one of the stops the train doors opened, and the quiet afternoon was shattered by a man bellowing at the top of his lungs, cursing obscenely and violently. He was big and drunk and his hair was crusted with filth. Screaming, he swung viciously at the first person he saw, a young woman holding a baby. The blow glanced off her shoulder, sending her and the baby, miraculously unharmed, into the laps of an elderly couple.

---

1. Terry Dobson, *Safe and Alive* (Los Angeles: J. P. Tarcher, 1981), pp. 128–29.

Terry stood up, determined to teach this man a lesson. He was in good shape and had been training in aikido every day for the past three years, but he had never tested his martial-arts skills in a real fight. However, he remembered his teacher telling him that aikido was the art of reconciliation: "Whoever has the mind to fight has broken his connection with the universe. If you try to dominate other people, you are already defeated. We study how to resolve conflict, not start it."

Although Terry had managed to avoid fighting, he still was dying to be a hero. He realized he had been seeking a legitimate opportunity to "save the innocent by destroying the guilty." The drunk on the train provided that opportunity. Terry convinced himself that if he didn't do something fast, someone might get hurt.

As Terry stood up, the man focused his rage on him. "A-ha!" the drunk roared. "A foreigner! You need a lesson in Japanese manners!" He punched a metal pole to emphasize his words.

Terry gave the drunk a look of disgust, summoning up every bit of nastiness he could. He pursed his lips and blew him a sneering kiss that was intended to hit him like a slap in the face.

"All right!" the drunk screamed, "You're gonna get a lesson."

Terry prepared himself as the drunk was about to rush at him. A split second before the drunk moved, someone yelled, "Hey!" It was an ear-splitting shout, yet Terry remembered a strangely joyous, lilting quality to it.

Both the drunk and Terry turned to see a little old Japanese man, well into his seventies. He took no notice of Terry but beamed with great delight upon the drunk, as though he had an important secret to share with him.

"C'mere," the old man said, beckoning to the drunk. "C'mere and talk with me."

"Why the hell should I talk with you?" the big man bellowed, planting himself threateningly before the old man.

The old man continued to beam at the drunk. "Wha'cha been drinking?" the old man asked, his eyes sparkling with interest.

"Sake," the drunk bellowed back, "and it's none of your god-damned business."

"Oh, that's wonderful!" the old man said. "You see, I love sake too. Every night, me and my wife warm up a little bottle of sake and take it out into the garden, and we sit on the old wooden bench that my grandfather's first student made for him. We watch the sun go down, and we look to see how our persimmon tree is doing. My great-grandfather planted that tree, you know, and we worry about whether it will recover from those ice storms we had last winter. The persimmons are so beautiful this time of year."

The old man looked up at the drunk, his eyes filled with happiness as he shared this experience.

The drunk's face had softened as he struggled to follow the intricacies of the old man's story. Even his fists had relaxed. "Yeah," he said. "I love persimmons, too."

"Yes," the old man said. "And I'm sure you have a wonderful wife."

"No," the drunk replied. "She died. I don't have a wife or a home or a job. I've got no money and nowhere to go."

"My, my, this is very difficult," the old man said. "Sit down here and tell me all about it."

Within moments, the drunk was sprawled in the seat next to the old man, his head on the old man's lap. The old man's face was filled with compassion and delight, one hand softly stroking the drunk's matted head. As tears rolled down the drunk's cheeks, a spasm of despair rippled through his entire body.

Standing there witnessing all this, in what Terry described as his "well-scrubbed youthful innocence" and his "make-the-world-safe-for-democracy righteousness," he said he felt dirtier inside than the drunk was outside. At about that time, the train arrived at Terry's stop and he pushed his way out.

After the train pulled away, Terry reflected on what he had wanted to do with muscle and meanness, and on what the old man had done with a few kind words. With his gentle voice, compassion, fearlessness, and love, the old man had accomplished what no amount of combative muscle could have done.

LOVE AND TRANSFORMATION

We have all had the experience of being influenced, to some degree, by the loving energies of other people, as portrayed in the story above. Perhaps the experience occurred with a loved one who helped us through a difficult time or with a professional counselor or therapist whose love and support gave us the extra energy we needed to resolve a problem.

Similarly, we have been in the presence of someone who is very angry, and have felt anger within ourselves, even though we had no apparent cause to feel that way. We have experienced having a person greet us openly and happily and recognized how that greeting tends to evoke those same feelings within ourselves. We have also experienced being with a person who is holding very focused, purposeful thoughts in mind, and have responded to that purposefulness.

In holoenergetic healing, it is important to go beyond appearances and to perceive each thought we have and each emotion we express as being energy in a particular form or pattern: the emotion of anger being one pattern, the emotion of joy another, the sense of purposefulness another, and so on. Through the energetic patterns that we shape with our thoughts and emotions, we can support the natural healing processes in ourselves and others.

To understand how our thoughts or emotions can affect our bodies, we must recognize that our bodies are not only physical, or material, as we usually perceive them to be. Einstein postulated that matter and energy are equivalent and interchangeable aspects of a single underlying reality or "universal field." This implies that everything is energy in various states of vibration and motion. Just as the ocean is made up of many currents and waves moving simultaneously in different directions and with different forces, so our bodies are made up of many pulsating, interacting energy fields. Although we may think of our bodies as solid physical matter, their mass is simply energy given that particular form.

Within this energetic system that we call the human body are a number of subsystems that help heal us and keep us well. These include the lymph system, circulatory system, nervous system, musculoskeletal system, immune system, digestive system, and endocrine system, all of which work interactively. Each of them is responsive to subtle energies coming from both inside and outside the body.

X Rays and Energy Fields

A friend broke her ankle and brought her X rays to me at my office. I took them into a different room where the lighting was better for viewing.

Out of curiosity, I wanted to see if by systematically scanning the X ray energetically, using a crystal, I could feel any subtle vibrations as I crossed the fracture site. I programmed my mind to be sensitive and open to the energy of this injury; then I closed my eyes and proceeded to scan. To my surprise, as I was scanning, my friend called out from the other room that her fractured ankle was starting to throb painfully. I opened my eyes and noticed that the crystal was pointed exactly at the fracture site on the X ray. I moved the crystal past the site and asked how she felt.

"The pain's gone," she replied.

I pointed the crystal to the fracture site again and she immediately called out, "It's back. Are you doing something?"

I went back to the room where she was waiting and explained what I'd just done. We repeated the process several times, with the same results each time.

Apparently, X rays not only show a physical representation

of events within the body—they also hold an energetic representation that can be consciously activated and brought into expression.

During this time, I was having regular meetings with physicians and clinicians at my home to experiment with healing through subtle energies. Wanting to explore further my observations with the X rays, I asked one of the physicians to bring X rays of various fractures to our next meeting.

At the meeting, I asked everyone to close their eyes. Then I gave each of them an X ray of a fracture and a pointed crystal with which to scan it. They programmed their minds to sense when their crystals activated the fracture sites. When their crystals came within two inches of the fracture site, eight out of ten felt a sensation such as tingling, warmth, or pulsation in the hand holding the X ray—even though their eyes were shut.

From these experiments, we speculated that if X rays and other photographs have energetic representations that are accessible in this way, not only could we derive information energetically, but it could potentially have therapeutic value.

Photographs have been successfully used as energetic "witnesses" by psychics to locate missing persons and for other police work. Some healers use photos as a focus for distant healing. Obviously, this area is both worthy of and ripe for scientific investigation. Later I'll discuss the use of photographs for exploring your own energy fields.

It is not too difficult to imagine, then, that since our thoughts and emotions are patterns of energy and our bodies are intersecting fields of energy, the energy of our thoughts and feelings is quite capable of affecting our well-being either positively or negatively. But how does the energy of our thoughts or emotions get transferred to other people, intersecting and perhaps altering the patterns of energy that make up their bodies? We don't yet know all the answers, but recent research has begun to provide us with some clues.

We know, for example, that every cell in the human body can transmit waves of electromagnetic radiation, which are measurable as light in the near ultraviolet range and light in the infrared range. These waves of radiation transmit information both inside the cell and outside it, to communicate data to other cells concerning its vital processes.

We also know that DNA (the blueprint of life) has piezoelectric properties, meaning that it can convert energy from one form to another. For example, if energy in the form of pressure or vibration is applied to a piezoelectric structure, it releases electrons. On the other hand, if electrons are introduced into a piezoelectric structure, it begins to vibrate. Almost all cells in our bodies, except mature red blood cells, contain DNA and therefore are piezoelectric. Nobel prize laureate St. Gyorgi reflected that transfer of electrons both within and between cells is the key to life processes. Thus, it is not surprising that certain energy field vibrations can be beneficial or deleterious to our health.

Experiments in Russia by Dr. Vlail Kaznacheyev, director of the Institute of Clinical and Experimental Medicine in Novosibirsk, suggest that the radiation (movement of energy) of cells may be a much more important mechanism for transmitting information than was once believed.[2] Kaznacheyev took healthy cells and separated them into two samples. The samples were then separated by either a quartz or a glass window. One sample was subjected to either a virus, a bacteria, a toxic chemical, or nuclear radiation. This led to the death of the subjected cells.

When the separating window was made of glass, the uninfected, unexposed cells on the opposite side of the window remained healthy. However, when the window was made of quartz, something unexpected happened. Seventy to eighty percent of the time,

---

2. V. P. Kaznacheyev, et al., "Distant intercellular interactions in a system of two tissue cultures," *Psychoenergetic Systems*, 1(3), March 1976.

disease was mirrored in the unexposed cells on the other side of the window, and they died shortly after the exposed cells died.

The results demonstrated that infected cells communicated information about their diseased condition to noninfected cells, and they did this through the transmission of energy that passed through quartz but not through glass. (Quartz allows passage of ultraviolet light, while glass blocks or filters it so that the signals sent by the cells are altered.) Further research identified the specific energy as that in the near ultraviolet range, the range of DNA radiation.

This research, involving over seventeen hundred experiments, demonstrates that the DNA in living cells can communicate with other nearby cells through the transmission of energy in the form of light. These results indicate that cells can communicate with one another independently of biochemistry and of organ systems such as the circulatory system, nervous system, or immune system.

THE WATERS OF LIFE

Scientists say that the human body is approximately two-thirds water. Changing the energy fields around water can alter its structure, which can have a profound influence on the body's cells.

Dr. Bernard Grad, biologist at McGill University in Montreal, demonstrated that the absorption spectrum, surface tension, conductivity, and acidity of water can be altered by focused thought or intent. When structured with healing intent, the hydrogen bond angles of the water molecules widen. The increased angle weakens the normal attraction of water molecules to one another. This causes a decrease in the surface tension and an increase in the solubility of the structured water, as well as an altered spectrum-absorption pattern.

In one series of experiments, Dr. Grad had an individual with a "green thumb" and one severely depressed mental patient each hold a sealed flask of water in their hands. He then regularly treated groups of plants with either the green thumb structured water, the negatively structured water of the mental patient, or plain water that had received no structuring. Plants that received green thumb structured water grew faster than those that received plain water. Plants that received water from the depressed mental patient grew more slowly than the plants that received plain water. (See Gerber, *Vibrational Medicine*, p. 295.)

Since we know that in structured water the absorption spectrum, surface tension, conductivity, and acidity are altered, it is very likely that by structuring water we can also change the electrical resistance and the permeability of the cell membrane, making it more receptive or less receptive to signals on a vibratory level.

It appears that structured water also stores information that living systems can "read." This has far-reaching implications for healing, since cells of the human body contain and are surrounded by water. If thoughts and healing energy can structure extra- and intracellular water, which in turn affects the distribution of electrical charges of cell membranes, this could clearly facilitate healing.

THE EFFECTS OF INTENTION

Physicists tell us that our very observation of an event changes that event. In quantum physics this is known as the *observer effect*. Physicist Fred Wolf defines observation as any action that causes a choice to be made. He has proposed that the observer effect is an attribute of consciousness and that it occurs at both conscious and unconscious levels.

Unconscious processes can be altered by conscious intent. Our conscious choice to change, to heal an infection, can alter patterns of energy in the immune system, for example, in either ourselves or another person. Because of this, the observer effect is most significant in holoenergetic healing.

William Tiller, professor of material sciences at Stanford University, reported at the 1986 annual Association for Research and Enlightenment Conference in Arizona that he had developed a device that releases electrons when subjected to healing intent.

Tiller sealed a layer of gas between two diode electrodes and introduced a high AC voltage across the electrodes. The voltage was low enough so that it did not separate the gas into its constituents. Although no charge was observed, small avalanches of electrons were released. Tiller used a counting circuit to keep track of the electrons emitted.

A Faraday Cage was placed around the instrument to eliminate any electromagnetic effects on the device. The instrument's threshold was set so that if someone merely stood near it, the device would emit a maximum of one burst of electrons approximately every five minutes.

Tiller next had someone intentionally focus healing energy into the device through his hands. There was no response for the first ninety seconds, but over the subsequent five-minute period more than fifty thousand bursts were recorded. When the healing energy transmission was discontinued, the energy bursts gradually subsided. Nothing was found that could shield the device from the effect of healing energy. The device could not be triggered with ultraviolet or infrared light, gamma rays, or high-voltage current. This suggests the influence of an energy beyond the frequency of electromagnetic radiation.

Tiller went on to research the effect of varying his thoughts on electrons emitted from the device. He focused his intention while using his hands to send healing energy. A count of twenty thousand to fifty thousand was registered. Then he placed his hands around the device again, but this time he neutralized his intent to send healing energy by focusing on mathematical calculations. No energy bursts were registered.

Tiller noted that when he allowed his mind to drift to the device, it would start counting. He also discovered that if he was ill or his mind was fuzzy, the counts came up much lower than those registered when he was in a healthier physical or mental state.

Tiller also demonstrated the effect on his device of visualization. Standing fifteen to twenty feet from the device, he visualized the device over his solar plexus; it registered between twenty thousand and fifty thousand counts.

After performing thousands of such experiments, Tiller concluded that there is an energy beyond the electromagnetic spectrum, emitted by humans, that can activate the release of electrons. This subtle energy can transfer information, directed by the mind and focused by intention, attention, and imagery.

The healing energy transmitted through the hands, intention, and thoughts of a healer, which is capable of releasing electrons in Tiller's device, may well be capable of affecting the charge balance of cell membranes and perhaps DNA and thus the health of living cells.

Since nonliving systems in Tiller's experiments could be affected by human energy, it seemed likely that living systems would respond similarly. I decided to find out for myself if this was so. Indeed, my own research confirms that our intention and imagery have an effect on living systems. In a series of experiments I found that, with imagery alone, I could induce an eighteen percent inhibition of tumor cell growth in culture relative to controls.

When I included the intention for the rapidly growing cells to return to the natural order of their normal growth rate together with imagery of reduced cell growth, the inhibitory effect was doubled to forty percent. In these studies it seems that imagery and intent each contributed equally in influencing the psychoenergetic inhibition of tumor cells in culture. For details, see appendix A.

ENERGY AT THE SUBATOMIC LEVEL

Physicists refer to another level of energy—the subatomic level—in terms of photon exchange. Photons are massless, chargeless packets of energy that constitute the basic unit of light and electromagnetic energy. When an atom releases a photon of light from an electron, it loses energy. When an atom absorbs a photon, it gains energy. The release or absorption of photon energy by an atom can be influenced by a more fundamental energy often referred to as the energy of the "void" (vacuum), or the zero-point energy state.

Researchers have traditionally postulated that potential energy is organized and stored in fields surrounding objects or living beings. Yet at the level of photons and subatomic particles, energy does not always behave as it would when it is in the form of a field. Particles disappear and reappear in unexpected places, violating the postulated law of conservation of energy.

David Bohm, one of the world's leading theoretical physicists, refers to the higher-order "quantum potential energy" of particles to explain why energy can seem to move faster than the speed of light.[3] When two photons are released from a single atom and spin away from each other in opposite directions, physicists have found that influencing the spin of either photon (by polarizing it) simultaneously affects the spin of the other.[4] Since the photons are traveling away from each other at the speed of light (photons are packets of light) any means of communication between the two photons would have to occur at twice the speed of light, defying all the known laws of physics. These experiments reveal that parts are connected to the whole at higher unifying orders, even when the parts (the photons) are separated from each other in space and time.

Some biophysicists studying the effect of higher-order quantum potential energy on the biological systems are calling it *scalar* or *non-Hertzian energy*. Non-Hertzian energies are thought to provide the mechanism by which "subtle energies" exert their influence upon and beyond the electromagnetic energy field.[5]

---

3. David Bohm and F. D. Peat, *Science, Order and Creativity* (New York: Bantam, 1987), pp. 89–93.

4. Abner Shimony, "The Reality of the Quantum World," *Scientific American*, January 1988: 46–53.

5. The application of these new quantum energies to biology, and their role in healing, is discussed in appendix A by Glen Rein, Ph.D., director of the Quantum Biology Research Laboratory.

HUMAN ENERGY FIELDS AND ENERGY CENTERS

Each physical body, composed of interacting, pulsating energy fields, has its own set of vibrating patterns, like musical notes, that are natural to it and with which it resonates. Since all notes have higher harmonics, we can assume that the body does as well. These higher harmonics of the body have been called *subtle bodies* or *subtle fields* (see fig. 1). Through interpenetration of the physical electromagnetic energy field, subtle fields enable consciousness to interact with the body.

The body's subtle energy fields are commonly divided into arbitrary groups that extend beyond the physical body. Clairvoyants perceive these as colorful auras surrounding the physical body. Biomechanical testing (dowsing) can also be used to detect the extent of these subtle fields.

Described below are five subtle energy fields associated with the human body-mind: bioenergy, etheric, emotional, mental, and intuitive.

The Bioenergy Field

The bioenergy field consists of both subtle and scientifically measurable energies and is partially the result of the body's cells growing, metabolizing, and dying, new cells being generated, and so on. It is made of carbon dioxide, tiny salt crystals, water molecules, ammonia, and other substances created by life's processes. It also consists of the electromagnetic, gravitational, acoustic, and subtle fields of the physical body. Some of these fields can be measured scientifically in the laboratory. It has been proposed that this collection of materials is excited by ultraviolet photons given off during cell division in the body. The overall effect is the presence of a cloud of ionized particles around the body, extending from two to four inches from the skin, with a clearly defined outer boundary. The state of our bioenergy field reflects the state of our physical health—expanding during periods of vibrant health, contracting during most illnesses.

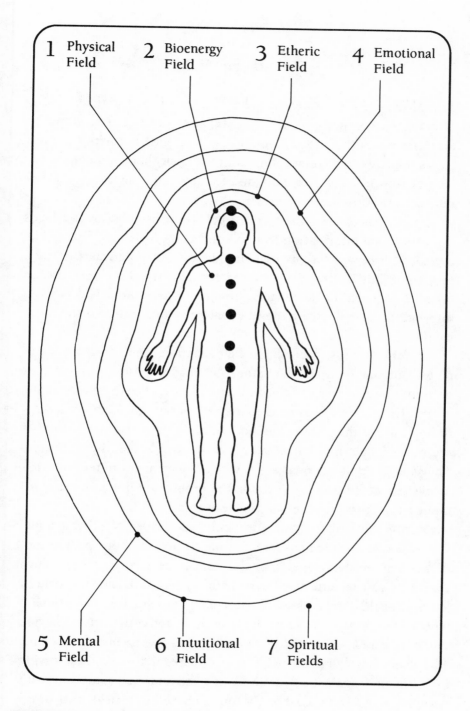

1 Physical Field
2 Bioenergy Field
3 Etheric Field
4 Emotional Field
5 Mental Field
6 Intuitional Field
7 Spiritual Fields

FIGURE 1 Your Subtle Fields

The Etheric Field

The etheric field, which extends beyond the bioenergy field, configures the energy pattern of the body, both its harmonies and its disharmonies. Of all the energy fields, it provides us with the most direct subtle-energy connection with the physical body, giving us the best picture of how our thoughts, feelings, and environmental influences are affecting our bodies.

I define the etheric field as distinct from the other subtle fields but containing information from all of them. The etheric field is like a radio station—it has its own frequency and broadcasts its own programs, but it also gives regular reports on every other station broadcasting within its range. Thus, the etheric field will contain information broadcast by the physical body-mind and all the other subtle-energy fields.

In other words, the etheric field contains the energetic "templates" of our lives. In the same way that we use a template, or pattern, to cut pieces of fabric to make a coat, the templates of the etheric field (themselves constructed of energy) guide the organization of energy throughout the body-mind. Some neurophysiologists are now speculating that memory exists outside the physical body. They suggest that brain cells—as well as elements of mind that exist as packets of information outside the brain—are holographic, containing a picture or template of the whole.

If you think about your life, and about those of other people, you will realize that there are certain constants about people that make them recognizable from day to day and year to year. Such constants can include their personalities, physical features, beliefs, levels of health, and so forth. You remain who you are, and I remain who I am, despite the facts that our cells are constantly renewing themselves and we are changing in other ways. The templates of the etheric field, and of other fields as well, make that possible, allowing us again and again to "cut the cloth" so that we come out with essentially the same coat each time. The etheric field also interacts with the genetic code to express its patterning physically. As

Richard Gerber says in *Vibrational Medicine,* "While the genes within the DNA direct the molecular mechanisms which govern the development of individual cells, the etheric body guides the spatial unfoldment of the genetic process" (p. 69).

Whenever we want to effect change, as in holoenergetic healing, we work with the templates described here. At the etheric level we get a composite picture of all the energetic templates that affect our lives. It is here that we begin our journey into the energetic source of our present circumstances, and it is from here that we first broadcast our healing programs.

In chapter 5, I will describe how to use your etheric field as a baseline for assessing information about your body-mind and all your corresponding energy fields.

The Emotional Field

Beyond the etheric field is the emotional field. It interpenetrates the bioenergy and etheric fields as well as the physical body. Feelings, emotions, and intentions affect the emotional energy field and influence the physical body.

Thoughts are always associated with feelings. Our feelings vary according to the nature of our thoughts, and vice versa. Emotions impel us to express our feelings through our actions, though sometimes we repress our actions. In a healthy state, our thoughts and feelings are aligned and integrated to guide our actions. Thus, when thoughts are in sync with feelings, and when thoughts and feelings are expressed through action, the emotional field is affected.

Our emotional health depends on our ability to be in touch with our emotions, feelings, and thoughts. Having an awareness of their origins and of their effects on us and on others enhances our sense of self.

The Mental Energy Field

The mental energy field is associated with intellectual functioning. Its higher frequencies interpenetrate and extend beyond the etheric and emotional fields. The mental field's interactions with other fields enable us to categorize, analyze, rationalize, synthesize, and create from our thoughts.

The brain, it seems, works by amplifying thoughts, which come through the mind. But where is the mind located?

Karl Lashley, a neurophysiologist, worked with rats to determine where memory resided. After teaching the animals how to run a maze, he began making lesions in different parts of their cerebral cortexes, destroying brain tissue. He found that it didn't matter where these lesions were made: the rats were still able to run the maze, because memory was not located in any one place. However, he did find that there was a critical minimum mass of brain tissue needed in order for the rats to remember the maze. After 20 percent or more of the rats' brains had been destroyed, they began proportionally to lose their ability to run the maze. Neurophysiologists learned from this and similar experiments that memory does not exist in only one place in the brain. Rather, our brains may function holographically—that is, each brain cell is capable of accessing a picture of the whole; it is as if each cell had available to it a sort of blueprint of the whole brain, even while performing a specialized function particular to the individual cell.

After three decades of research, Lashley concluded: "It is not possible to demonstrate the isolated localization of a memory trace anywhere in the nervous system."[6] Similarly, biologist Rupert Sheldrake supports the hypothesis that "our brains are like televisions"—that is, tuning devices—while the storage of information takes place outside the brain and body.[7] This implies that memory itself is at least in part nonphysical.

---

6. Karl S. Lashley, "In Search of the Engram," *Symposia of the Society for Experimental Biology,* 1950, 4:454–82.

7. Rupert Sheldrake, "Can Our Memories Survive the Death of Our Brains?" in *Proceedings of the Symposium on Consciousness and Survival* (Sausalito, CA: Institute of Noetic Sciences, 1987), p. 67.

The normal or above-normal performance of some hydrocephalic children also suggests that the mind exists outside the brain, rather than being limited to the brain cells. With hydrocephalus, ventricles of the brain that contain cerebrospinal fluid are blocked in the fetus, causing a dramatic swelling inside the head. As a result, brain tissue is compressed against the inside of the skull by a buildup of fluid pressure, leaving, in some cases, less than a millimeter of brain tissue. Despite this reduction in brain mass, some hydrocephalic children are able to learn complex mathematical operations and excel in school.

Both Lashley's experiments and the behavior and capacities of hydrocephalic children suggest that we must look beyond brain tissue itself to understand the mind. Candace Pert, formerly of the National Institute of Mental Health, proposed that there is a complex communication network that sends information back and forth between the nervous system, immune system, and endocrine system. The messengers carrying this information are molecules called *neuropeptides,* which are produced by our brain, kidneys, intestines, and blood cells. This communication system joins virtually every part of our body and mind, making us, in a very real sense, like a single large brain. The stuff of thought is everywhere, not limited to the "gray matter" in our heads.[8]

One implication of this is that our thoughts and feelings stimulate the cells of the immune system. These cells are then guided by neuropeptides to repair wounds and to decide which cells to protect and which ones to kill, as in the case of cancer cells. Thus, our thoughts and feelings literally result in the generation of physiological substances. In allopathic medicine, the study of these connections is the newly emerging field of psychoneuroimmunology.

In the view of Candace Pert, the brain and body are simply a physical substrate of the mind. But the mind cannot be explained in

---

8. Candace Pert, "Neuropeptides, the Emotions and Bodymind," in *Proceedings of the Symposium on Consciousness and Survival* (Sausalito, CA: Institute of Noetic Sciences, 1987), p. 79.

physical terms alone; it also consists of a nonmaterial substrate, composed of the information that is flowing in and around it. The physical brain might be likened to a radio receiver, while the information that constitutes the mind is like the radio waves around it.

Clearly, not all communication and understanding occurs at the mental or intellectual level. There are additional levels of awareness, which we call the intuitive and spiritual, that help us complete the picture.

The Intuitional Field

Sometimes known as the causal field, the intuitional field bridges the spiritual with the emotional and mental (personality) fields. It is through this level that we experience direct knowing, subsequently registered in the form of thoughts and feelings. At the intuitive level we can tap in to knowledge that transcends intellectual and rational thought. Existing beyond and interpenetrating the intuitional field is the spiritual realm.

THE CHAKRAS: HOW THE DIFFERENT ENERGY FIELDS ARE LINKED

The biophysical, etheric, emotional, mental, and intuitive energy fields are not separate, with clearly delineated boundaries. Rather, they intermingle, each one affecting the others, moving together like a great sea of energy. Imagine the various movements of an ocean, with currents moving along one axis as waves roll in another direction, and turbulence being created around land forms; include in your mental picture the movements of fish and animals, the movement of the earth through space, and so on. We can plot the general direction of a current or of the waves as they roll up on shore, but to understand how each current affects the whole is quite another matter. It is even more difficult to form a mental picture of all the various movements representing energy forms in the ocean.

Similarly, it is not easy to get a complete picture of the human body's energy fields and their interactions. One of the most helpful models we have for this is the *chakra* system, developed thousands of years ago. Over the centuries this "map" of human energy has continually been revised and refined, and it is still widely used today in acupuncture and various other healing and spiritual systems.

According to this ancient system, the bioenergy, etheric, emotional, mental, and intuitive fields are linked to the physical body through seven major energy centers called *chakras*. In Sanskrit, chakra means "wheel of energy or fire." According to ancient spiritual traditions, these whirling vortices assimilate, transmit, and distribute subtle energy. The chakras have been likened to an antenna array that can be tuned to the information contained in multidimensional space. When subtle energies are downstepped, the body is vitalized and imbued with consciousness. Specific yogic meditation and breathing practices further activate these centers, bringing about renewed energy and enhanced conscious awareness.

Each of the seven centers is associated with an endocrine gland, a color, and a sound characteristic of its spin frequency. Each center also corresponds to a major nerve plexus in its particular area of the body. Specific body areas are vitalized and nourished by their associated chakras (see chart on page 48). Pathology in any area of the body is directly related to its corresponding energy center.

Our chakras continuously expand and contract, reflecting our daily experiences, feelings, and emotions. At the same time, there is a part of them that changes very little. Like a tree, a chakra may have deep roots that appear physically to move or change only in very small increments over its lifetime. However, a tree's branches respond to every breeze, to changes of the seasons, to the movement of the sun across the sky, and even to the scurrying about of wildlife in its branches; a chakra, too, responds to many influences. In evaluating a chakra, the information you get depends upon which of its dimensions you are choosing to look at.

At the physical level, a diseased organ may influence the state of the chakra associated with it. For example, a gastric ulcer may affect

Major Chakras and the Area of the Body They Nourish

Chakra	Color	Endocrine Gland	Area of Body Governed
7-Crown	Violet-White	Pineal	Upper brain, right eye
6-Head	Indigo	Pituitary	Lower brain, left eye, ears, nose, nervous system
5-Throat	Blue	Thyroid	Bronchial and vocal apparatus, lungs, alimentary canal
4-Heart	Green	Thymus	Heart, blood, vagus nerve, circulatory system
3-Solar Plexus	Yellow	Pancreas	Stomach, liver, gall bladder, nervous system
2-Sacral	Orange	Gonads	Reproductive system
1-Base	Red	Adrenals	Spinal column, kidneys

Source: Adapted from David Tansley, *Radionics and the Subtle Anatomy of Man,* p. 29.

the third chakra quite directly. Interestingly, the third chakra is also associated with emotions such as competitiveness and control. While self-control and self-mastery bring inner peace and harmony, the need to control the external world—other people and situations outside us—creates distress, which experts in behavioral medicine have correlated with ulcers and other diseases of the digestive tract.

In the holoenergetic healing process, each chakra is represented by a level of consciousness expressed in terms of psychological or esoteric function (see fig. 2). The esoteric level reflects the state of evolution of the chakra at the moment and can lead us to the source of an illness or disease.

The esoteric functions of the first three chakras can be distorted by deep-seated beliefs, which affect our thoughts and feelings, and by events occurring in the present. Since the first three chakras represent the foundation of this energy system, anything based upon them will obviously reflect their influence.

✸ EXERCISE: SENSING SUBTLE ENERGIES

This exercise will allow you to experience subtle energy for yourself. While most people will be able to sense this energy on the first or second try, some will not. If you do not sense the subtle energies, don't be discouraged. You'll have other opportunities to experiment as we go along.

1. Rub your hands together vigorously, as if you were washing them.

2. Hold your hands comfortably in front of you, palms facing each other, about six inches apart.

3. Slowly move your hands closer together while focusing your attention on the sensations in your palms.

4. Allow yourself to sense what seems a buildup of pressure as your hands draw closer. You may experience this as a tingling or coolness, a warmth or pulsation, or perhaps a combination of these.

5. When you identify one of these sensations, however slight, and even if you think it is only your imagination or the result of my suggestion, drop one hand and see what happens to the sensation. Does it change when you take your hand away?

6. Now bring the hand back up and notice if the sensations resume as before.

Chakras—Esoteric Functions

Each Chakra is a witness containing energy, images, and information.

Functions:	Qualities	Distortion
7 Spiritual Awareness		
6 Intuitive Knowing, Will to Know		
5 Creative Expression		
4 Love	Unconditional Giving, Caring, Compassion	
3 Emotion	Conditional Giving, Caring, Compassion, Empowerment	Power Over, Manipulative Control
2 Sensation	Pleasure, Creativity	Stimulation, Possession
1 Security, Will to Live	Life Force	Survival

FIGURE 2 Chakras and their Esoteric Functions

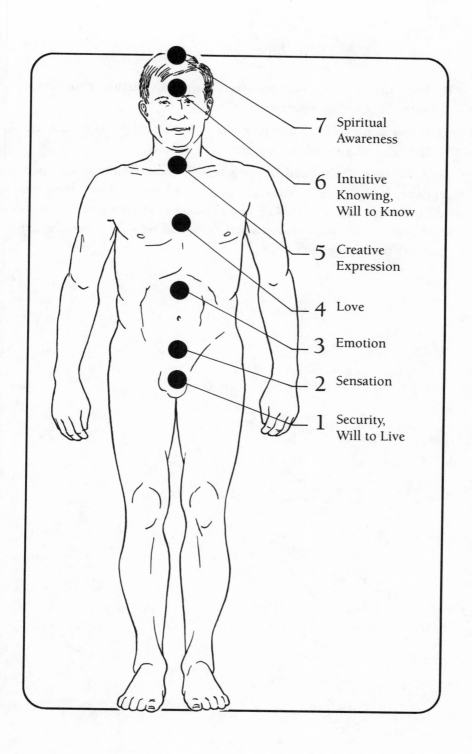

7 Spiritual Awareness

6 Intuitive Knowing, Will to Know

5 Creative Expression

4 Love

3 Emotion

2 Sensation

1 Security, Will to Live

7. Vary the distance between your hands to further experiment with these subtle energies.

8. If you don't feel the energy at first, try again, perhaps in a different setting or when you are more relaxed.

Note: Because doubts and limiting beliefs create filters to our perceptions, many people require a number of trials before they are satisfied with the results. The key to success in this exercise is to trust your senses while momentarily suspending your preconceived thoughts and judgments.

3

Love and Holoenergetic Healing

Love is a form of knowledge . . . we truly know any thing or any person, by becoming one therewith, in love. Thus love has a wisdom that the mind cannot claim, and by this hearty love, this becoming one with what is beyond our personal borders, we may take a long step toward freedom.

—THE YOGA SUTRAS OF PATANJALI

There comes a time in the seeker's life when he discovers that he is at once the lover and the Beloved. The aspiring soul which he embodies is the lover in him. And the transcendental Self which he reveals from within is his Beloved.

—SRI CHINMOY

Writing about love has been done grandly by such psychologists as Erich Fromm and such poets as Walt Whitman and Elizabeth Barrett Browning. The powers of love have also been explored by physicians such as Bernie Siegel, M.D., in *Love, Medicine and Miracles*, and Deepak Chopra, M.D., in *Quantum Healing*. The fact that so many authors, from all professions and all walks of life, have written about love attests to its great universal power. In *Femininity Lost and Regained*, Robert A. Johnson notes:

Sanskrit, the basis for most East Indian languages, has ninety-six terms for love . . . English has only one. English does not have the breadth, scope, and differentiation for the feminine and for feeling experiences of Sanskrit. . . . If it did, then we would have a specific word to use in our appreciation of father, mother, sunset, wife, house, mistress, or God. Having only one word to apply to these many levels of experience makes it difficult to understand the complexity of our inner lives and emotions. The Eskimo language has thirty words for snow. This reflects the need for clarity in a complex relationship to snow. When we are as interested in relationship . . . as the Eskimo is in snow, we will evolve a differentiated and focused language for that dimension of our lives.[1]

To focus on the ways that love relates to holoenergetic healing, I must emphasize *unconditional love,* which goes beyond judgment and comparison and has a most powerful effect on the healing process.

The power of unconditional love is evident to us in many areas of our lives. I remember reading in 1987 about the Golden State Warriors' Sleepy Floyd. At the start of the fourth quarter of the National Basketball Association playoffs, the Warriors were trailing the Los Angeles Lakers by fourteen points. As the quarter began, Floyd looked up into the stands and saw a sign: "Win or lose, we love you."

"That really touched me," Floyd said. "I felt I had to give everything I had. . . . I didn't think about the points. I just played instinctively, and the crowd got into it."

Sleepy Floyd went on to score a record-setting twenty-nine points, which gave the Warriors a victory. The fans' unconditional acceptance and love touched him in the heart of his being, triggering in Floyd a source of energy and power that allowed him to realize his greatest moment and the best individual scoring record for a single quarter in the history of professional basketball.

---

1. Robert A. Johnson, *Femininity Lost and Regained* (New York: Harper & Row, 1990), p. 2.

LOVE AS A HEALING FORCE

The new healing model I present here is based on love, expanded awareness, and the empowerment that comes from a conscious choice for change. It provides us with directions and tools for consciously evoking loving energy and intentionally transferring that energy to another person, or to a particular area of our own bodies, with tangible effects that can be sensed as well as measured in the laboratory.

While love can take many forms, its essence is relatedness. We can become aware of this relatedness or nonseparation, which always exists. We can experience and feel it as the impulse toward unity, and we can express and manifest it through our actions.[2]

Love is the most powerful healing energy and catalyst for transformation. Our inability to love ourselves or to receive love from others is the source of most of our maladies. Our difficulties with love often result from early childhood experiences or perceptions of betrayal, abandonment, humiliation, or rejection, which lead to feelings of unworthiness, shame, and guilt. These deep-seated feelings result in a sense of separation from self, from one's own body and spirit, and from other people. While this perceived separation may at first be the psyche's effort to defend itself from fear, isolation, and pain, it eventually becomes the source of continual feelings of separation, alienation, and anxiety.

When illness is manifest in our beings, we can choose to remain focused on symptoms and treatment, or we can go to the source of the disorder and transform it. This entails "going into ourselves," to that part of our being that maintains the sense of separation, isolation, and pain.

Traditionally, Western allopathic and homeopathic medicine has left to psychotherapists and the clergy the task of getting to the sources of illness. In psychotherapy, finding the core information

---

2. The exercise "Transpersonal Alignment Process" in this chapter gives you an opportunity to experience this.

and releasing it often involves protracted therapy. However, in holoenergetic healing, we engage the symptoms, intermediate causes, and deeper sources of distress and disease as holoenergetic patterns, or holoforms, located in and around the body-mind. Once this core information is accessed energetically and experienced, it consciously needs to be acknowledged. To acknowledge the source of a disorder as a perceived separation requires that we come into resonance with it, become at one with it, and accept the truth of its existence. We can then assume responsibility for having contributed to the existence of the illness, by virtue of our perspective at the time we formed the core belief. In other words, if in infancy you formed the belief that you were unworthy of being loved, you would take responsibility for having created that belief from your limited understanding of yourself and others at that time.

I use the word *responsibility* not in a moralistic or judgmental way but to connote a particular ability that we all have. Responsibility has, unfortunately, been interpreted to mean "I am to blame for my disease; I caused it." In holoenergetic healing, however, responsibility means the ability to *be responsive* and *to understand and accept our contribution* to our ailment, without self-blame or self-judgment. It's not what others did to us but the way in which we responded that is our "response-ability."

To accept responsibility is a tremendously empowering experience. When we do so, every illness or reversal, and every healing, becomes a source of self-discovery, another step on the transformational journey.

SYMPTOMS, CAUSE, AND SOURCE

In holoenergetic healing it is important to be able to distinguish among the symptoms, causes, and sources of an illness. With the common cold, for example, the symptoms may include sniffles, coughing, and fever. In modern Western medicine, we still deal primarily with symptoms: take a decongestant, cough medicine, or homeopathic remedy. Obviously, we still aren't getting at the cause or source.

Recently we discovered that the common cold is "caused" by a virus. Then, further investigation revealed that even when we are well we harbor viruses. Therefore, viruses, in and of themselves, cannot be viewed as the sole cause of colds. If the immune system's functioning is compromised, the viruses that are always present seem to emerge and attack. So the real cause of a cold must be the state of the immune system. However, more recently we've learned that stress compromises the immune system. So wouldn't stress be the real cause? But wait—there's more. We are now finding that fear of losing control is at the root of most stress. So perhaps this fear is our real cause? Causal links will continue to build in complexity until we get to what we call, in holoenergetic healing, the *source* of an illness.

The First Level of Source

The first level of source consists of *perceptions and interpretations* of events, which establish a holographic pattern of beliefs, thoughts, and feelings. I call these patterns *holoforms* because they give form to holographic entities, which have their own order and natural frequencies of vibration. Such entities have the capacity to cause unmanifest energy to manifest in our lives. In other words, holoforms can produce harmony or disharmony.[3] Until we perceive something, we have no experience or felt awareness of it. For example, anger is regarded as a state of physiological arousal in response to a perceived threat. Research shows that the hormones that trigger anger (epinephrine, norepinephrine, and thyrotropic hormone) unleash other emotions such as fear, grief, and even joy. What makes one emotion different from another is not the physiological arousal pattern but our *perceptions and interpretations* of

---

3. Vernon Woolf, in *Holodynamics*, also works with these holoenergetic entities, which he calls "holodynes."

the causal events. For instance, if you are standing in a crowd and suddenly feel a hand on your shoulder, you experience an adrenaline rush and turn to see who it is. If it is someone you don't know, you may experience fear or anger; if it is a friend, you will probably experience relief or joy. The salient point is that you identify your emotion according to your perception and interpretation of the event, even though the hormones involved are the same in both cases.

Our perceptions are conditioned by the messages, beliefs, and behaviors we were exposed to from the prenatal and perhaps even the preconceptual period on. Interpretation involves a choice— conscious or otherwise. We perceive what happened and we interpret what it means to us. In other words, it's not what happens that creates our experience of the event, it's our perception and interpretation of it.

I refer to certain events and their interpretations as the "critical incidents" and "critical choices," because they lead to the establishment of disharmonious core beliefs and holoforms, which later become disease patterns. A critical incident could be anything from misunderstanding a parent's laughter during the early, egocentric years to actual physical abuse. It might even be a fetus's awareness of its parents' wanting a child of the opposite sex.

Critical incidents involve feelings such as abandonment, fear, betrayal, humiliation, and rejection. These are immediate reactions to present events. We then give meaning to these feelings: "Because my father left, I must not be good enough," or, "My parents wanted a boy (girl). There must be something wrong with me. I'm a mistake." The meaning we give represents the critical choice of interpretation.

Shame, guilt, or both are frequently associated with critical incidents. Shame is the deep-seated feeling that frequently comes from the perception that there is something fundamentally wrong with you, while guilt is the feeling that commonly results from the perception that you have *done* something wrong.

The various elements of each critical incident are usually formed simultaneously, not gradually.

At the moment of a critical incident, we give meaning to our perception of the event; that interpretation becomes crystallized as a core belief, which has a lasting effect, influencing choices that serve to support the belief. These experiences are received through the physical senses and stored in the mind as multi-dimensional images or holoforms. They develop their own causal potency and resonate with their own frequency. If a crystallized belief is in conflict with the body's natural patterns of balance and harmony, it can be said to be the source of disease patterns—the source of illness in our lives. Thus, to find the source of an illness, we need to get to the critical incident and the core beliefs that are causing it.

The Second Level of Source

The second level of source involves *love, worthiness, and a sense of value.* The deeper meaning beneath the core belief "I'm not good enough" is the belief "I'm not good enough to love, or to be loved." This causes shame or guilt, which leads to the belief "I'm unforgivable." This in turn leads to the choice to remain separate, by refusing to be loved or to love and by engaging in numbing addictions, self-pity, self-punishments, and more guilt and shame.

In holoenergetic healing we begin to become aware that the source of our illness is our sense of separation and alienation—a lack of relatedness of self to self, self to others, self to the world, and self to the One.

The Third Level of Source

The third level of source deals with the realization that *we have a choice.* At this point we discover our individuality. Along with this may come a sense of our power and freedom to choose, or a sense of our separation and alienation when we don't express our choice.

The Fourth Level of Source

The fourth level of source deals with *the choice to be separate from or at one with spirit or God*. We are free to become whole and healed to the extent to which we know and relate to something greater than ourselves.

After we access and resonate with an unhealthy energy pattern—which emanates from these sources, be it in the form of a sensation, an image, a thought, a feeling, or a core belief—we can change or "unform" that pattern. In holoenergetic healing we learn specific, highly effective techniques for unforming these undesirable energy patterns; we literally release the body-mind from the disease templates that are influencing it. By working with this disharmonious energy field (the disease holoform or template) and its physical, emotional, mental, and spiritual expressions of disease, our awareness, loving energy, and conscious choice can bring about dramatic change, facilitating transformation and healing.

The feeling of forgiveness of ourselves and others lies at the heart of our healing work. It is important to understand that we often choose before we learn to discern. We tap in to this level of source when we begin to understand how and when we made the choice to separate from our loving feelings. Once we have holoenergetically accessed the issue, we can release the undesirable pattern it created.

TECHNIQUES FOR CHANGE

We can effect change in the energy forms within our body-minds in many ways. One way is through thoughts, feelings, and imagery, which have a direct physiological effect on the body, causing changes in the immune, endocrine, digestive, musculoskeletal, circulatory, and nervous systems. For example, fear and stress are quickly translated into muscular tension. This can affect blood circulation, resulting in headache, heartache, digestive problems, and lowered resistance to infections. We can reverse the symptoms in these cases by learning new ways of responding to stress.

Another powerful way to produce physiological change involves our breathing patterns. (Please see chapter 4 for more detailed information.) Breath—that which carries the life force—plays a major role in holoenergetic healing. Breathing builds an energy charge physiologically, and when focused and appropriately directed, that energy can be given form—that is, it can be moderated consciously by the mind to transfer information to an area of the body or even to another person. In natural childbirth, breathing is used to reduce pain and focus the mother's attention to synchronize her efforts with the normal reflexes of the birth process.

In holoenergetic healing we use breath in many ways. For instance, imagining and focusing on your breath moving in and out of a specific area of your body energizes that area. The energy fields that surround and penetrate your body register that attention and intention. Once activated, the area is prepared for change, ready to access and release old information and receive new information. Holding your breath at certain critical moments gains the immediate attention of your subconscious mind and brings your body into harmonious resonance with it through a slowing of the heart rate. Pulsed breath—blowing in short, forceful spurts—can facilitate the disruption of undesirable energy patterns and enhance the transformation of energy from one form to another.

THE ACTIVE INGREDIENT OF HOLOENERGETIC HEALING: LOVE

In holoenergetic healing it is essential that we be able to relate to or interact with those aspects of ourselves or others that we wish to change. Such interactions occur through our energy fields, through the life force that manifests itself as a biosphere in and around our bodies.

Every structure, animate or inanimate, has a set of energetic vibrations or frequencies that are unique and natural to it. When a structure is vibrating in a way that is characteristic for it, it is said to be in resonance. That resonant frequency, or set of frequencies, is the tune to which it dances best. Every structure, including every atom in the universe, is also responsive to other energy fields around it, so there is significant interaction among the vibrating fields produced by each structure.

When one structure vibrates at the natural frequency of another structure, *resonant coupling* occurs. Then a number of things happen. First, the intensity of the interaction builds because the vibrations of one reinforce those of the other. You may have experienced the effect of such reinforcement when, as a child, you had someone push you on a swing. If he or she pushed you at exactly the right moment, the arc grew larger and you swung higher. The same thing can occur with energy in resonance—each person's resonance in effect amplifies the other's. Another effect of resonant coupling is that the energies of the two structures become linked as one, moving together in unison.

We can demonstrate unison in resonant coupling with the use of two tuning forks. Take two tuning forks tuned to the same note, say C. Holding one fork still, strike the second fork so that it begins vibrating. Now set the second fork a few inches from the first. After a few moments, the first fork will pick up the vibrations of the second and begin resonating with it, sounding its note in unison.

In holoenergetic healing we utilize love, which is the universal harmonic, to help ourselves or others release energy patterns of separation and move into energy patterns of wholeness.

The essence of love is relatedness—to a person, a place, an object, a food, one's self, the universe, or God or an undefined Higher Order. We can look at relatedness in a very literal sense: to relate means "to carry back together." What I mean by relatedness, then, is that love brings back together what was once one but seemingly became separate. It is a coming home. We can become aware of this nonseparation, or relatedness, for it always exists. We can experience it as a sense of wholeness, completion, peace, and the impulse toward unity. And we can express and manifest it through our actions. When we relate fully to what is so, love becomes known as Truth or Pure Consciousness; perceiver and perceived become one.

Love creates an energy field that affects all that enters it. It is said that the loving fields of Christ and Buddha were so powerful that people were healed in their presence. Both of these great avatars taught that loving energy is the energy of oneness, harmony, balance, and peace. In the presence of a powerful loving field, if there is the intention and willingness for healing to occur, the body's inherent self-healing capabilities will be stimulated and augmented.

To use an analogy, in modern medicine there is a technique called MRI (Magnetic Resonance Imaging), which uses a magnetic field, rather than X rays, to produce computer-generated images for diagnosis. In the blink of an eye, a magnetic field brings all the protons of the hydrogen atoms in the body into alignment, causing them all to spin and move as one; a radio wave resonant with the hydrogen proton is then pulsed through the body, producing signals that a computer translates into visual images.

In the presence of a coherent magnetic field, such as that produced by MRI, the hydrogen protons spin in concert as they align themselves with the field. In effect, they all dance the same dance; they become one. Similarly, when you create a coherent loving field, everything within that field begins to vibrate as one, to dance to the same rhythm.

When all begins to vibrate as one, separation disappears and there is only oneness. Time and space disappear, because they are measures of separation. The end merges with the beginning and the spinning circle is complete. Finite becomes infinite. In this state of oneness, the natural order and harmony inherent in the tissues, cells, molecules, atoms, and subatomic particles reassert themselves. The cells remember the higher order and balance of health and wholeness. Love is their reminder.

How can a seemingly ethereal energy like love remind our cells of their natural order and harmony? In *The Body Quantum*, physicist Fred Alan Wolf speculates that feelings such as love could be described in terms of the quantum properties of matter, light, and transformation (p. 266–67). Wolf is not alone in his beliefs; many physicists now believe that all matter is composed of trapped light. This belief is embodied in Einstein's famous equation $E = MC^2$. Wolf further speculates that love can be viewed in terms of the quantum statistical behavior of light particles—that is, photons. He points out that all photons tend to move into the same state, dancing the same dance, if given the opportunity. In this sense, the natural impulse of photons is a move toward unity, toward oneness. Thus, the age-old association between light and love reflects a profound wisdom.

In his book *Theories of the Chakras,* Dr. Hiroshi Motoyama reported detecting photons emitted from the heart chakra of an experienced meditator when she projected loving energy with intention (p. 276). Although the research is not yet conclusive, at this point it is reasonable to speculate that photons respond to a variety of mental and emotional states, particularly to love. How de*light*ful!

To become the light, or to be enlightened, describes and honors that quantum state of the massless, chargeless photon, which recognizes, relates, and becomes one with all.

Thanks to our inherent self-healing mechanisms, our bodies know how to heal themselves and will do so with or without the conscious expression of love. However, there are many ways that we can hinder or support these natural healing processes. As a surgeon, I can facilitate healing by paying attention to asepsis, antisepsis, and homeostasis, by carefully approximating the incised skin, and by using the appropriate suture material. What I say during the surgery, while the patient is unconscious, and how I relate to the patient following surgery can also have an effect on the patient's natural healing processes.

Knowledge, skill, attitude, belief, intention, will, laughter, love, and human caring can all facilitate the healing process. Thus, we can enhance or interfere with the body's inherent healing process. In my practice I have seen again and again how the energy of love and the creation of a loving field can profoundly enhance healing, not only physically but mentally, emotionally, and spiritually. Love is not only the stuff of poets and mystics but a tangible, transmittable energy that can produce healing.

THREE ASPECTS OF LOVE

Love, as I refer to it here, has three aspects: awareness, feeling, and action. Love is our *awareness* of the inherent connection that we share with everything else; we experience it as a *feeling;* and we express it as an *action.* Thus, love is the felt sense of knowing we are a part of everything, a recognition that each of us is a part of a vast, universal order. These connecting, unifying qualities make love the subtlest and most powerful of all energies, which is why it lies at the heart of our healing work.

Behind and between the awareness, feeling, and action of love is the energy of being—the energy of the Self. When these three aspects of the energy of love become coherent, your being universalizes, extending beyond itself to become one with All.

If we view love as a universal pattern of resonant energy, we begin to recognize it as an energetic pattern that can influence other energies to move toward wholeness and healing. Our universe can be thought of as a matrix of consciousness that emerged out of the void. Love is the connecting glue of unifying consciousness in the universe and is ever-present whether we are aware of it or not.

In discussing love, I often use the term *resonance.* When we begin to resonate lovingly with another person or thing, we become aware (consciously or unconsciously) of two vibrational systems: the self and the other—I and thou. Each separate individual or thing can operate as both a sender and a receiver as it vibrates at its particular frequency. When the waves of energy of each system vibrate at the same frequency, the result is a *coupled resonance.* With resonant awareness comes a felt connection, an awareness that you have been met.[4]

---

4. The loving feelings we experience toward another person are directly related to

Although resonance is a quality of love, merely coming into resonance with others is not to be mistaken for love. For example, you can resonate with another person's anger, fear, or sadness. Love includes but is not limited to resonance. With love there is also the feeling and awareness of being connected with another in a way that moves us toward harmony and unity.

Love can also become our state of being, characterized by the feeling and awareness of relatedness. Through the energy of love we are able to resonate not just with a special person but with our own self, with all others, with nature, and with everything else in our universe and beyond. The sense of wonder we experience when we regard a spectacular mountain vista is a felt awareness of and a resonance with nature. When love becomes second nature to us, it becomes our state of being.

LEVELS OF LOVE

Love can be experienced at the physical level, the personality level, and the higher levels of the transpersonal self. Love at the spiritual level filters down to the personality and physical levels, where it is expressed in thoughts and feelings, words and deeds. The quality of the experience of love is different at each of these levels.

When we begin to experience love at the spiritual level, the heartfelt love of our soul merges the lower and higher levels of loving awareness. At these transpersonal levels, love is characterized by resonances such as compassion, caring, peace, gratitude, and joy. As these levels evolve, our feelings and thoughts gradually dissolve

---

the resonant link we establish with that person. When in resonance with another person (or thing) you may experience a pleasant or even profound sense of your connectedness with her or him. Resonance with another person is often accompanied by a strong sense of what the person is thinking and feeling, along with empathy for him or her. It is as if a silent communication conveyed a special understanding and warmth that transcends the exchange of words; so it is that communication is established at an energetic level.

into a transcendent awareness of oneness, a state of bliss, no longer aware of the object of our relatedness but only its energetic essence. This state of love is *unconditional love.*

Unconditional Love

Unconditional love is inherent in our consciousness. We become aware of this, and of the ways in which we are all one, only as we learn to recognize the boundaries of our individual selves. We become aware of how we're one with all others in the universe only when we can see the differences that make us think and feel we are separate. Thus, your sense of separation is like the outward bound part of your journey home.

The full realization of one's self and one's value allows for the dissolution of conditional boundaries, which include our fears, our beliefs, our desires, and the state of our bodies. When these boundaries are dissolved, self and nonself come into resonance and become one. This boundless love has the capacity to resonate with all others—that is, it has a universal "frequency." In this respect, unconditional love expresses the innate harmony of the universe, the common chord that is heard in every individual song, be it the song of the atom or that of the entire universe.

Because unconditional love is inherent in the consciousness of every person, we all have had flashes, moments, or even extended periods when we experienced it. These flashes of bliss often come to us during significant events in our lives, such as a birth, the death of a loved one, the overcoming of a life-threatening illness, or a near-death experience.

For most of us, our awareness of unconditional love evolves as we grow to value and love ourselves; then we begin to relate and resonate with others through that new set of vibrations—a chord of self-value. When we relate from our sense of value and self-love, we are able to connect with the authentic self of other people, a self that is beyond the level of personality. With this resonance of unconditional love, we say "yes" from the heart.

Conditional Love

Although we all are capable of unconditional love, loving with conditions is far more common. When we love another because he or she meets our needs, we are loving conditionally. Similarly, when we give to get, we are placing conditions on our love. This is the way love is usually defined and the way most of us are brought up to understand it. Conditional love is but a pale reflection or dim remembrance of the universal force we call unconditional love.

"Falling in love" is conditional love, a projection onto our loved one of our own idealized image of him or her. In effect, our attraction to the other person is primarily our attraction to our own projection. While falling in love in this way is not unconditional, it can give us glimpses of unconditional love; through it we may be able to come to know and to relate to the essence of our own and another person's being. Having "loved and lost" is not in vain when we have allowed ourselves to seek and sense the qualities of unconditional love that lie between and beyond our projections. Such experiences illuminate the world for us through a deeply heartfelt oneness, leaving us with a new perspective from which to view all things.

Loving Expressions

Respecting others by seeing and accepting them as they are is an expression of unconditional love. When we give unconditional love, we provide people with a mirror that reflects back their own image so they can know themselves. We love unconditionally when we allow intimacy with others, granting them the freedom to be and to express themselves in new ways each day. Being committed to our own growth and that of another person is another expression of unconditional love. It is giving and caring and responding without concern for getting something in return. By expressing in these ways, you provide yourself and your loved one with feelings of security, pleasure, trust, acceptance, room for creativity and change, and permission to be vulnerable, honest, and intimate. Thus, feelings of separation, fear, shame, and abandonment are greatly reduced.

Feelings of separation that result from the feared inability to love or to be loved frequently bring illness into our lives. Illness is often a cry for help, a call for love and a deeper sense of connectedness in one's life.

Through love, we can heal and become whole again. With loving actions and felt awareness, we can experience our oneness, our universal relatedness. When we begin to love ourselves, a link is established between us and all else, and fear is dissipated. When the illusion of separation dissolves at a spiritual level, love allows us a state of oneness that harmonizes even the seemingly dissonant patterns of illness and injury. In her book *The Inward Arc,* Frances Vaughan comments:

> Wholeness is based on a balance and integration of opposites, not on getting rid of what we don't like. When we feel an inconsistency or conflict between inner experience and outer expression, between persona and shadow, fear and love, life and death, body and mind, or any other pairs of opposites, we experience pain and tension. According to ancient Hindu scriptures, the Upanishads, wherever there is other there is fear, for fear is born of duality. We can be released from fear only when we recognize the unity of opposites and learn to balance the polarities of emotional experience in a context of healing awareness (p. 66).

THE POWER OF LOVE

Unconditional love is the most readily transmittable of all the universal energies. Any information or energy pattern, any thought or feeling, that is conveyed or linked with loving energy will have a greater effect than any other transmission of subtle energy. Thus, its multidimensional pervasiveness and its capacity to serve as a universal vehicle for information makes love the most powerful of all healing energies.

Through conscious awareness of the relatedness that comes with unconditional love, the sense of separation disappears. Without separation, time and space dissolve, because they are simply measures of separation that we have structured and imposed on the universe. Similarly, without separation there is no loss of energy, no entropy. The suspension of time and space allows for the natural order and harmony inherent in the subatomic particles, atoms, molecules, cells, and tissues to unfold. Thus, unconditional loving energy is the most potent force in the cosmos.

THE TRANSPERSONAL ALIGNMENT PROCESS

The Transpersonal Alignment Process, described below, allows you to experience sending and receiving love with a partner and to experience alignment with the higher aspects of yourself. In this exercise, you evoke a loving attitude, thinking love, feeling love, and then you transfer to your partner whatever love means to you. Your feelings of love, whatever they may be, are what you'll be working with here. When your intention is to transfer loving energy there is no way you can fail with this exercise, because in the subtle realms intention is action.

 EXERCISE: TRANSPERSONAL ALIGNMENT

This exercise can be done with another person, or alone, by working with a mental image or photo of yourself or with your mirror image. Although I recommend that you do it with another person, much can be learned from both methods.

Choose a partner with whom you feel comfortable and secure. Make sure that you each give the other permission to work together. In addition, ask your partner if he or she is willing to receive love.

To begin, designate who will be the receiver of love and who the sender. The instructions below are addressed to the sender. The receiver need only sit in a relaxed position with eyes closed, receiving your loving energy. (You will reverse roles later.)

1. Sit facing your partner, close but not touching, both of you in comfortable, relaxed positions with your eyes closed.

2. Recall a time when you felt most loved or loving. Bring this moment vividly to mind, recalling details that enhance your felt sense of love.

3. Focus your attention for a moment on the center of your chest. Let yourself experience feelings of love in your heart center.

4. Shift your attention to your throat. Allow feelings of love to fill this center.

5. Shift your attention to the center of your forehead and then to the top of your head (collectively the head center). Allow feelings of love to fill this center.

6. Now imagine a radiant sphere of light, six to eight inches above the top of your head. This is the transpersonal space, the interface between your spiritual being, or higher Self, and your personality and physical form.

7. Imagine a ray of light moving down from the transpersonal space, through your head center, then down through your throat center to your heart center. In this part of the exercise you are aligning the energy centers, or chakras, above your diaphragm with your transpersonal space.

8. After aligning your energy centers in this way, focus your attention on your partner, mentally aligning his or her energy centers in the same way. To do this, focus on your partner's heart center, then throat and head centers, and finally the transpersonal space. Now imagine a ray of brilliant light from your partner's transpersonal space passing down through the energy centers to his or her heart center.

9. Link each of your own aligned centers with your partner's centers by sending a steady beam of light to each—heart to heart,

throat to throat, head to head, transpersonal space to transpersonal space.

10. Visualize intensifying the beams of light you are sending. As you do, *think loving thoughts* about your partner. In your mind, repeat three times, "I love you," using your partner's name. Try using your breath to enhance this process, breathing out each time as if you were breathing energy from your heart center to your partner's heart center.

11. Allow yourself to *feel love* from your heart to your partner's; reinforce your love by recalling, once again, how you felt when you were most loved and loving.

12. While still aligned and linked, imagine the radiant sphere above your head descending like the sun through the top of your head to the center of your chest. Allow yourself just to *be love*. You may wish to enhance this process by visualizing or imagining transparent, shimmering wings of light emanating from your shoulders, gently enfolding your partner.

13. Take a few minutes to complete this process, then withdraw the beams of light back to your centers. You may allow the light link with the transpersonal space to remain. By disconnecting in this way, you can avoid picking up thoughts and feelings that you do not want to experience.

14. Silently thank your partner for receiving this love. Open your eyes and gently touch your partner's hand, letting him or her know you are finished.

15. Now reverse roles, with the sender becoming the receiver and the receiver the sender.

16. When you are both finished, discuss with each other your experiences in this exercise.

EXERCISE: CREATING A DOUBLE
(OR USING A MIRROR)

You can do the Transpersonal Alignment exercise alone by sitting in front of a mirror or by creating a mental image of yourself sitting opposite you. Treat your mental image or your reflected image just as you did your partner in the above exercise. You can also place a photo of yourself, or another person you want to send love to, in front of you. Mentally magnify the image when you close your eyes, and go through the exercise as described.

THE PROCESS OF HEALING WITH LOVE

To use the holoenergetic healing model, we start with the premise that we have the power to choose and that change is possible. In holoenergetic healing, the intent of the observing consciousness (either the healer or the "healee") determines the forming perception and initiates the transformation of energy into matter and matter into energy. It is the observer's intent, whether conscious or unconscious, that converts the affected area of the physical body to its unifying energy or wave form, making it accessible to holoenergetic change.

Intent is a mental process; specifically, it is a planned choice. Conscious or unconscious intent brings us into resonance with what we want to access or influence. Consciousness, in this sense, is related to the "void" or fundamental field, that primordial ocean from which are formed localized whirlpools of energy called matter. In the words of Albert Einstein:

We may regard matter as being constituted by the regions of space in which the field is extremely intense. . . . There is no place in this new kind of physics both for the field and matter, for the field is the only reality.[5]

The key principle here is that the void or fundamental field, given structure by consciousness, creates the form. It is the field that becomes structured as matter. Once structured, it becomes self-organizing, able to perpetuate itself.

Health is the ability to maintain a dynamic, multilevel, multi-dimensional balance of the harmonious energy patterns of our body-minds. Healing is intended to restore this balance and harmony, thus leading us to wholeness. The template for healing—that is, the energy pattern that produces it—is inherent in the body-mind and can be accessed through choice. This inherent order and harmony can be stimulated by invoking love and by aligning with our spiritual essence.

We can work with energy in a way that heals. The principles underlying holoenergetic healing actually flow into one another; however, in order to understand the transformation, it is helpful to consider the transformational process as having four basic steps:

1. Recognition
2. Resonance
3. Release
4. Reformation

Step 1: Recognition

Before we can transform something, we must first determine what it is that we want to change to another form. In other words, we need to gain information about it. How does it look to us? Feel to us? Sound to us? What images, thoughts, emotions, or memories do we associate with this form?

We must also ask ourselves, "Why change?" Frequently the motivation to change comes out of a desire to diminish pain and fear

---

5. Albert Einstein, *Ideas and Opinions* (New York: Crown, 1954), p. 84.

in our lives. Less commonly, the motivation is to experience more growth and joy or to unfold some hidden potential. These feeling states, when brought to awareness, reach to the source of the conscious desire for change. Although we may not consciously know the ultimate source of our desire to change, that knowledge is inherent within us. Consciously, we need to know only that we want to change and what it is we want to change to initiate the holoenergetic healing process.

Step 2: Resonance

After determining what we desire to change and acquiring the necessary information, we then focus on the target through resonance, in effect blending and becoming one with it. We can resonate with the form by (1) focusing on the affected area of the body-mind or on the issue to be changed; (2) reexperiencing selected physical and emotional events associated with the issues involved; and (3) addressing the cause and source by assuming responsibility and accepting our self and the truth. We can also be inducted into a healing state by breathing techniques, by touch, by the presence of a loving, healing person, or by a heart center induction, as described in the Transpersonal Alignment Process.

Choosing to take responsibility for an event or for your life is a profound way of coming into resonance, even though you may not be consciously aware of all the causal dynamics involved. I have noticed, through my healing work, that as people begin to take responsibility for contributing to the cause of their illness, their attitude toward the whole of life starts to change. In fact, these sweeping life changes are what prompted me to call this process holoenergetic healing.

Assuming responsibility supports the belief that if you have the ability to cause an event, you also have the ability to change it. Taking responsibility in this way is empowering and, in my experience, facilitates healing. Acknowledging that at some critical point you chose how you would respond in a given situation, that you played a role in it, can be profoundly transformational.

I once met a wealthy American businessman who asked me for help while we were traveling together on a train in India. He had suffered for five months with severe back pain, despite visits to an orthopedic surgeon, a chiropractor, and an acupuncturist. I took him to an empty compartment on the train and, by using the information access processes described in chapter 12, found that his problem was related to basic survival issues. While I focused on his heart center he got in touch with an overwhelming fear of impending financial disaster. When I asked him to look at the source of the problem and his willingness to let go of it, he saw an image of his own face smiling back at him from the base of his spine. As we energetically released the image, he screamed, collapsed on the bed in the compartment, rolled up into a fetal position, and rocked back and forth for a while. When he next spoke, he reported that not only was his back pain gone but he had had a major revelation. *He was the cause of his own back pain*, he said. He was afraid of business failure and fearful that his overwhelming time commitment to business left him no time for spiritual growth. He held the subconscious belief that he would have to cause his business to fail so that he would have time to grow spiritually. He had made a choice to respond in this way, and it had manifested in pain.

Eight months later, back in the United States, I met the man again. His back pain had never returned; he had put his financial affairs in order and created time for his spiritual growth. His whole life had changed.

It is important to realize that responsibility carries no blame, with its associated judgment, guilt, and punishment. Blame implies wrongdoing and censure. There was no wrongdoing involved in our having made particular choices that may have been best under the circumstances at the time, but in the present those choices no longer serve us and function only to generate disharmony.

We can come into resonance with something by accepting it as it is; accepting the truth rather than denying it. You come into resonance with yourself by accepting and loving yourself as you are. In order to change, you have to become one with what you want to change.

When you accept and love the parts of yourself that you want to reject or to change, you create opportunity to discover the positive life force behind them. Beneath all that we do and are, beneath all of the distress and disease, no matter how deeply buried, lie seeds of positive intention; that is, in some way, at some time, the part that you now want to change or reject was intended to serve you. It allowed you to survive or seek love, or it freed or protected you. When the seed of positive intention is uncovered, it can become an ally, transforming distress and illness into health and harmony.

In a workshop, a woman with asthma told of how, at her birth, her parents tried to strangle her. They were extremely poor and "did not want to bring a child into the world to suffer as they were suffering."

In adulthood, the woman became involved in abusive relationships. Twice, people she was involved with tried to strangle her. After several painful relationships, she joined a religious group. At the time of the workshop, she'd spent six years serving others.

As she told her story, the woman began to sob, saying, "I gave to others and gave and gave, until I felt suffocated."

At this point she realized that she had always felt she didn't deserve to be alive. To justify her existence she'd had to give to others, sacrificing herself. With this realization, and holoenergetic activation, she was able to get in touch with her original positive intention, which was to experience being loved for being herself. For the first time she was able to give to and love herself. Having gotten to the source of her asthma, she could "breathe easily" for the first time in her life.

Step 3: Release

Once you have targeted the information and focused on it through resonance, you need to unform the cause of the imbalance. When you unform something, you release its present form. This represents the "death" of the form. Releasing it, whether by unforming it or absorbing it, is an inherent part of all transformation. This disintegration or change represents the law of the Hindu god Shiva, the destroyer who creates space for the new form.

Frequently, because they fear the unknown, people feel reluctant to give up the present form. ("If I give this up what will it be replaced with?") They may prefer the familiarity of the pain and disharmony to the risk and uncertainty entailed in releasing that pain. We can bridge this fear of the unknown by determining the positive intention behind the present form.

Another reason why it may not be easy for us to change is that the unformation process also involves the death of many treasured wounds, secondary gains, or payoffs. Frequently, our illnesses serve us. Sometimes the benefit can be financial, as when a person receives disability payments and as a result lacks the incentive to get well. Sometimes there are functional benefits, such as receiving help and attention from others in ways that make ill health more desirable than wellness. In addition, illness can preoccupy us and prevent us from being bored. And of course, there are the emotional benefits, which are more difficult to identify. For example, when as children we were hurt and began to cry, we got attention. From such experiences, we may have learned the value of manipulating out of weakness and our roles as victims. Under these conditions we may look at illness as an opportunity to get attention and to avoid responsibility for our growth, and an excuse to continue to blame and punish ourselves and others and then feel sorry for ourselves. The martyrdom of silent suffering can also be used to punish ourselves and induce guilt in others as a way to punish and control them.

In addition to the ways that illness can offer benefits, the healing process can be further inhibited by psychoenergetic blockages, such as shame, fear, anger, guilt, doubt, and self-pity. These emotions need to be addressed. Once we become aware of our resistance and blockages to change, we have the opportunity to make growth or fear choices.

Step 4: Reformation

Finally, we need to reform what we have unformed. Using holoenergetic techniques, we allow the body and its energy fields to return to their natural harmony or to form a new energy pattern that promotes wellness and wholeness. This is the rebirth, the resurrection, the Phoenix rising from the ashes. Responsibility for healing is taken by making the conscious choice to change and then acting on that choice. During reformation, you align your healthy, new image with your positive intention. If at that time you can take it further and align with your purpose, your vision or dream, and the higher aspects of yourself, a process of change occurs that transcends transformation. A change takes place in the way you experience the world. Your whole vibrational set is shifted to another level, where the reality created is totally different and new. At that point, you have engaged the transcendent process.

Corresponding to Recognition, Resonance, Release, and Reformation are the four guiding principles of holoenergetic healing.

Guiding Principles for Holoenergetic Healing

1. *Knowing:* Locates and illuminates what we want
2. *Loving:* Links us to what we want
3. *Willing:* Acts upon what we want
4. *Spirit:* Guides our knowing, loving, and willing

LOOKING AHEAD

Before going on to explore the four R's of holoenergetic healing in more detail, we will be turning to breath as a way of harnessing and augmenting healing energies.

4

The Breath of Healing

Every change in the physiological state is accompanied by an appropriate change in the mental-emotional state, conscious or unconscious, and, conversely, every change in the mental-emotional state, conscious or unconscious, is accompanied by an appropriate change in the physiological state.

—ELMER AND ALYCE GREEN

Breathing is often taken for granted. We can live for weeks without food and for days without water, but without breath, we would survive only minutes. Fortunately, breathing takes place automatically, without our consciously thinking about it.

Breath is life. The Latin word for breath is *spiritus,* an animating or vital principle that gives life to physical organisms. This life-giving force is reflected in the English words for breath: respiration, inspiration, and expiration. In Chinese, the word *chi* has similar dual meanings of "life" and "breath." And for the Egyptian, the symbol of the *ankh* means "the breath of life." "Life force" in Sanskrit is known as *prana.*

The ancients were well aware of the connection between spirit, life force, and breath. According to these traditions, when spirit imbues matter with its essence, life force is created.

The inner spirit inspires many to seek to identify and understand what the life force is and how it is intimately connected with breathing. If we try to understand life force at the physical level of matter, we see its effects, rather than its essence. Life force is not tangible. It cannot be captured by machines or measuring devices and thus leads much of the scientific community to deny its existence. The effect of spirit can be only sensed or intuited. To know spirit we must operate in its medium: consciousness.

The yogis have been exploring the relationship between breathing and consciousness for more than two thousand years. Some years ago, during a deep meditation, I became aware of the profound value of breathing in healing. I realized then the usefulness of controlling breathing to build and transfer energy and to create the resonance for healing to take place.

Through my study of breathing in Eastern traditions and Western scientific literature, as well as electroencephalograph (EEG) research I engaged in at a university medical center, I developed the use of controlled breathing as a major factor in my work.

In this chapter you'll find seven simple exercises introducing you to breathing techniques I found to be valuable for healing. I recommend that you pause to experience these exercises as you go along. I will be referring back to this material in succeeding chapters, so these exercises will be directly applicable throughout.

NINE KEY FUNCTIONS OF BREATH

There are nine key functions of breathing that make it a vital force in healing:

1. *Nourishment.* Breath provides our cells with oxygen, facilitating the life-giving process. Just as food nourishes the physical body, breath also nourishes the energetic aspect of the body-mind.

2. *Building energetic charge.* Breath can energize the body by building a charge, which I will describe later. In this capacity, breathing is instrumental in the intentional transfer of healing energy.

3. *Directing attention.* Breathing can help us focus and direct our attention. This is expressed in the following principle: energy flows where attention goes.

4. *Accessing information.* Controlled breathing allows us to more readily gain access to information from the subconscious mind.

5. *Altering feelings and thoughts.* Changing the way we breathe allows us to change our feelings and thoughts.

6. *Reflecting feelings and thoughts.* By observing our breathing patterns we can become aware of the effects of certain feelings and thoughts.

7. *Shifting and reflecting consciousness.* Controlled breathing, such as in meditation and some forms of psychotherapy, enables us to shift to nonordinary states of consciousness.

8. *Inducing resonance.* Breathing can facilitate coming into resonance with other energies, which is vital in transforming energy patterns of illness into patterns of health.

9. *Linking conscious and unconscious mind.* Breathing provides a gateway between the conscious mind and the physiological functions that are generally controlled by the subconscious body-mind.

BREATH AND THE NERVOUS SYSTEM

Breathing into deadened or disconnected parts of our body image is perhaps the surest way to awaken and reanimate them.

—RALPH METZNER

The nervous system is divided into two main components: the involuntary, or *autonomic,* system and the voluntary, or *somatic,* system.

The voluntary nervous system is at the service of your will or volitional expressions; that is, it comes into play whenever you move your body or express yourself in any way.

The involuntary nervous system controls bodily functions such as the beat of your heart, the release of hormones, digestion, the flow of blood, the contraction and dilation of the pupils of your eyes, and, of course, your breathing. These self-regulating functions normally occur outside your conscious control; that is, you don't have to remember to control your heartbeat or your breathing. The involuntary nervous system automatically sends out signals for all these to work interdependently and in harmony.

The autonomic nervous system can be further subdivided into the *parasympathetic* and *sympathetic* branches:

- The parasympathetic branch is associated with a state of re-laxation. Stimulation of the parasympathetic nervous system slows heart and respiration rates, via the vagus nerve, facil-itates digestion, and dilates (opens up) blood vessels, thus lowering blood pressure.
- The sympathetic branch is associated with arousal. Stimula-tion of the sympathetic branch arouses the body, increasing heart and respiration rates and bringing increased blood flow to the "big muscles" of the arms, legs, and back. The sym-pathetic branch is associated with the "fight-or-flight" re-sponse to certain kinds of personal threat or stress.

Every system of the body is part of a vast communication net-work that maintains harmony between one area and another. No organ of the body works entirely independently; rather, it receives and sends signals throughout the rest of the body. Because of this interdependence, changes in breathing patterns are registered throughout. Every organ will have a response to any changes we make in the rate or rhythm of our breathing.

Normally, you don't consciously intervene in the functions of the autonomic nervous system. You don't tell your heart how to beat or your endocrine system how much and what kinds of hor-mones it is to produce. However, you can intervene where breathing is concerned. There are a number of ways you can do this: You can hold your breath, or change how quickly, slowly, or deeply you breathe. You can emphasize specific parts of the breathing cycle over others—breathing out more quickly, breathing in slowly, or vice versa. You can breathe deeply or shallowly.

By consciously altering your breathing cycle you can profoundly affect your energy field and open yourself to expanded states of consciousness. And since breath is closely associated with life itself, changes in your breathing patterns can influence your subconscious mind, which is intimately linked with the natural healing processes of your body-mind.

Altering breath is one of the few ways you can establish an interface between the voluntary and involuntary nervous systems that together coordinate the functions of every system of the body.

Patterns of breathing reflect emotional, mental, and physical states. Each emotion and significant thought has an associated breathing pattern. When stressed or fearful, we chest breathe with shallow, rapid breaths, sometimes even holding our breath. When acting agitated we may overbreathe, that is, we hyperventilate. When being cautious we underbreathe. When we are startled we gasp, and when we are relieved we sigh. If we are suppressing sadness or grief we exhale incompletely and may limit our breathing to control the deep emotions we're feeling.

It is possible to change your breathing patterns consciously to influence your thoughts and feelings and even alter your state of consciousness. In addition to enhancing the healing process, controlled breathing can be a valuable complement in stress management and in meditation.

THE PHYSIOLOGY OF
DIAPHRAGMATIC BREATHING

The act of breathing in is accomplished primarily through the sympathetic nervous system; breathing out is generally passive and is thus influenced by the parasympathetic system.

When you breathe in, your diaphragm and the muscles between your ribs contract. As the diaphragm (a dome-shaped muscle between the chest and abdominal cavities) contracts, it flattens and moves down, causing the chest cavity to expand, drawing air in. A downward motion of the diaphragm exerts pressure on organs of the abdomen, causing the abdomen to expand.

During normal expiration the diaphragm relaxes and air is released from the lungs. Expiration can, however, be assisted by contracting the intercostal and abdominal muscles, forcing air out of the lungs.

The stressful environment of contemporary life has led to the habit of rapid, irregular breathing that takes place predominantly in the upper chest. This breathing pattern stresses the heart, limits blood flow, accounts for lower oxygenation of the blood, and tends to keep us emotionally stressed. We can reduce this form of stress through diaphragmatic breathing, which provides us with an example of the potential healing effects of breath.

A number of benefits are derived from employing diaphragmatic breathing. Deeper breathing brings air to the lower lobes of the lungs, which are more richly endowed with blood vessels than the upper and middle lobes. This means that more oxygen can be absorbed into the blood. Chest breathing, which expands primarily the middle lobes of the lungs, results in less air coming in and thus less oxygenation of the blood.

Deep breathing also lowers pressure within the chest cavity, improving blood circulation and making it easier for blood to return to the heart. This reduces the load on the heart.

Continuous deep breathing generates considerable body energy, which can build up at areas of blockage or tension. This confluence of energy may activate repressed images and feelings, creating discomfort until it is released.

✤ EXERCISE: DIAPHRAGMATIC BREATHING

1. Sit on the forward edge of a comfortable chair and lean back so that you are slightly reclining.
2. Place one hand, palm down, a few inches above your navel. Place the other palm on the center of your chest.

3. Start by exhaling completely, as though you were breathing a sigh of relief, releasing as much of the air in your lungs as possible. This allows you to breathe more deeply and fully on your next inhalation.

4. Draw in your next breath while imagining that your lower chest and abdomen are expanding like a balloon, being filled with air, and notice that your abdomen is expanding more than your chest.

5. As you breathe out, imagine this balloon deflating and flattening.

6. After three to four diaphragmatic breaths, become aware of how you feel.

Is your body more relaxed?

Are you feeling more peaceful?

Is your mind more calm?

Frequently, people experience all three of these feelings when they practice diaphragmatic breathing.

HOW BREATHING BUILDS ENERGY

One of the major functions of breathing is to energize the physical body. Breathing charges the body in several ways: through cellular respiration, through the inspiration of ionized air, and through the shearing action of blood flow, which I'll explain in a moment.

During inspiration, oxygen is absorbed from the atmosphere. This oxygen is transported via the bloodstream to the cells, where it undergoes a process in which electrons are released as a way of transferring energy; this process is called *cellular respiration*. It serves to increase the body's electrical charge. A by-product of cellular respiration is the release of carbon dioxide, which is carried away from the cells to the lungs, then expelled from the body. Interestingly, it is not the need for oxygen but rather the level of carbon dioxide (waste products in the air inside the lungs) that stimulates the next breath.

Breathing also allows for the absorption from the air of electrically charged particles known as negative and positive ions. Research has shown that negative ions facilitate the removal of carbon dioxide from the body as well as the passage of oxygen through the air sacs of the lungs into the bloodstream. Positive ions seem to have the opposite effect.

Waterfalls, rain, a moist environment, and electrical storms all produce negative ions, which energize our systems. Conversely, dry, hot winds and air conditioners can produce positive ions, which tend to devitalize our systems.

As blood flows through the body, blood cells rub against one another and against blood vessel walls. This tumbling, rubbing action shears electrons from the surfaces contacted. As you breathe, the movements of your chest and diaphragm alter blood flow in the major vessels of the chest and affect the heart rate. These beneficial fluctuations in blood flow augment the shearing effect, which enhances the body's electromagnetic field. The acceleration-deceleration of charged particles, resulting from alternating blood flow, further amplifies the electromagnetic field, as I will describe in the following section.

Physiology of the Pulsed Breath

The pulsed breath is one of the most important techniques used in the Release and Reformation phases of holoenergetic healing. Through the pulsed breath we can release unwanted energy patterns, making room for the new.

There are two types of pulsed breaths. They are

- *The Ex-Pulse Breath.* To ex-pulse, draw your breath in and hold it. Then sharply exhale through your nose while forcefully contracting your abdominal muscles.

- *The In-Pulse Breath.* To in-pulse, take in a short, sharp breath through your nose while contracting your abdominal muscles.

You can ex-pulse your breath to clear your body from unwanted charges, negative thoughts, feelings, discomfort, or pain. The technique can also be used to rid yourself of other people's energy when you feel it is affecting you adversely.

You can in-pulse your breath to release, reform, or withdraw an energy pattern. The short, sharp pulses of this type of breathing create an electromagnetic flux that facilitates all the processes of holoenergetic healing.

When we unform or release something through the pulsed breath, we free ourselves of it. There are three ways of doing this. One is to put so much energy into a structure that it can no longer contain it (ex-pulse) and explodes like an overinflated balloon. A second way is to withdraw so much energy from a structure that it can't sustain itself (in-pulse) and collapses like a deflated balloon. A third way is to envision the transfer of energy from a structure with the intention that it become absorbed and transformed into another existing structure.

In self-healing work you generally use the ex-pulse, that is, a sharp outward release of air, to disrupt a disharmonious pattern in your own energy field. In doing healing work on others, the in-pulse breath, a sharp inhalation, is more frequently used for the withdrawal of the energy pattern being transformed.

✪ EXERCISE: BREATHING FOR INCREASED AWARENESS

Body Awareness

1. Sit in a comfortable position with your back straight. Take a few moments to become more aware of your breathing, an activity that only a moment ago you were engaged in without thinking about.

2. While you're still aware of your breathing, focus your attention on your breath itself as it passes in and out through your nostrils. Notice if the air seems to move more easily through one

nostril than the other. Notice how your nostrils move slightly as you breathe. Notice the coolness of the air as it enters and the warmth as it is released.

Emotional Awareness

1. To become aware of how your thoughts and feelings influence your breath, take several diaphragmatic breaths.

2. Next, think of a situation or person you associate with stress or anxiety in your life. Vividly imagine that situation or individual and allow yourself to feel related emotions. Observe any change in your breathing—its rate, depth, location.

3. Then resume diaphragmatic breathing. What do you notice? Did the feelings associated with the anxiety dissipate?

With practice, people find they can shift their emotions at will through breathing.

Awareness of Change

You are probably aware that your breathing pattern changes with physical activity. To sense the effect that even a small change in posture has on breath, try the following exercise:

1. Sit in a comfortable position with your back straight. Close your eyes to enhance awareness.

2. Place your hands on your knees, palms up.

3. Notice what part of your body moves as you are breathing. Is it the upper, middle, or lower chest or abdomen that moves most?

4. Now, turn your hands palms down on your knees and notice any change in location of breath movement.

You may notice that with your hands turned palms upward your breath seems to move lower in your chest and may even include abdominal movement. The palms-down position is often associated with midchest movements. Some people find just the opposite to be true, with deepest breathing occurring when the palms are down.

Simply note the differences in the patterns of your breathing when you make even these subtle changes in posture.

THE FOUR PHASES OF HOLOENERGETIC BREATH

Breathing is normally an automatic function, a two-phase cycle of inspiration and expiration with no conscious intervention. In holoenergetic healing, we also employ a four-phase breathing cycle, one that yogis have used for thousands of years in their meditative practice (see the chart on p. 92). In the East, the control of breath forms the basis for the practice of *pranayama,* literally, the science of withholding the breath.

The four phases of holoenergetic breath are as follows.

1. Pause—The Rest Before Inspiration

Since all processes begin by creating space, a breathing cycle begins when you exhale completely, evacuating air from your lungs, thus creating space for the next inhalation.

This space can be regarded metaphorically as being the void, a state of no motion, or absolute motion, from which everything originates and unfolds. Space is not empty. It contains enormous energy. Physicist David Bohm calculated that the energy contained in one cubic centimeter of space is more than the energy of all the matter in our known universe.

When you have completely exhaled and are in a state of conscious awareness at rest, a tension starts to develop and you begin to focus your awareness as attention. The basis for your attention is the desire for inspiration; the desire to breathe, to move, or to change. This building of tension from the void is the source of creative energy for change.

Metaphysically, the void is the space from which desire arises and vibration begins. Vibration sets up electromagnetic, gravitational, and acoustic patterns that we may perceive through our nervous system as "substance" in the form of sensation or physical matter. Similarly, we perceive the "substance" of our mind as thought and feeling.

2. Inspiration—Drawing Air into the Body

Inspiration is the doing or active phase of breathing. It involves the contraction of the muscles of respiration, influenced by the sympathetic nervous system. During inspiration your body takes in the "spirit," the life-giving component of the air. This is where you build power and the ability to act. This is where your "energy battery" is charged. In Eastern traditions, inspiration is associated with the yang energy of the breathing cycle known as our masculine or active side (see fig. 3).

It is inspiration that gives us an idea. An idea is the substance of desire beginning to take form—it is an emerging thought and feeling.

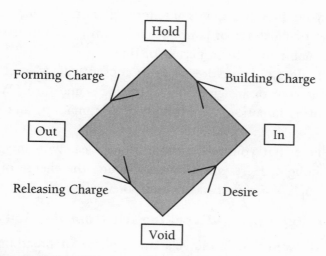

FIGURE 3 Building Charge with Breath

The Four Phases of Holoenergetic Breathing

REST/PAUSE	INSPIRATION	REST/HOLD	UNASSISTED* EXPIRATION
Awareness	doing	Retention	allowing
A-tension	active	Re-tension	passive
Attention	contraction	Intention	relaxation
	diaphragm	In-tension	yin
	intercostals		parasympathetic
	yang		influence
	sympathetic		
	influence		
Being	>Becoming	>>Becoming	<Becoming

*Expiration can be assisted by abdominal and intercostal muscles or unassisted with expulsion of air due primarily to elasticity and surface tension of the lungs. Expiration normally occurs when respiratory muscles relax.

3. Hold—The Rest Between Inspiration and Expiration

Holding your breath requires intention. It is the energy of desire given a particular form or plan. When breath is held in tension, the charge is maintained for a period of time.

The holding phase expresses your chosen will. Metaphorically, your will is your desire given persistent focus and form. Will often takes form as intention, determination, imagination, and expectation.

It is here that you give form to your idea, with imagery and focused thought. Here you are transforming the energy of an idea into a thought form that has causal potency.

4. Expiration—Expelling Air from the Body

Unassisted expiration is the relaxation phase of breathing and is influenced by the parasympathetic nervous system. Air is allowed to be released passively, primarily by the elasticity of the lungs. When you breathe out with intention, you can energize that toward which your breath is consciously directed. Directing the release of built-up tension allows for the transfer of energy and information.

Relaxed expiration is the polar complement of inspiration and as such is considered part of our feminine side or yin.

Upon releasing your breath you manifest in action the feeling, thought, or idea that you have formed and charged with energy and intent in the Holding phase of breathing. For example, a weight lifter lifts upon expiration, and gymnasts time certain precise movements with exhalation.

After expiration, you again enter the void. If you did not take another breath you would soon die and de-part in the void. In the void your receptivity to information and creative energy is enhanced. This is also a time when you are more vulnerable to external influence (see fig. 4).

When a desire first comes out of the void it conveys the potential choice. At this stage it is substance without form, energy in motion. You may become aware of the vague desire to move, to go for a walk. As this feeling grows, you build the inspiration or idea. As you hold that idea you begin forming the thought, giving the substance structure, depth, and breadth, finally transforming it into action.

You can focus the thought and give it more and more form: "I will go for a walk up the mountain and walk to the summit to watch the sunset. I will take a jug of water with me." As you release the thought, you manifest the action, transmitting the energy of thought to your creation—taking the walk. Like the decision to go for a walk, the four-part breath cycle takes us through the conscious creation, formation, and transmission of a thought or feeling from energy to form to action (see fig. 5).

In his book *The Power of Myth*, Joseph Campbell elaborates on the metaphysical aspects of the four-phase breath cycle expressed in the AUM sound in meditation (p. 231). AUM is regarded in several ancient traditions to be the oldest sacred sound. In the Bible it is

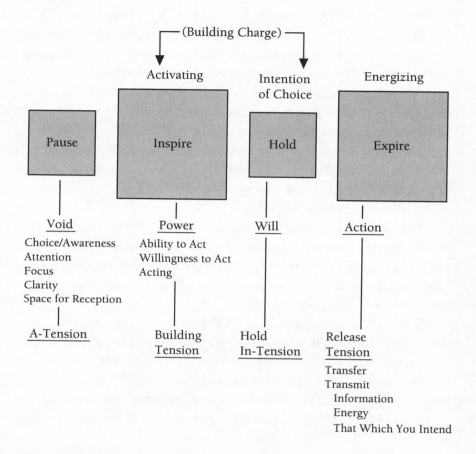

FIGURE 4 Energizing Breath

written: "First there was the word." Some mystics interpret that cosmic word to be AUM:

"A," the birth, corresponds to the action of inspiration.

"U," the becoming, corresponds to the holding after inspiration.

"M," the dissolution, corresponds to expiration.

Finally, AUM returns to the silence out of which it arose. This is the void that corresponds to the pause.

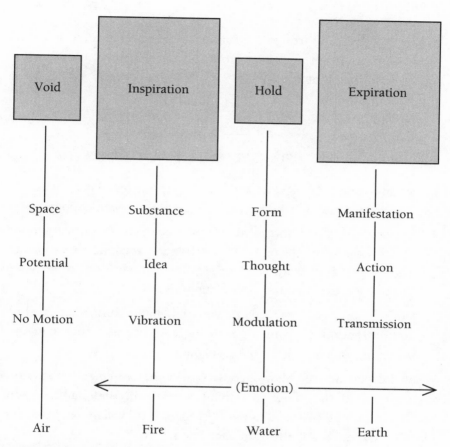

FIGURE 5 Esoteric Functions of Breath

FOCUSING ATTENTION THROUGH BREATH

Attention is focused awareness, which allows you to define and refine a specific content or subject of that awareness. Through awareness you develop your ability to make choices. Only when you are aware of the present circumstances, as well as your alternatives, can you take charge of your life.

You can learn to focus and shift your attention consciously and purposefully, using the following breathing exercise. By practicing attention you gain the capacity to direct your energy simply by choosing what to focus on.

As you proceed through the following exercise, become aware of how your attention energizes your body and how adding your breath amplifies that energy.

✹ EXERCISE: FOCUSING ATTENTION WITH BREATH

1. Sit in a relaxed position with your eyes closed. Focus your attention on your left hand. Become aware of what happens.

2. Imagine breathing into and out of your left hand, with your breath coming in through all five fingers. Imagine that you are drawing the breath up your wrist, then release it again out your fingers. Repeat this and notice any effects.

3. Draw your breath in through your left hand. Immediately shift your attention to your right hand and imagine that you are breathing out through your right hand.

What did you notice? Many people report that when they focus on their left hand they feel warmth or tingling in that hand. When breath and attention shifts to the other hand, they also experience a sense of the energy shifting to that hand.

Experiment with this exercise. Use your imagination to add form to the energy created by your attention and breath. You could, for example, add the image of warmth by picturing your hand igniting into flame from your breath, just as the burning embers of a fire burst into flame with a gust of wind. Or you might imagine your palms cooling as you bring your breath through them. The use of imagery can thus add form to the energy created by your attention and breath.

Some biofeedback trainers have found that headache symptoms are often reduced when people master the technique of warming the hands, particularly the palms.

Energizing and Relaxing Breaths

By emphasizing inspiration over expiration, you enable your body to build energy, or to build up a charge. Conversely, when you extend expiration so it is longer than inspiration, you allow your body to feel more relaxed.

- Emphasized inspiration—builds charge
- Emphasized expiration—releases charge

⊛ EXERCISE: ENERGIZING BREATH

Begin by exhaling completely. Then, inhale through your nose about twenty times with short, forceful breaths. Don't be concerned about expiration—just let it occur as it will. When you do this correctly it sounds like a steam locomotive. Note the effects of this kind of breathing on your body. What affect does it have on your feelings? People in my workshops generally report sensations of tingling, warmth, lightheadedness, and increased vitality; all of these are expressions of energy.

⊛ EXERCISE: RELAXING OR RELEASING BREATH

1. Begin by exhaling completely.
2. Then inhale gently and easily through your nose to the count of three. Then let the breath out to the count of six.
3. Do this three times and notice its effects, as you did at the end of the Energizing Breath exercise.

Most people report that this exercise helps them feel more relaxed.

ACCESSING INFORMATION FROM THE SUBCONSCIOUS MIND

Controlled breathing can be used to gain access to long-forgotten memories or new information held in the subconscious mind. By

---

voluntarily holding your breath in the way described here, you can directly gain the attention of your subconscious mind. One of the functions of the subconscious mind is to help your body maintain physiological balance, or *homeostasis,* so it is sometimes called the "body-mind." Controlled breath can be particularly useful for the Release and Reformation stages of holoenergetic healing.

Holding breath for healing, however, needs to be distinguished from the chronic form of breath holding associated with the suppression or dulling of fear or anxiety. Holding breath as an attention-focusing form of breathing becomes a valuable tool for healing because it is the subconscious mind that mediates the healing response.

In my workshops I describe the interaction as follows:

> We're going along and everything is fine. Then we take a deep breath and hold it. The carbon dioxide level starts to build up in our system, and the subconscious mind, which speaks mostly through images, symbols, and physiological communication with the autonomic nervous system, says: "Hey, the carbon dioxide level is building up. What is going on? What are you doing? What do you want?" Now you've gotten the attention of your subconscious mind. You say, "Listen, this is what I want you to do. I want you to mobilize white blood cells to this specific area." The subconscious mind then replies: "Yes, I get the message and I'll do it." You say, "Good, now I will breathe again."

Once you have the attention of your subconscious mind, you can tell it what you want it to do. The subconscious mind acts as a filter between the unconscious and the conscious mind. Beliefs and attitudes have representations in the subconscious to which we must gain access for healing. Retrieval of deep-seated information and reprogramming are both facilitated by using breath in specific ways. You can do this by simply holding your breath as you consciously request desired information.

COMING INTO RESONANCE

In his book *Stalking the Wild Pendulum,* Itzhak Bentov writes that when you hold your breath your heart rate slows and your heart and aorta together become a resonant system. Normally, when blood is pumped from your heart into the aorta it travels, under the pressure of the heart's pulse, down the trunk of your body to your pelvis. Near your pelvis, the aorta bifurcates, or separates, into two large blood vessels carrying blood into your legs. When this pressure pulse strikes the bifurcation it rebounds back up the aorta like an echo, colliding with the new pulse moving down. A dissonant interference pattern is created, much like two waves crashing into each other, creating turbulence, resulting in irregular micromovements of the body.

However, when you hold your breath, your heart slows so that the echo and the pressure pulse become coordinated and travel together in synchrony. Such a system is said to be *in resonance.* The body is now resonating in a rhythmic pattern of approximately 7.5 cycles per second. At the same time, this rhythm comes into resonance with two other important rhythms, notably the brain wave patterns of the deeply receptive state between the alpha and theta waves (between 7 and 8 cycles per second), and the natural pulsations of the earth-ionosphere cavity, which is about 7.8 cycles per second.

By holding our breath, we bring our body into resonance with itself, with the rhythms of the brain in its most receptive state, and with the rhythms of our planet. This synchrony greatly facilitates the reception and transfer of information and energy, both of which are critical components of healing.

✦ EXERCISE: ACCESSING INFORMATION

- To experience the enhanced receptivity of the Pause phase of breathing, first clearly formulate in your mind a question you want to ask. You may prefer to write the question down on paper.

- As before, begin with an exhalation. Then draw air into your lungs as you close your eyes.
- Hold your breath and ask yourself for the information you want.
- Now, completely relax your chest and abdomen, silently releasing your question along with your breath.
- Then free your mind of effort and thought and allow information to begin coming in during a five- to ten-second pause before the next inspiration.
- If you do not receive the information you asked for the first time, suspend for a moment all judgment of, or attachment to, the content of the information and be open to whatever comes. Then repeat the exercise.

THE BALANCING BREATH

While doing research at a university biofeedback laboratory on the relationship of breath to brain wave activity, I discovered a breathing technique that I found to be of great value in healing work. I refer to this as the *balancing breath*. Its value to us is that it allows us to rapidly expand and elevate consciousness by synchronizing the right and left hemispheres of the brain. Balancing of the brain hemispheres brings the mind into a state of resonant coherence.

As part of my early research, I explored an ancient yogic technique for balancing the brain hemispheres. The technique, called alternate nostril breathing, involves alternately compressing and releasing the nostrils with the fingers while breathing, thus first inhaling on one side, then exhaling on the other.

I did this exercise while being monitored by an electroencephalograph (EEG), which measured activity in the right and left hemispheres of my brain. I noticed that the use of my hand to perform the balancing breath technique, as prescribed by the yogis, created an unbalanced hemispheric pattern. But then, when I kept my hands

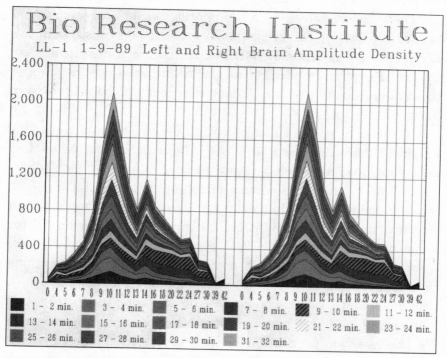

FIGURE 6 Left and Right Brain Amplitude Density

relaxed in my lap and simply imagined air moving in one nostril, then out the other, and so on, an interesting thing occurred. The EEG showed that the right and left hemispheres of my brain came into synchrony, producing what is referred to as hemispheric coherence. My brain wave activity displayed a synchronous alpha brain wave pattern (about 7 to 8 cycles per second) for both hemispheres (see fig. 6).

This state of resonance, brought about through the balancing breath, enhances performance on many levels, and is especially valuable for healing work. Initially, however, it isn't easy to stay in this state of balanced hemispheric coherence for long periods of time.

Balancing breath is most effective when practiced just before healing yourself and others, or as preparation for meditation.

There are several ways breathing brings us into balance. Rhythmic, even breathing can bring about autonomic nervous system balance because inspiration arouses sympathetic nervous system activity, while expiration elicits parasympathetic activity. Breathing in through one nostril and out through the other adds another level of balance.

When we achieve a balance between the two hemispheres of the brain, it is known in the East as the balance of yin and yang. How does your body accomplish such a balance?

In your natural automatic breathing pattern, the air flow through one nostril predominates for about ninety minutes; then a switch occurs and air flow is greater through the other nostril for about ninety minutes.

You can determine which nostril you are primarily breathing through by wetting the palm of your hand and breathing into it to determine which side is cooler. Or you can compress each nostril while breathing in to determine which is easier to breathe through.

The switch in nostril dominance every ninety minutes is mediated by the hypothalamus, which essentially controls the autonomic nervous system. Blood vessels that supply the mucous membrane of the nasal passages are under the control of sympathetic and parasympathetic portions of the autonomic nervous system. Through alternate sympathetic constriction and parasympathetic dilation of these small blood vessels, the nasal passages either allow more air flow or become congested.

Nasal dominance can have a significant effect on our thinking, as well as on our moods and our state of consciousness.

When we breathe in through the left nostril, the right brain hemisphere is stimulated. Conversely, when we breathe in through the right nostril, the left brain hemisphere is stimulated. D. A. Werntz, a researcher conducting a study at the University of California at San Diego School of Medicine, demonstrated that breathing through one nostril generated EEG activity in the opposite brain hemisphere.[2]

The right and left hemispheres of the brain have different functions. Characteristically, the left hemisphere is associated with verbal, linear, rational activities, while the right hemisphere is generally associated with spatial, nonlinear, intuitive activities. Werntz showed that when nostril dominance was forced to a particular side of the brain, the task performance associated with that side was enhanced. Right nostril breathing, for instance, improved the verbal skills associated with the left hemisphere, while left nostril breathing improved the intuitive or spatial skills associated with the right hemisphere.

Moods and emotions often thought of as negative or contractive, such as anger, depression, or fear, seem to focus in the right hemisphere of the brain. More positive or expansive emotions, such as joy and gratitude, focus in the left brain.

You can change dominance, regardless of which side is dominant at the moment, by directing or imagining breath coming in through the opposite nostril. If, for instance, you want to stimulate more intuitive activity, you can start breathing in through your left nostril several times by compressing the right nostril, or by simply imagining your breath coming through your left nostril.

David S. Shannahoff-Khalsa, a colleague of Werntz's, states that appetite and digestion are greater during right nostril/left brain dominance. He also points out that left nostril emphasis is more beneficial for receiving new ideas, while right nostril emphasis facilitates speaking abilities.[3]

2. D. A. Werntz, R. G. Bickford, D. S. Shannahoff-Khalsa, "Selective Hemispheric Stimulation by Unilateral Forced Nasal Breathing," *Human Neurobiology* 6: 165–171.

3. D. S. Shannahoff-Khalsa, *Energy Medicine Around the World*, T. M. Srinwasan, ed. (Phoenix, AZ: Gabriel Press, 1988), pp. 89–110.

Nostril dominance affects our autonomic nervous system so that not only one side of the brain but one side of the entire body will have greater sympathetic activity at any given time.

Studies with volunteers have shown that when blood is drawn from each arm at regular intervals, the level of norepinephrine produced by the sympathetic nervous system is always significantly higher on the side correlating with nostril dominance. This demonstrates that the body, as well as the brain, switches dominance at regular intervals.

By breathing through both nostrils simultaneously after the balancing breath, you can further enhance balance between the two hemispheres of the brain and the functions associated with them. Breathing through both nostrils at the same time may also help generate a natural crossover of dominance. When a ninety-minute cycle ends, it takes about ten minutes for nostril dominance to change naturally from one side to the other. This crossover period correlates with peak task performance of the skills associated with both hemispheres and with balanced nostril dominance. By breathing through both nostrils simultaneously, you can generate this crossover at will.

Although normally we achieve a balance between the two hemispheres over a period of time, it is useful to achieve this balanced state in the moment. The balancing breath can be used before and during meditation, healing, or counseling to shift consciousness into the transpersonal dimension.

The following exercise allows you to bring both hemispheres into balance.

✦ EXERCISE: THE BALANCING BREATH

1. Assume a comfortable, relaxed position.
2. Gently close your eyes.

3. Exhale, allowing your lungs to empty and relax.

4. As you breathe in, imagine your breath coming in through your left nostril, then up to the center of your forehead.

5. As you exhale, imagine your breath coming out your right nostril.

6. Next, inhale through your right nostril, up to the center of your forehead. Exhale through your left nostril.

7. Breathe in the way described for seven cycles. (Each inhalation followed by an exhalation is one complete cycle.)

8. On your eighth cycle, breathe in through both nostrils simultaneously. Hold that breath for a moment and focus your attention on the center of your forehead.

9. Release your breath as if you were exhaling it through your forehead. This opens up your sixth chakra, or energy center, the center of the intuitive functions of your mind.

As you do this exercise, try to involve as many senses as you can. For example, as you breathe in, notice that the air flowing through your nostrils feels cool. Notice how it feels warmed in your nostrils as you exhale. As you breathe, air moves the tiny hairs that line your nasal passages. Allow yourself to sense these movements.

You might also imagine that you are breathing in light or color, or even a fragrance, such as that of a rose. If you want to balance or increase the energy of a certain chakra, you might now refer to the chakra chart in chapter 3 and imagine yourself breathing in the color that corresponds with that particular chakra. Or you can breathe in the seven chakra colors during the seven cycles, which helps to balance your entire subtle energy system.

What's exciting about the balancing breath is that it enables you to make one brain hemisphere more dominant, or to bring both hemispheres and your autonomic nervous system into balance as you choose. Through your breathing, you can consciously influence your body, your feelings and thoughts, and your state of consciousness.

The balancing breath links you with your spirit, and it helps to bring healing into the realm of conscious choice.

THE BALANCING BREATH AND TRANSPERSONAL STATES

When both hemispheres are brought into balance, as happens with the balancing breath, consciousness is shifted into the transpersonal dimension. This balanced and synchronous state may be accompanied by a release of energy, sometimes seen as light. The release of energy may be sensed as a blue light; in Eastern traditions, this light is sometimes referred to as the Blue Pearl.

As I explored the balancing breath, I realized that when I saw the Blue Pearl, there had been a subtle energetic fusion of my right and left hemispheres. Along with the light I experienced a sense of inner peace and unity. My consciousness at that moment seemed to expand to an area just above my head, which is often referred to as the *transpersonal space*.

In this inclusive state of consciousness, it became obvious to me that it takes energy to maintain the illusion of separation, just as it takes energy to maintain a separation of charge across cell membranes or in a battery. Therefore, when whatever is held to be separate is unified, energy is released. This is the energy of synergy, the energy of the unified whole that is greater than the sum of its parts. To the extent that we open ourselves to the transpersonal realms of consciousness—through such activities as meditation and conscious breathing—the energy we use to maintain the illusion of separateness is no longer needed, and is released as light.

In ordinary states of consciousness, where one brain hemisphere or the other is dominant, the illusion of separation is maintained. This illusion frequently causes us to feel alienated from our center or source; we experience this as a fear of loss or abandonment and as a sense of being out of touch with our true nature. We are not, at that time, in resonance with our own bodies, our own minds, or our own selves, nor are we in a resonant relationship with the universe. Conversely, in those moments when we experience oneness and come into alignment with our source, or true nature, we no longer feel alone or abandoned. We are coming home, in resonance with our source.

If we remain misaligned or separated from our source, we eventually become ill, which reminds us to come back into resonant unity. The essence of healing, then, is to become one with the source of our being.

I like the way the Gospel of Thomas addresses the illusion of separation and duality and the unity of matter and spirit:

> *Jesus saw children who were being suckled.*
> *He said to his disciples:*
> *These children who are being suckled*
> *are like those who enter the Kingdom.*
>
> *They said unto him:*
> *Shall we then, being children,*
> *enter the Kingdom?*
>
> *Jesus said to them:*
> *When you make the two one,*
> *and when you make the inner as the outer*
> *and the outer as the inner,*
> *and the above as the below,*
> *and when you make*
> *the male and the female into a single one,*
> *so that the male will not be male*
> *and the female not be female,*
> *then shall you enter the Kingdom.*[4]

---

4. Gospel of Thomas, II, 2, 22.

SPECULATIONS ON ENERGY, BREATH, AND HEALING

In the study of energetic systems we find that when a wave of a particular frequency and amplitude meets a wave coming from the opposite direction of the same frequency and amplitude, a standing wave occurs at the point where they meet and resonate. The pattern created by the two waves at this juncture then becomes self-organizing; it becomes a template that tends to seek like forms and to perpetuate itself.

To use an analogy: in a pipe organ, the length and size of the pipe determines the form of the standing wave; when air is pumped through the pipe it sets up a standing wave (which we experience as sound) characteristic of that form.

When frequencies merge to create resonant standing waves, they generate the formation of geometric energy patterns or templates that are capable of storing and transmitting information to other forms that resonate with them. This is how the interactions of two or more energy fields create form.

When the right and left hemispheres of the brain come into synchrony, they energetically fuse to create a standing wave form that resonates with the transpersonal space. This shifts our perceptions from the body-mind realm to the spiritual realm.

Within the energetic model of holoenergetic healing, beliefs, thoughts, and feelings have energetic signatures; that is, a particular individual's feeling of unworthiness would have a specific, recognizable form that is as unique to that person as his or her hand-written signature. When we believe or feel something, that belief or feeling creates a specific energetic form. That form exists within the energy fields of our own body-mind, but it can also extend outward, like a radar system seeking and/or creating matching forms with which to resonate in the external world.

The energetic templates or holoforms of our thoughts and feelings seek out circumstances (other people, experiences, physical forms, etc.) that are supportive of those templates. In other words, the energetic forms of our own beliefs, thoughts, and feelings tend to find other people or situations that confirm, validate, prove, or justify them. If our energy configures as a victim form we'll tend to gravitate toward circumstances that make it appear that the world is our victimizer. And if our energy takes a more active and self-actualizing form we'll tend to gravitate toward circumstances that make it appear that the world is filled with opportunity and re-sources. The resonance between the external world and the forms established within our own energy fields creates what we perceive as our individual reality.

In holoenergetic healing, we use breathing to focus and amplify desire, will, intention, and imagination (mental imagery). Controlled breathing reinforces the chosen conditions by creating a standing wave resonance (organizing energy field) within us that attracts to itself, from the world around us, forms like itself.

For example, we might have a fear of intimacy that we want to heal because we have met someone with whom we would like to share a long-term relationship. We begin with the desire to change the energy pattern that expresses that fear. Then we discover the source and the positive intent behind the fear. We create the mental image of a new form in which we see ourselves as freely receiving and giving love. However, just having created that new form is not enough; we then commit our will to maintain the form in which we are ready to freely receive and give love. Then we employ intention to establish a plan for moving forward with this new form, express-ing it and maintaining it as an organizing energy field to attract like forms from the world around us.

At each step, from desire through forming a mental image and on through developing a plan to assertively move that new form out into the world with us, we use the breathing exercises described in this chapter to focus and amplify our endeavor. This process, am-plified by the appropriate conscious breathing methods, sparks the energy that moves us toward change, both inner and outer—toward our desired reality.

Also, by consciously using breathing we can balance the hemispheres of our brains and create a sense of unity within ourselves: a sense of balance between the polarities of the inspirational breath of life and the expirational breath of death; of the active and the passive; of the sympathetic and the parasympathetic; of the masculine and the feminine. All these polarities can be brought into balance through a rhythmic pattern of breathing.

Thus, balancing the hemispheres of our brains with the balancing breath coheres a state of consciousness that profoundly facilitates the healing process.

✸ EXERCISE: STRUCTURED WINE OR WATER

We can demonstrate the transference of loving energy in a practical way by restructuring wine. This simple exercise in energy transference forms the basis for distant healing, telepathic communication, and blessing food and wine.

This exercise can be performed with water by those who prefer to abstain from alcohol.

1. Open a bottle of wine or mineral water and pour it into two glasses, labeling them A and B. Remove B from the area.

2. Set glass A down in front of you. Place your hands around the glass without touching it or touching your hands together.

3. Recall a time when you felt most loved or loving. Feel that sense of love in the center of your chest. Breathe in and out through your chest as you allow the feeling of love to expand.

4. If you are using wine, take a moment to become aware of the source—grapes once living on vines. Allow yourself to feel a sense of gratitude toward this fruit that, instead of dying on the vine, sacrificed itself for your nourishment and enjoyment. Allow yourself to imagine the possibility that these grapes have a consciousness, and let your love and gratitude acknowledge their

sacred gift of life energy. Allow yourself to sense these feelings of love and gratitude. If you are using water, allow yourself to feel gratitude and love for the gift of life that water gives us.

Breathing Cycle

1. Focus your attention on the wine or water and breathe its essence in through the center of your chest. If you close your eyes as you breathe in, it will be easier to do this. Hold the image or sense of the wine or water in the center of your chest. Feel your love and gratitude merging with the essence of the wine.

2. Now, using intention, transfer your loving energy by releasing your breath as if from the center of your chest into the wine or water in the glass.

3. Once again, breathe the essence of the wine or water into the center of your chest. As you inhale, imagine your breath moving up into your shoulders. As you exhale, imagine your breath moving down your arms, through your hands, into the wine or water, infusing it with your love and gratitude.

4. Repeat the breathing cycle three times.

5. Wait at least ten minutes. Then compare the aroma and taste of the wine or water in each glass. Note any differences. Sometimes tiny bubbles form in the structured wine or water. Most people say the quality of the structured wine or water is enhanced. As a matter of individual taste, some prefer the nonstructured wine or water.

To demonstrate the effectiveness of energy transference at a distance, repeat this exercise but omit the step using your hands. The wine or water can be placed across the room or even in another room. Transfer your energy from your heart center to the wine or water as described.

The energy field of the structured wine or water will persist for days, even months, after the wine or water has been "blessed." You can also bless food this way. Not only does the act of blessing energize you directly, but the food and drink now become additional sources of loving energy. Your own love is fed back to you through whatever you structure in this way.[5]

With overviews of the holoenergetic healing process and breath in mind, let us now move forward to examine each of the Four R's in detail. In the next two chapters, we'll be exploring Recognition, the first R. It consists of two chapters because there are two phases to Recognition. Phase One involves rational knowing; it uses verbal processes to begin to discover and explore the forms of the present energy you desire to change. Phase Two is intuitive; in this phase, you'll be using intuitive methods to access information at an energetic level.

---

5. In chapter 6, I will explore biomechanical testing with L-rods to measure energy fields. You may want to save these samples to later test the energetic levels of the wine or water. You will find instructions for how to evaluate structured wine or water in the same chapter.

PART TWO

5

Recognition—Rational Knowing

Truth is whole and cannot be known by part of the mind.
—A COURSE IN MIRACLES

You are now ready to put into practice the principles presented in part 1 of this book. In this and the next five chapters I describe holoenergetic healing in terms of how you would use it for self-healing. However, these same techniques can be applied for healing others. Where it is not immediately obvious how to apply these processes to others, I have included brief descriptions to assist you.

I recommend that you read through this and the next seven chapters before you begin an actual healing session. By doing so you'll be able to form a mental picture of the entire holoenergetic healing process. Near the end of chapter 12, you'll find a box that lists all the steps of holoenergetic healing in a simplified outline. These steps will serve as an easy guide when you actually start the process.

Keep in mind that, as it is presented here, Recognition is a two-phase process. The first part is Rational Knowing; this is a verbal, mostly left-brain process, wherein you call forth information about your present circumstances by asking yourself questions and listening quietly for answers—which will come from your conscious mind and memory. The second phase of Recognition is Intuition; it is mostly a right-brain process in which you access nonverbal information.

You may find that if you are working alone, it is helpful to use a tape recording of the steps, especially for those sections after you have been asked to close your eyes. You can, of course, make your own tape, using the short outline at the end of this section as your guide. In taping the self-healing instructions, allow a time interval for your response. When playing the tape, stop it as is necessary to complete each step. With a small amount of experimentation you'll be able to establish a pace that works well for you.

You will also want paper and pencil close by so that you can make notes as you go along. In most cases, brief notes are best so that you don't interrupt the flow of the session. After completing a session, you may wish to go back and fill in any details you missed the first time around.

You can also work with a partner or witness who asks you the questions, reads you the steps, and records your responses. When working with another person you need not respond aloud to the questions; you can silently note the answers to yourself and record them in your notebook. Discover the form that suits you best.

IDENTIFYING THE SOURCE OF DISEASE

The first step in holoenergetic healing is Recognition, the information-gathering step in which you'll be identifying the energy forms that you are consciously or unconsciously maintaining in your life. This information-gathering or recognition phase is an essential first step in all treatment systems and in all systems of conscious change. The process of recognition is important: only by recognizing the forms our energy has taken is it possible to consciously transform them.

In *Awakening Intuition,* Frances Vaughan points out that "the more completely you identify with (get to know) your inner experience, the deeper you will be able to penetrate into the creative wellsprings of your intuition," wherein healing occurs. For this reason, she recommends that you "own and experience your feelings consciously before attempting to transcend them" (p. 89).

As you begin, it may be helpful to think of the word *information* in a somewhat new way. When you break down the word, you find the root words *in* and *formation*. For our present use, think of formation as the manner in which energy is currently stored in our body-minds. To recognize these in-formations is to bring them more fully to our awareness.

WELLNESS AND INFORMATION

Gathering information is an essential first step in every treatment system, be it modern medicine, dentistry, psychotherapy, homeopathy, acupuncture, bodywork, or holoenergetic healing. In modern Western medicine, the information is derived primarily through a biographical medical history, a physical exam, and laboratory tests. Modern medical diagnosis focuses on organ system pathology. It asks, "What are the physical signs and symptoms of diseased organs and systems in the body?" In holoenergetic healing, our focus is on the energy field of the person's body-mind where patterns of information are held. Before we can transform an energy pattern, we need to know (that is, recognize) its present form. In other words, accessing these energy patterns is essential for the holoenergetic healing process. Although an imbalance of energy may be manifest in our bodies as illness, its source reaches into emotional, mental, spiritual, or all of these levels.

The holoenergetic history, along with intuitive diagnosis and subtle energy assessment, are our tools for identifying patterns of illness. Many of the techniques I will describe here draw on our intuitive capabilities to bring information from its diffuse, subconscious state of awareness up into more defined levels of consciousness, where they may actually be articulated.

We begin the holoenergetic healing process by focusing our attention on the issue, or issues, we choose to change. That work begins on a verbal level, in which we utilize a personal holoenergetic healing history.

Holoenergetic Healing History

The personal history we take in holoenergetic healing asks us to reflect on the past, present, and future. It allows us to recognize wounds that we hide from the world, and it helps us recognize how hiding these wounds, for whatever reason, often prevents us from changing. This same format gives us an opportunity to identify the energy patterns we are holding within ourselves on both conscious and unconscious levels.

Five Key Questions

Ask yourself the five key questions that follow. You may wish to record your answers with a tape recorder, jot them down, or have a friend act as a witness to ask the questions and jot your answers down for you.

1. What do I want to change?
2. What is prompting me to change now?
3. How do I see myself as contributing to the present circumstances?
4. What does having this illness (or situation) keep me from doing, being, or having? What does it allow me to do, be, or have?
5. Where do I want to go from here? What result or inner experience do I really want to create?

Once we ask about a condition, our intuitive mind interacts with our rational mind to explore the information requested. In this way, the holoenergetic history begins to establish the planes of energy where the healing work will occur. This process plants the seeds for that healing to progress.

Each question in the holoenergetic history is an important step in the healing process. This history can be used both for self-healing and for assisting others in their healing. The entire process takes about fifteen to thirty minutes.

Question One: What Do I Want to Change?

What circumstances, conditions, symptoms, feelings, thoughts, attitudes, or beliefs do you want to change?

This question focuses your attention on your perceptions of your present circumstances and your feelings about it. For example, you may say, "I have severe back pain. It's just making my life miserable. It also prevents me from working and having fun."

Question Two: What Is Prompting Me to Change Now?

Ask yourself, "Why do I want to change now?" and, "Is the pressure I am feeling to change coming from within me or from external sources?"

Here you are identifying your motive for changing. At first, the answer may seem obvious. "I have pain and I want to get rid of it." Look deeper. See if the desire to change comes from within or without. For instance, one may seek change for the approval or love of others, so the answer might be, "My husband and children need me and this pain keeps me from taking care of them." Such external motivation does not, in my experience, carry a high likelihood for holoenergetic change, unless you are willing to go more deeply into your own dissatisfaction. An internal motivation for change might be, "I am unhappy with my family's constant demands on my time and energy. I want to be loved for something other than my ability to keep house for them and fix their meals."

By asking yourself to identify your motives for changing, you can get in touch with some of the sources of the illness itself. Look for particular patterns, or themes, in your life.

For example, is there a victim pattern? Not everyone has this particular pattern, of course, but many people have had the opportunity to experience being victims as children. They found that when they hurt themselves they got special attention. They may have realized that weakness through illness and suffering allowed them to get what they wanted, perhaps to feel nurtured or to stay home from school and play. That was part of the growing up process. They then chose this pattern as a way of controlling others through weakness and guilt, attempting to fulfill their own needs in a way that worked during childhood.

Is there a theme of codependence? That is, do you constantly defer to others, putting their needs before your own? Another pattern might be that you are constantly hurting yourself, perhaps following an old tendency toward self-punishment that you learned in childhood.

The patterns you are looking for are as many and varied as there are people. Yet there are commonalities. Several of the more common patterns are described in the section in this chapter on recognizing five patterns of illness.

The issues that come up when you ask yourself "What and why do I want to change?" may be simple, or at times they may be complex. Although the patterns you seek may seem obscure, there is a part of you that understands. By asking the questions, you begin seeking on that intuitive level of mind, the level that knows. By actively searching in this way, you create the opportunity for coming into resonance with that dimension of your intuitive mind that recognizes patterns within that are not always apparent to you in your everyday consciousness. Thus, even without your conscious effort, your deeper levels of mind are preparing for the holoenergetic work to follow.

These questions help you to look for patterns that may be operating in your life and allow them to come to light. You need not explore or resolve what emerges at this time. Just recognize and sense that you are the source of your desire to change.

Question Three: How Do I See Myself As Contributing to the Present Circumstances?

Ask yourself how you are contributing to your present circumstances. In this question you increase your awareness of how the choices you made in the past, or are currently making, contribute to the circumstances you want to change. In asking this question, you are not looking for blame or fault; rather, your goal is to identify what choices you did make, either consciously or unconsciously, so that you can choose once again. Realizing you had and still have choice shifts you back into the seat of your power.

Bear in mind that the part you played that led to the present situation may have occurred long ago, when you were a toddler with limited knowledge of your options. For example, Beth, a young woman who suffered from severe headaches, recognized a choice she made: her parents had fought frequently when she was a child, and she had found she could reduce her anxiety about this by tensing the muscles in her neck, as if to elevate her shoulders and duck her head for protection. Though it was not a conscious choice at the time, it had been a choice nevertheless. Not everyone in the same situation would have responded in the same way. Another child might cry or run and hide.

Beth saw that this choice led to the habit of tensing up her neck and shoulder muscles whenever she was under pressure, and this tension, over time, brought on her headaches. When she became aware of this, she was able to take responsibility for her contribution to the situation she wanted to change; she was able to make a new choice and holoenergetically release the old form. Responsibility here refers to one's level of awareness of how one is responding to the present circumstances, and leads one to ask what other, more beneficial, ways one might respond.

Although you may not have been aware of it in the past, there was a point when you made a choice to believe something about yourself and your world, a choice to act or allow certain things to occur. We make choices even in the most coercive and unjust situations. In a deeply moving recollection of his experiences in a Nazi concentration camp, Victor Frankl wrote the following in *Man's Search for Meaning:*

> The experience of camp life shows that a man does have a choice of action. There were enough examples, often of a heroic nature, which proved that apathy could be overcome, irritability suppressed. Man can preserve a vestige of spiritual freedom, of independence of mind, even in such terrible conditions of psychic and physical stress. We who lived in concentration camps can remember the men who walked through the huts comforting others, giving away their last piece of bread. They may have been few in number, but they offer sufficient proof that everything can be taken away from a man but one thing: the last of the human freedoms—to choose one's attitude in any given set of circumstances, to choose one's way. The way in which man accepts his fate and all the suffering it entails, the way in which he takes up his cross, gives him ample opportunity—even in the most difficult circumstances—to add a deeper meaning to his life.[2]

Life exists; how we respond to it is our choice, and our choice creates our experience of it. The more conscious we are of our responsibility for creating our experience, and the more responsibility we take, the more power we have to change our experience. Accepting responsibility allows us to forgive ourselves as well as others and to begin to heal.

I cannot overemphasize the importance of your asking how you have contributed to your current circumstances in a gentle way that is neither accusative nor blaming. We all contribute to our reality through our thoughts and feelings; our perceptions, interpretations,

2. Victor Frankl, *Man's Search for Meaning* (New York: Simon & Schuster, 1984), p. 86.

and beliefs; our actions; and what we allow to occur. Healing is initiated when we compassionately recognize our participation and regain the belief that choice is possible and that we can choose to heal.

Question Four: What Does Having This Illness (or Situation) Keep Me from Doing, Being, or Having? What Does It Allow Me to Do, Be, or Have?

Ask yourself, "What is the present situation keeping me from doing, from being, from becoming, or from having?" It is also important to ask, "What am I currently doing, being, and having that I would not have if I were healed? What might I be gaining from this situation?"

We often find that before healing can take place, we must make a conscious choice to identify and release the benefits that come to us through the present situation, however uncomfortable that might be. These secondary gains of illness create resistance to healing. I recall a man who had been in a rehabilitation center following a stroke; he had to recognize that he had come to depend on the shelter and security of the center. To take the next step in his healing, to go home and resume full responsibility for himself, he first had to choose to give up that external sense of security. He saw that security as a benefit of the situation he wanted to heal.

Asking the questions described here allows you to evaluate the meaning of illness for you. In other words, how has it changed your life? You begin to get a sense of what resistances you might have to healing; what might you be gaining by not releasing what you want to change? What's blocking you from changing? What needs are being met by your illness that you did not know how to satisfy in other ways? Secondary gains frequently fall into three categories: financial, physical, or emotional.

Are the circumstances of your present illness taking the place of your being loved in a more satisfying way, experiencing a truly nurturing relationship, or enjoying success? Has the comfort, care, and security become more important than getting well?

By identifying these secondary gains of illness, and the sources of our blockages, we are discovering real and legitimate needs that can be met in more beneficial and satisfying ways.

Therapists who work with attitude and imagery in treating cancer have come to believe that we develop our diseases for honorable reasons. It's our body's way of telling us that our physical and emotional needs are not being met, and the needs that are fulfilled through our illnesses are important ones.[3]

Question Five: Where Do I Want to Go from Here? What Result or Inner Experience Do I Really Want to Create?

If, as a consequence of this work, you were to be spontaneously and instantaneously healed and filled with vital energy and a sense of aliveness, what would you do next? What would you do with this released energy? Imagine what it would be like to already have what you want.

Here you address the meaning of your true desires and sense of purpose. There is still another way of asking this question: If you knew that in whatever you tried you could not fail, what would you do? What would you have? How would you be? This question releases the fear of failure, humiliation, and shame, allowing, at least for the moment, a chance to get in touch with a sense of your path based on true desire. Asking this is different from asking, What do you think you could or should do? It is clearly asking, What do you really want? What is your destination on this journey? What brings you joy, peace, freedom, and fills you with love? What is your bliss and your ecstasy?

By asking these questions (see fig. 7 for a summary), you begin to recognize that there are many choices and that it is possible to choose; the choices you identify are between what your life attitudes are now and what you would like them to be. As you identify these

---

3. Carl O. Simonton, Stephanie Matthew Simonton, and James Creighton, *Getting Well Again* (Los Angeles: J. P. Tarcher, 1978), p. 121.

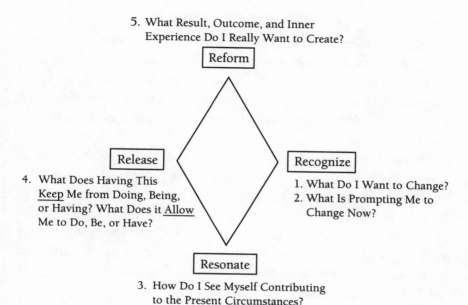

5. What Result, Outcome, and Inner
Experience Do I Really Want to Create?

Reform

Release

4. What Does Having This
<u>Keep</u> Me from Doing, Being,
or Having? What Does it <u>Allow</u>
Me to Do, Be, or Have?

Recognize

1. What Do I Want to Change?
2. What Is Prompting Me to
Change Now?

Resonate

3. How Do I See Myself Contributing
to the Present Circumstances?

Summary of Recognition: Rational Knowing.
Each question, integrated with the Four R's,
is related to a step in the holoenergetic process.

FIGURE 7 Recognition Questions

choices, you come to recognize that you are truly seeking change
and that consciously or unconsciously you have a picture of how
you would like things to be. You begin to recognize the form taken
by the old energy pattern and you recognize a new pattern, drawing
you toward your future.

RECOGNIZING FIVE PATTERNS OF ILLNESS

In the course of my early research involving holoenergetic healing
and herpes, I observed five key disease patterns that maintain illness
or other energy forms that people want to change.

1. Difficulty Receiving Love

People may have difficulty receiving love for a number of reasons. They may fear the associated vulnerability, obligation, or responsibility of being loved. Many of us feel vulnerable when we're loved because we feel obligated to the one who loves us. When someone loves us we sense that person's openness and vulnerability, and we feel responsible for that.

What better way to avoid receiving love, with all the sense of responsibility it seems to imply for so many people, than to have a communicable disease like herpes, for which no cure has been found? The disease, while not life-threatening, provides a justified reason to avoid contact with others. This is not to imply that herpes is the only disease that serves such a function. A wide variety of situations, from other infectious diseases to financial difficulties, can achieve the same results.

Frequently, the source of this pattern can be traced back to our earliest years. When we were children we may have been told that we would be loved by our parents if we would just do what they wanted us to do. Such love was conditional, and we may have felt manipulated by the threat of having love withdrawn. In this way, love became identified with manipulation. "Thanks, but no thanks" is often the response of those who have learned to think and feel in this way. When our parents or others who are close to us express their disapproval of our actions by withholding their love from us, we quickly develop feelings of betrayal, abandonment, humiliation, or rejection. That sets the stage for shame. With shame, we feel not just that our actions are unworthy or even bad but that we ourselves are unworthy or bad. If we have been "shamed" early in life, it is easy to understand why we are afraid of being loved or receiving love.

Fear of intimacy also makes it difficult to receive love. Each of us has a mask, or persona, that we present as our face to the world; this mask consists of aspects of ourselves that we feel are acceptable or admirable. Often, beneath the mask lies a hidden part, an aspect of ourselves we want to keep secret because we believe it to be undesirable or shameful. The prospect of receiving love may cause us to feel fearful that another person will discover what's hidden beneath the mask and then we'll be abandoned or humiliated—an experience that we believe would be devastating to us. Having our mask rejected is easier to handle, and so we put out signals, through our masks, that we are not willing to receive love. They may be very subtle signals, but others have no difficulty detecting them on a conscious or unconscious level.

I found that many herpes sufferers, though certainly not all of them, stated the source of their difficulty in receiving love (and the source of their recurrences) in one of three ways: (1) "What's wrong with me?"; (2) "I am not good enough to love or be loved"; and (3) "I'm a mistake." Behind these sources are usually perceptions or realities of abandonment, abuse, and/or betrayal at an early age.

2. Difficulty Receiving Pleasure

Similar to our difficulty in receiving love is our difficulty in receiving pleasure. It is often associated with the belief that there is always a price to pay for pleasure. This belief, generally formed in childhood, was commonly learned from parents, society, or religious teachings. I frequently found that beneath the belief that a price must be paid for pleasure lay the shame-based belief "I don't deserve pleasure."

In my gynecological practice, the price many patients paid for pleasure included chronic vaginal infections, such as herpes, and unwanted pregnancies.

3. Difficulty Expressing and Releasing Anger

The ways we experienced anger when we were very young often affect our ability to express it in our adult lives. Possibly our first experiences were that our parents ignored or belittled our expressions of anger, so we quickly learned to suppress angry feelings whenever they arose. Or perhaps our expression of anger produced such frightening reactions in our parents and others around us that we became fearful of those feelings. Any combination of these reactions can make us fearful of anger, whether we are the one expressing it or it is being directed toward us by others.

It is interesting to note that the inflamed herpetic lesion is red. When people have an opportunity to look at that lesion intuitively and are asked to allow themselves to experience the feelings it evokes, they often associate it with anger or rage.

Many people equate anger with the loss of control, and the loss of control suggests that someone is going to get hurt. This anger or control-hurt pattern is especially prevalent with people who were harshly punished as children, either physically or emotionally. Although anger, loss of control, and hurt are not of necessity linked, we frequently do link them with one another. This threatening belief limits our expression of this powerful emotion, anger.

In and of itself, anger is not a negative or contracting emotion as long as it is expressed without the intention of hurting or manipulating others. Frequently, we get angry when our ability to choose or act has been restricted. This restriction may happen because our lack of experience or knowledge results in our making a choice in which we end up giving away our power. Or it may occur when someone who has given us power over them suddenly withdraws that "right" from us. An example would be the anger parents often feel when their children begin to challenge their authority. Any perceived loss of power over another can elicit the experience of losing control, with all its attendant feelings of anger.

Whenever we suppress our anger, for whatever reason, it becomes what is often called a negative or contracted emotion. When suppressed, the energy of the emotion known as anger is turned inward, leaving us with a sense of isolation or separation.

Cancer patients often turn their anger inward and acquiesce to other people's desires and wishes. They don't want to offend others or to incur other people's anger, so they deny their own feelings and subordinate their own desires and feelings to those of others. It has been found that cancer patients who allow themselves to express anger appropriately, and thus attain or regain a sense of personal control and power, have higher survival rates.

When herpes patients I worked with started expressing and releasing their anger appropriately, their disease symptoms were substantially reduced. One can release anger appropriately by expressing it without the intent to hurt or manipulate, simply by stating, "This is what I feel," instead of turning what one feels into an accusation or attack on another person. The intent of expressing anger is to communicate and release our feelings, not to get even. Sometimes it is not appropriate to express anger directly to another person, because to do so would have obvious negative consequences. An example might be the anger you might feel toward a boss whose immediate reaction to your honest expression of anger would be to fire you. Under these circumstances, it is still possible to express anger adequately by bringing to mind an image of the person toward whom you feel angry, then communicating your feelings to that image. In certain methods of therapy, this is augmented by pounding a pillow with your fists. The forgiveness process described in chapter 9, "Release," provides another way to express anger and internally resolve the issue with forgiveness, leaving us with peace of mind and heart.

4. Difficulty Forgiving

Another behavior often associated with disease is holding on to blame as a way to punish others or to protect oneself from further hurt. Herpes sufferers often direct blame toward the partner who presumably introduced the virus, or even toward themselves for contracting the infection. Just as often, this clinging to blame is a way to punish parents and others who are perceived as the source of one's resentment.

Often, along with blame and lack of forgiveness comes self-pity. Self-pity, so often expressed in a kind of silence that speaks louder than words, is another way of punishing oneself and other people.

The question becomes "Who is it you're punishing when you feel sorry for yourself?"

One expression of blame involves self-punishment and self-destructive choices that punish one's parents. In their healing work, people exhibiting this pattern often discover the source of it in very early relationships, when they consciously or unconsciously learned that their own self-denial or self-abuse resulted in their parents' feeling distressed. Beneath the creation of distress was a call for love and attention.

Discovering patterns of blame and punishment led me to develop the forgiveness process that allows people to release themselves from their own reluctance to forgive.

5. Difficulty Trusting

Most of us wonder, to some degree, how our loved ones would respond if we became ill. But for some people, getting ill is a way of testing a partner's love, fidelity, reliability, or degree of responsibility. This kind of testing is often a substitute for trust; in the tester's mind it takes the place of investing trust in the other person. Instead, the tester asks that person to pass a specific test to "prove" that he or she can be trusted. While some people use testing to make certain they won't trust, others succeed in building trust based on testing. However, this testing doesn't produce the same results as the other form of trust. On the contrary, it usually leads to an endless chain of new tests, each one invented when the tester has doubts or fears, or is feeling unloved or unworthy of love.

Testing other people's love is a common pattern with many illnesses. In my research with herpes sufferers, many asked the underlying question of their partner: "How much do you love me? Do you love me enough to relate to me even though I have a communicable disease, one that you could have for the rest of your life if you caught it?"

One of my herpes patients was sexually abused by her father, and she continued to fear and despise other men as a result of this exploitation. As if to prove to herself that she didn't have to fear them, she set up a test for them. In effect, she was saying, "I've got herpes. Let's see how much you really do love me. Are you willing to risk getting this?" If a man passed the test by risking the infection, she felt that he could be trusted, that he would not exploit her as her father had.

During a healing session, this same woman was able to go to the source and transform the energy of her anger into love. She subsequently reported that the severity and frequency of her herpes outbreaks diminished significantly.

I have found that herpes sufferers who test their partners in these ways frequently have a past history of sexual, emotional, or physical abuse. For them, herpes serves an important function, protecting them from a recurrence of the abuse they experienced in the past.

Any of these patterns block the flow of energy, creating an imbalance that will be reflected in the etheric field. This imbalance, in turn, lowers immune function and in the case of herpes leads to recurrent outbreaks.

While it is true that these five patterns were uncovered in the course of my research with herpes, they are clearly not disease-specific. In my work I have continued to find it useful to look for them regardless of the reason that people seek healing assistance. Identifying the patterns we use to block loving energy is a most important step in all healing. Releasing ourselves from these patterns opens the way for us to receive the healing energy of love.

In presenting these five patterns, I do not mean to imply that these are the only patterns there are or that the patterns you find will coincide with these perfectly. I believe it important to look at these typical patterns, or combinations of them, because they focus on receiving love, the healing force of holoenergetic healing. However, keep in mind that these are only models, presented here to give you some clues about the kinds of energy patterns we are looking for in the Recognition phase of this healing process.

By learning to identify the patterns of illness, you start to seed your intuitive mind in preparation for the healing work. These questions give you an opportunity to review your past, look at your present, and attune to your future. Although the questions may not lead to immediate answers, to the extent that they are honestly addressed the answers will emerge into conscious awareness. When these questions are coupled with a process I call holoenergetic activation, they can produce profound insight to and resolution of physical and psychospiritual distress.

As you ask yourself these five questions, keep in mind that there are no "right" or "wrong" answers. Recognition is an ongoing process that will continue throughout the remaining three steps of your holoenergetic healing and even beyond that. As many people have said, there is a subtle magic here that continues throughout the healing process, bringing change and comfort and deeply touching our everyday lives.

6

Recognition—Intuitive Knowing

I did not arrive at my understanding of the fundamental laws of the universe through my rational mind.

—ALBERT EINSTEIN

We should not pretend to understand the world only by the intellect; we comprehend it just as much by feeling. Therefore the judgment of the intellect is, at best, only the half of truth, and must, if it be honest, also come to an understanding of its inadequacy.

—C. G. JUNG

In this chapter you will be accessing subtle energy levels of your body-mind. Here you'll be focusing on your etheric energy in order to get a gestalt, or overview, of your energy fields and their effects on your body-mind. Then, for more targeted information, you'll be focusing on your chakras. In assessing both your etheric field and your chakras, you'll be using biomechanical testing, or *dowsing,* a tool I've adapted for measuring these subtle energies. I've included detailed instructions in this section for both constructing and using dowsing rods. The construction is a simple project requiring two wire coat hangers and a pair of pliers.

You'll want to make the dowsing rods and practice with them before doing a healing session. That's part of why I suggested that you read this and the following chapters on Resonance, Release, and Reformation before actually applying the information contained here.

Intuitional biomechanical testing is an optional part of the holoenergetic healing process. However, intuition itself is an integral and natural part of your healing work, so I would encourage you to develop your skills in this area. As we shall see in the chapter on Resonance, which follows, your intuitive sense will provide insight into the nature and meaning of the form and source of the issue or illness you want to change. The intuitive skills you'll be developing through your practice with biomechanical testing will later be invaluable in the process of holoenergetic activation, during which you'll focus attention on an object such as a lesion, a symptom, an emotional disturbance, a traumatic experience, an affected chakra, or the thymus.

INFORMATION STORED IN SUBTLE ENERGY FORMS

Much information that is valuable for holoenergetic healing is stored in our body-minds nonverbally. One way it can be identified is by examining its expressions in the subtle energy that extends beyond the body. This information, which may affect us mentally, emotionally, physically, and spiritually, exists within us as an energy form that subsequently manifests as a verbal message, a physical symptom, or even a mental image.

To access information in these forms, you'll be using your own intuitive sensing capabilities to assess two key sources of information: (1) the etheric energy field and (2) the chakras. Using biomechanical testing, you'll also be able to establish when the present circumstances began and how the energy centers are affected by emotions, specific allergens, foods, and environmental factors.

BIOMECHANICAL TESTING

One of the ways subtle energy can be biomechanically evaluated in holoenergetic healing is with *dowsing*. (Dowsing means "to seek or search.") This approach is among the oldest of recorded methods of intuitive information acquisition, appearing in ancient cave drawings in Europe. Traditionally, dowsers have detected water sources for wells and for agricultural purposes. Dowsing has not been limited to water detection, however. It has also been used for discovering minerals and archaeological artifacts, locating missing persons or pets, finding lost objects, and detecting oil. Marines in Vietnam even used it for locating land mines, booby traps, and enemy ammunition caches.

In recent studies of experienced dowsers at the SRI, a research institute in California, physicist Hal Puthoff found that, by a probability factor of more than a million to one, successful dowsing results were not a chance occurrence. Yet scientific explanations for why it works are inadequate at best.[1]

I use biomechanical testing in holoenergetic healing because I have found these techniques most valuable for tapping into the vast repository of information we each hold within our subconscious mind. Here's how that probably works:

Your subconscious mind picks up every visual detail, sound, smell, and other sensory impression in your environment. For instance, as you read this, you are paying attention to the words on this page. You may not notice the sound of traffic on the street, the humming of a fan overhead, or the smell of dinner cooking in the kitchen. But this unnoticed information is entering your subconscious mind and it remains there, potentially available to you if you ever want to have access to it.

A hypnotist once did experimental work to determine how much information we subconsciously store in our minds. One of his

---

1. Reported at the conference of the American Society of Dowsers at the University of California, Santa Cruz, July 1987.

subjects was a man who had been a university student about twenty years before. The hypnotist took this man back to that earlier time and asked him to count all the bricks on the facade of a certain building on the university campus. The man saw the building in his mind and counted the bricks. Then they went to the campus and counted the bricks on the facade of the building. To their amazement, they found that the man's count had been right.

The point of this story is that we each have the capacity to summon up information, even minute details about our lives, that are not possible to recall in ordinary states of consciousness. Biomechanical testing is one way of making this information available to our conscious mind.

When you perform biomechanical testing you become the sensing instrument or detector. But, just as do electronic devices such as radios, most of us require a way of amplifying the information we access. With most electronic devices we can amplify and translate the information we've detected to the movement of a needle on a dial or a wiggly line on an oscilloscope. For our purposes here, we will use L-rods, a traditional dowser's tool.

As we proceed, keep in mind that L-rods do not directly give us access to the information. Rather, they can be regarded as psychomotor extensions of our subconscious minds, amplifying the minute neuromuscular responses triggered by that part of our unconscious mind that already has access to the answer. These tools focus our attention and provide us with a visual signal of specific intuitive knowledge.

Here's how L-rods work: You hold two L-rods, one in each hand, with both of them in the neutral position, that is, pointing straight forward (see fig. 8). You then focus your attention on exactly what you want to know about. This might be your own image in a mirror, or another person. You may do this by mentally asking a question, such as "Where does this person's etheric energy field begin?" or by making a statement, such as "Show me the present extent of this person's etheric energy field." Thus, you can "pro-

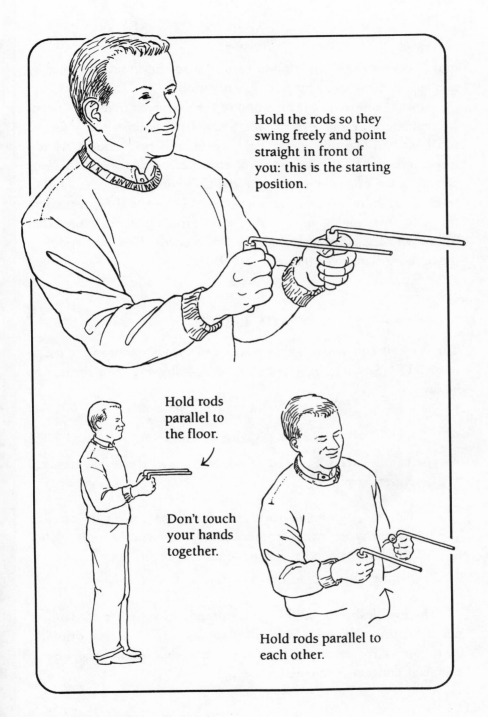

Hold the rods so they swing freely and point straight in front of you: this is the starting position.

Hold rods parallel to the floor.

Don't touch your hands together.

Hold rods parallel to each other.

FIGURE 8 Holding the Rods

gram" your subconscious mind to search for information either by giving a command or by posing a question.

You then move in the direction of the person or object you want to evaluate. For our present purposes, let's assume you want to move into an invisible energy field around a person's body. As you move into the field, the rods will either cross and form an X or spread apart, one swinging to the right, the other to the left. Either response is valid, but for the sake of simplicity I will be describing the rods as swinging open rather than crossing in the pages that follow. In the case of an imbalance in the energy field, one rod may move more than the other (see fig. 9).

THE L-ROD

The L-rod is commonly a thin piece of metal wire bent in the shape of an "L." (See fig. 10.) Use two L-rods, following the instructions below.

How to Make L-Rods

All you need to make a pair of L-rods are two wire coat hangers and a wire cutter or pliers.

1. Cut the bottom of each hanger so that one part of each hanger is ten inches from the bend. Now cut the ends so that you have a handle that is about five inches long.
2. Adjust each rod so that it forms a right angle.

The handles must be able to turn freely in your hands. To best allow for this movement you can place sections of plastic drinking straws or narrow cardboard tubing (such as that found on some dry cleaners' hangers) over the handles.

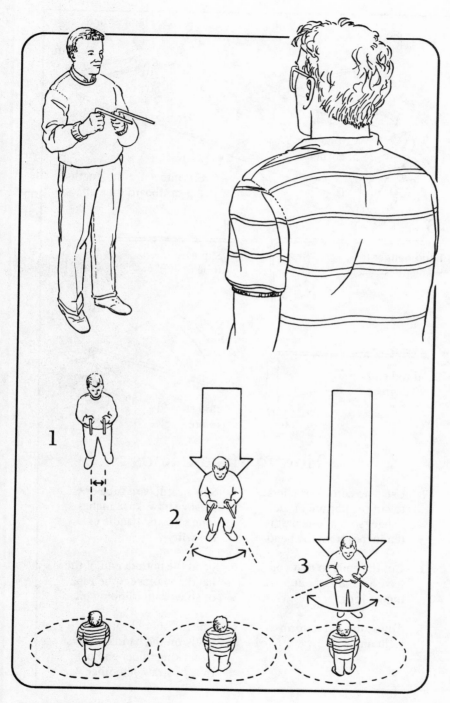

FIGURE 9 Using the Rods

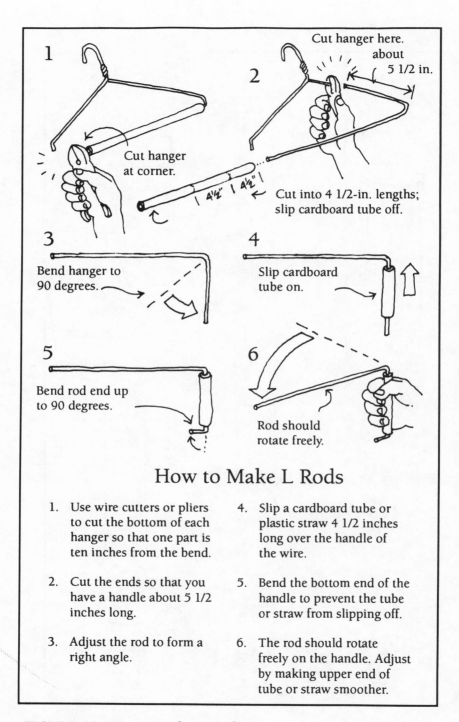

1 Cut hanger at corner.

2 Cut hanger here. about 5 1/2 in.

Cut into 4 1/2-in. lengths; slip cardboard tube off. 4½″ 4½″

3 Bend hanger to 90 degrees.

4 Slip cardboard tube on.

5 Bend rod end up to 90 degrees.

6 Rod should rotate freely.

How to Make L Rods

1. Use wire cutters or pliers to cut the bottom of each hanger so that one part is ten inches from the bend.

2. Cut the ends so that you have a handle about 5 1/2 inches long.

3. Adjust the rod to form a right angle.

4. Slip a cardboard tube or plastic straw 4 1/2 inches long over the handle of the wire.

5. Bend the bottom end of the handle to prevent the tube or straw from slipping off.

6. The rod should rotate freely on the handle. Adjust by making upper end of tube or straw smoother.

FIGURE 10 How to Make L-Rods

Holding L-Rods

- Hold the L-rods so that they can swing freely in their handles. The upper part of the rod should not be touching any part of your hands.

- Hold the rods parallel with the ground and parallel to one another. They should be pointed straight out in front of you. This is the starting position. Practice getting the rods to stay in this basic starting position, which we will refer to throughout this chapter.

- Try walking slowly across the room with the rods in the starting position. Mentally focus on maintaining the rods parallel to each other and to the ground. If your mind wanders, so will the rods.

- Hold the rods as level as possible. If you point them down they will not be able to detect the minuscule neuromuscular responses you want them to detect in your body, because they will have to overcome gravity. If you point them up they become overly sensitive. When you find your rods are too sensitive and are spinning around, you can lower the tips slightly, but remember they are less sensitive when they have to work against the force of gravity.

Programming the Rods

Always begin an evaluation by taking a moment to get very clear about what it is you want to know. This is the object of your focus. It is important not only to ask the right question but to hold within your mind the clear intention of getting an accurate answer.

Asking a clear and accurate question brings you into resonance with the subject of your inquiry. When you come into resonance with something, you vibrate at its frequency, or at a harmonic of that frequency. This is analogous to what happens when you sound an "A" on a piano; other strings will also resonate with that note, namely, the strings that are twice its frequency, half its frequency, one-quarter its frequency, and so on. When you come into resonance there are many levels or octaves that you can tune into that give you access to information.

Every thought, belief, and feeling has an energetic signature that is as unique as our faces or our fingerprints. So whenever we hold thoughts, beliefs, or feelings in our minds, we are creating specific energetic patterns. Those patterns exist within the energy fields of our own body-mind, but they also extend outward, seeking like forms with which to resonate in the external world.

When we work with the L-rods, the energetic templates that are formed by our intentions, questions, and programs seek matches of those forms in the external world. When a match is found, we have a standing wave: we have been "met." This is then recorded by our subconscious body-mind and reflected as minute neuromuscular movements of our whole body and thus transmitted to the L-rods. At the point when we get the resonant match, resulting in a standing wave, the L-rods move, providing us with a visual readout that tells us that we have the match.

Once your question is formulated, you must be able to detach yourself from the results. Any emotional attachment to getting a specific desired answer at this particular time will prevent you from receiving a reliable answer. For example, if you are a physician asking for information about the state of a person's immune system and you have a vested interest in seeing that immune system as fully capable of handling a present infection, you will see that person's immune system as fully functional, but you may not be right. Your own investment in seeing it healthy blinds you to the reality of its weakened state.

In the case of marines in Vietnam, it was found that those who were able to detach themselves from the result, allowing neither their fears nor their hopes to influence them, were able to dowse accurately for land mines. Evaluating with your intention clearly focused teaches you to let go of these inner controls and approach the information-gathering process with detachment. It allows you to create an open space in your consciousness for receiving the information you requested, clearing the way for intuitive feelings to flow freely through your subconscious.

As I mentioned earlier, a clear, detached program can be created in the form of a question or a command. For example, as we begin this phase of the healing work, we want to assess the person's (or our own) overall energy or vitality level. So we might ask, "What is the extent of this person's (or my) etheric energy field right now?" When formulating your program, identify the parameters of time and space—in other words, be sure to state that you want information about the person's energy levels right now and right here. Your subconscious mind needs to understand that you are asking about a person's energy field at the present time, since it is equally possible to use this method for accessing information that was true an hour ago, days ago, or even years ago. Remember, it is your conscious mind that is programming your subconscious to search for the answers.

When you are ready to do the actual assessment, you'll want to keep your clearly stated question in your mind; then take a deep breath and hold it for a moment. Holding the breath helps build a charge to energize your program. Then release your breath slowly and gently, and you will move into a receptive state, ready to tune in to the answers.

The Many Uses of L-Rods

In my workshops I show people how to use L-rods for identifying energy states and other information about themselves and other people. I also encourage them to practice using the rods for other purposes, for example, finding lost objects such as keys, jewelry, and so on. Exploring and using the L-rods in one's daily life offers one the opportunity to gain confidence in one's intuitive abilities. Once that confidence is gained, the L-rods can be set aside.

The following letter from a workshop participant illustrates the extent to which our intuitive abilities, as reflected by the L-rods, are often superior to our rational minds:

Dear Dr. Laskow:

I would like to share with you an experience I had with dowsing. One weekend when my parents were visiting me I decided to try out the L-rods I brought home from your workshop.

I had my mother hide her wedding ring somewhere in my living room, dining room, or kitchen. All of these rooms are open to one another, extending the full length of the house. I went to another part of the house while she hid the ring and my father looked on. Upon returning to dowse for the ring, I programmed my search with "Show me where my mother's wedding ring is." I also held a clear image of the ring in my mind.

I began by trying to narrow down which end of the house the ring was in. The rods registered a response as I walked toward the far end of the living room yet closed before I reached the wall or any furniture. Assuming this meant the ring must be hidden at the opposite end, toward the kitchen, I turned around and proceeded in that direction. Again the rods registered a response but then immediately closed before I reached any place the ring could be hidden. I tried dowsing around this open area, and watched as the rods opened and closed while I passed back and forth across it. I was quite confused. The rods were indicating the ring was not on either side of the room, yet I could see no place the ring could be hidden. My parents looked on in fascination. My mother finally said, "I think the rods know more than the dowser." At that point, I looked down at the floor and noticed one of my socks. I reached for it and inside was the ring! I had been walking directly over it, getting the appropriate response, never realizing it was right there all the time.

Because of this letter and other stories that workshop participants have shared about their experiences with the L-rods, I encourage you to experiment with them in similar ways in your life. You may want to do so even before you go on to use them for collecting information about your etheric energy field and your chakras.

ESTABLISHING A BASELINE

In chapter 2, I explained how we each consist of interpenetrating energy fields, all of which are represented holographically in the etheric field. The bioenergy field is associated with the physical body and can be measured scientifically. For the other fields, our intuitive abilities continue to be the most effective means of perceiving and measuring.

At any given moment, your etheric energy field reflects your core beliefs, as well as any physical disorders you might have, environmental influences, and your thoughts and feelings. This field also represents the harmonic composite of all the body's chakras; each chakra, in turn, reflects your physical, etheric, emotional, mental, and spiritual energy levels. And each of these energy levels is also influenced by each of the chakras. Just as in a hologram, whose smallest part contains all the information of the visual whole, so in our subtle energetic makeup each energy field contains the information of the energetic whole.

I have chosen to focus chakra evaluation at the etheric energy field level because I have found that this etheric level gives me the best readout of the interactions between our physiology and our subtle energy system.

The etheric energy field can change in energetic intensity—it can become stronger or weaker, like a light dimmed or brightened by a rheostat in your house—or it can change its pattern slightly—it can become stronger in one area than in another, greater on the left than the right—depending on the physiological, emotional, mental, or spiritual circumstances a person has experienced in the past or is experiencing now. Our program or question determines what aspect of the holographic field we will access.

A healthy etheric energy field both supports and reflects normal cellular and physiological functions. A disharmonious etheric field interferes with normal functions and, in turn, reflects circumstances that can be improved. (Fig. 1 represents a normally functioning etheric energy field.)

When we say that we want to establish a baseline for the etheric energy field, we are saying that we want to identify the intensity, as well as the balance between left and right, of this etheric field at the moment it is being measured. Within that field, as we know, there are many interacting energy fields. Just as with light or radio waves, energies of different frequencies can coexist in the same space at the same time. There are no actual levels, in the sense of up or down. Rather, there are only kinds of energy that interpenetrate. Focusing on any one of them will give us one reading, while focusing on all the different fields at once will give us quite another reading. Let me use an analogy:

There is a place in San Francisco, not far from my home, that provides a vantage point where I can stand on a cliff and look out over the ocean. It is a spectacular view. From this vantage point I can see the waves crashing in along the shore. I can see eddies and whirlpools around rock formations just a little way out from shore. And I can see the movement farther out at sea of the offshore current, a cold stream that comes from the north and flows south. All these waves, currents, eddies, and whirlpools make up the overall energy field of the ocean I see from that vantage point. In addition, the ocean responds to the environment with high tides during the full moon and huge ground swells during storms.

If I wanted to establish a baseline for the etheric energy field of the ocean, I would ask myself for an overall impression of my experience of the ocean at that moment. I would program myself to assess not just a single current or eddy but the whole dynamic of the ocean, within my perceptual range. On a stormy day, I might focus on the waves crashing in on shore. These waves might be turbulent and powerful, yet far out at sea the offshore current might be quite placid. If my impression were based solely on one or the other of these, it would not be an accurate baseline measurement. That baseline should take all the various energy fields into account rather than focusing on any one area of energy.

Similarly, when we are seeking the baseline for our own or another person's etheric energy field, we are seeking a composite, or overall level of energy, the total interaction of the subtle and physiological energies. Thus we must study the holoenergetics.

It is important to note that energy expands and intensifies or diminishes and contracts in a particular area for a moment, then returns to a baseline, in response to thoughts and feelings, and also to events in the immediate external environment. For example, if a car backfired outside, we might have a startle response, causing our energy to expand or contract for that moment. But after a few moments, we would relax and our energy level would return to the more stable baseline we had previously noted. The same might happen if we started thinking about an unresolved encounter we had with someone or began to imagine an idyllic place in nature.

Ordinarily, we can get a sense of another person's energy field when we stand between two and four feet from them. Depending on the person, the etheric energy field may normally extend from about two to four feet from any point in the body. It is this vitality baseline that we want to establish before we go on to collect more specific information about the chakras.

If all this sounds difficult, rest assured that it is much easier to do than to say.

Identifying the Baseline of the Etheric Energy Field

Our goal here is to identify energy fields that affect our health. Healthy energy field patterns support normal cellular and physiological functions. Disharmonious patterns interfere with these functions and create blockages to the flow of subtle energies, leading to imbalances, which eventually manifest in illness.

1. To establish your baseline (the intensity and balance of your etheric energy field), stand in front of a mirror. Regard the surface of the mirror as the plane from which to measure the energy fields and chakras; ignore the illusion of depth in the reflected image. If you do not have a mirror to work with,

turn to "The Transpersonal Alignment Process" in chapter 3 and find the exercise entitled "Creating A Double," which allows you to do your biomechanical evaluation. Note that when you use a mirror, the right and left sides of your image will be reversed. However, with "Creating A Double," the rods will respond to the image you create just as if you had another person sitting in front of you.

2. At a distance of about eight feet from the mirror, hold a pair of L-rods in the starting position, as explained above. Take a deep breath and, while holding the position, silently ask, "What is the present extent of my etheric energy field?" To be sure that you are picking up your etheric energy field, in your mind focus on and ask for a readout of the totality of your interpenetrating energy system as represented in the etheric field.

3. Now exhale slowly and gently, releasing the question you have asked as if into the space between the tips of the rods. Begin walking slowly forward, toward the mirror. As you are starting to move forward, release your mental control of the rods. You no longer need to think about holding them parallel to one another. Allow them to respond to the influence of the energy fields you want to measure. In my workshops I often tell participants to take what they get, that is, to experiment with the rods until they get a feel for the way they work. Take your time. Remember that this learning process requires practice to improve your ability. Be sure to walk slowly enough so that the rods have time to react when they reach the interface of your mirrored energy field.

4. At the point where the rods begin to swing apart, at least forty-five degrees from midline (see fig. 9), you will have reached the approximate outer limit of your reflected energy field. Generally you will find this point at about two to four

feet from the surface of the mirror itself. The average is about three feet.

An interface less than two feet from the surface of the mirror (or the other person's body) will indicate a relatively contracted etheric energy field. An interface of more than three feet indicates an expanded etheric energy field. Simply note these distances for now, without attempting to interpret what they mean.

How Immediate Thoughts and Feelings Influence Subtle Energy Fields

Positive and negative thoughts and feelings have an effect on the energy fields of both the person doing the evaluating and the person being evaluated. These thoughts and feelings are of two kinds: (1) baseline and (2) transient. Baseline feelings are those that are steadily reflected in the etheric field; they are thoughts and feelings associated with the holographic patterns we discussed in chapter 5. In other words, they are thoughts and feelings that are associated with our personal histories and are more or less constant. Transient feelings are those that we express in response to a more immediate experience; for example, the joy we feel upon receiving an unexpected visit from a friend we dearly love, or the feeling we have when we are pulled over by the police for a driving violation.

In biomechanical testing it is therefore important to be clear about what we're testing. Are we looking for baseline measurements, or are we looking for the influence of transient thoughts and feelings on ourselves or another person at that moment? The following exercise can help you understand the difference between baseline and transient.

Evaluating Energetic Effects of Thought Patterns

1. Begin by measuring your own or your partner's baseline etheric energy field using the L-rods as described above.

Mark the interface—that is, when the rods swing open at least forty-five degrees from midline, indicating the outer boundary of that field.

2. Still holding the rods in their open position at the interface, have your partner think negatively about someone or something. While your partner focuses on these transient thoughts, use the L-rods to determine any change in his or her energy field. Reprogram the open rods by holding your breath and silently asking, "What is the present extent of my partner's etheric field, as influenced by his or her transient thoughts and feelings?" As you release your breath, you should find that the energy field has contracted inward.

3. Next, have your partner ex-pulse sharply, with the intention of stripping the negative information, a transient thought or feeling, from the body, releasing it completely, and allowing it to dissipate. (More than one ex-pulse may be necessary.)

   Whenever there are negative thoughts and feelings, they first affect the energy field of the person who thought and felt them. (The same holds for positive thoughts and feelings.) You may want to follow negative thoughts and feelings by seeking something positive about the person or situation, or yourself, and sending a blessing of positive thought and feeling. It's like looking for the silver lining and feeling blessed once you find it. Holoenergetically, "What we give, we receive."

4. After your partner finishes clearing the transient thought with ex-pulses, evaluate him or her again with the L-rods. Observe how the energy field begins to expand to its previous size. If it does not expand, have the person ex-pulse again and once again use the rods to measure the results. The negative thought will be cleared at the point that the rods reveal a return to the original baseline.

5. Finally, let's examine the effect of positive transient thoughts. Have your partner think of someone, something,

or a particular situation that evokes thoughts and feelings of joy, love, and happiness. Ask your partner to allow those thoughts to expand and fill his or her entire being.

Again, use the L-rods to evaluate this person's energy field. Be sure you start sufficiently far away. You will usually find that when positive thoughts are being held in the mind, the field expands beyond the extent of the original baseline you established.

If you are too close to the person when you test for the positive feelings, the L-rods may act erratically, oscillating and vibrating but not opening at the moment you release the program to measure the field. Or the L-rods may open shortly after you've released the program but before you've started to step forward. This occurs because you are within the envelope of the now-expanded etheric field. Step back a few feet and try again.

You can determine the affects of your transient thoughts on your own energy field by evaluating yourself in a mirror with L-rods, as described above.

Whenever you start programming for biomechanical testing, take the time to monitor your own transient thoughts and feelings. If you are testing another person's energy fields, take the time to become aware of his or her transient influences as well. If you feel it necessary to do so, clear your own transient thoughts, or have the other person clear theirs, using the ex-pulse method I describe above. Then, for the most accurate readouts, set your program to read the baseline energy without the effects of the more immediate and transient positive or negative thoughts.

For example, if you are feeling self-critical, judging yourself as too heavy or too thin, you can clear that part of the judgment that is coming in as a transient intrusion in the same way you've learned to clear negative thoughts and feelings. Ex-pulse to release that judgment in the moment. In this way you can counter the adverse effects of your own thoughts on your energy field.

People occasionally become judgmental when evaluating energy fields and slip into negative thinking, which itself affects their etheric field and can affect the results of the evaluation. So when evaluating subtle energies, keep in mind that rather than judging right or wrong, good or bad, you are simply collecting information about the energy value of *what is*.

Energy value (E-valuation) can be defined as the life-enhancing, spiritually enhancing quality of a person. Where healing is concerned, the purpose of evaluating this energy is to help make conscious choices about how to improve our health or our quality of life.

To summarize, whenever you do an energy evaluation using intuitive processes, pay attention to your own thoughts, feelings, and desires. If you feel they are interfering with the reading, use the techniques and ideas we've discussed to focus your attention: (1) keep the program focused on evaluating the baseline etheric energy field, rather than the transient thought, feeling, or judgment; (2) if you are feeling negative or judgmental, ex-pulse and release the negativity; and (3) focus on identifying *what is* from the vantage point of the observer self.

Be detached; that is, suspend your desire for certain results—positive or negative—and take what you get. Be a detached witness, caring for yourself or the other person without attempting to impose your own desires on your evaluation. Identifying *what is* as accurately, objectively, and caringly as you can is the best way to begin transforming and healing a situation you want to change. If we make *what is* worse than it is by projecting negative judgments, we obscure the information and get limited results. If we try to protect ourselves or others by projecting a positive judgment on the information, we also get distorted results. The old golfing rule "Play it where it lies" is as applicable to holoenergetic healing as it is to golf.

EVALUATING THE CHAKRAS

In chapter 2, we discussed the chakras, that is, the multidimensional subtle energy centers interfaced with the body-mind. Each of the seven centers is responsible for maintaining the energetic health of specific organs and bodily functions. One way to determine the degree of your physical health, or your emotional state, is to measure the energy field of each chakra. We can use biomechanical testing to gather information about these energy centers.

Just as in measuring the etheric energy field, you can use biomechanical evaluation to assess the relative expansion or contraction of any chakra field.

Expansion or contraction only reflects relative differences in energy. For instance, with issues of survival-based fear, you may take one of two actions: fight or flight. A reaction of flight through withdrawal will frequently be associated with contraction of your first chakra. If, on the other hand, you flee actively or fight, your first chakra may expand. Thus, both fight and flight can result in either expansion or contraction. Your intuition is able to identify the most prevalent pattern. Similarly, when you express anger it usually expands your third chakra—commonly, the chakra most involved with anger. Or you can repress or block your anger, which contracts the associated chakra. (Other factors, such as chakra rotation, can also be associated with expansion or contraction, but we need not be concerned with these more complex dynamics right now.)

The intensity or activity of the energy of a given chakra influences its relative position in the overall pattern. Generally, one or two chakra fields will be at or within the baseline, which you established when you measured the etheric energy field. If a number of chakras are expanded significantly beyond the etheric field baseline, one or more will usually be found within its boundary and may carry enough intensity to dictate even the location of that baseline.

Evaluating the Quality of Chakras

It is important to understand that the expansion and contraction of the chakras, as described above, reflects their activity, not their development or the quality of consciousness associated with them. To

The Seven Chakras

CHAKRA	LOCATION	ESOTERIC FUNCTIONS	ORGANIC FUNCTIONS	COLOR
First	At the base of the spine or area of the tailbone	Associated with security, the life force, and our will to live	Governs the adrenal glands (located over each kidney), which are associated with the "fight-or-flight" syndrome, as well as hormones associated with relaxation. The adrenal glands respond to events an individual perceives as being a threat to emotional or physical survival. Stress, stimulated by survival concerns, usually affects the first chakra.	Red
Second	Mid-pelvic area, just above the pubic bone	Associated with sensation, pleasure, creativity, procreation, and sexuality. When distorted, it reflects a focus on external stimulation and material possessions. Associated with attitudes toward money, work, relationships with other people, and balance.	Identified with the genital organs and gonads	Orange
Third	Solar plexus area	Emotional development. Our changing emotions tend to be reflected primarily through this chakra. Third-chakra energy plays a role in conditional giving, caring, and nurturing, as well as empathy and issues of self-control and empowerment. When distorted, the third chakra is associated with seeking power through manipulating and controlling others rather than self-mastery and self-empowerment.	Associated with the pancreas	Yellow

Chakra	Location	Description	Association	Color
Fourth	Center of the chest	Love, compassion, unconditional giving, caring, and acceptance. Sometimes described as the "fulcrum" or "turning point" between the lower three chakras, which are concerned with issues of security, creativity, and self-empowerment, and the upper three chakras, which have to do with creative expression, intuitive knowing, spirituality, and unconditional love. All distortions of this chakra and those above it are reflections of distortions in the lower three energy centers.	Associated with the thymus gland and heart	Emerald green
Fifth	Throat area	This is the chakra of creative expression. Creative energy of the second chakra is brought to the fifth chakra, giving it form and expression. Energies here are directed toward self-actualization, self-expression, and communication.	Associated with the thyroid gland	Electric blue
Sixth	Middle of the forehead	Intuitive knowing. Raw energy of the will to live, associated with the first chakra, is drawn to the sixth, where it becomes a personal expression of one's will. Activity of this chakra brings direct knowledge from intuitive and higher spiritual sources.	Associated with the pituitary gland of the brain, sometimes called "the third eye" in conjunction with the pineal gland	Indigo
Seventh	Top of the head (sometimes called the "crown" chakra)	Reflects an awareness of one's spiritual essence, life purpose, and meaning. When fully developed, the crown chakra integrates all other chakras in accord with spiritual values.	Associated with the pineal gland	Violet

determine the quality of consciousness, you need to program yourself to intuitively sense that quality by shifting to your observer self
(see chapter 7), linking with each chakra, and asking for impressions
of its highest level of development at this time. You can use the
Transpersonal Alignment Process (see chapter 3) as a basic format
for such inquiry. Remember to ask permission first.

Generally, the energy of the chakras will extend out from the
body in progressively larger circles, from the first up to the seventh.
Thus, with the first chakra the smallest and the seventh the largest,
the overall pattern would be that of a cone. Sometimes the energy
of the chakras is approximately equal, so that instead of a cone
shape the overall pattern is barrel shaped.

Discontinuity in sequence does not necessarily indicate disease,
illness, or the existence of a negative issue; a discontinuity may be
of a positive nature. When a chakra is out of sequence, it is appropriate to look at the meaning. For example, the heart chakra may be
expanded out of sequence when a person has been sending loving
energy or doing healing work. Someone actively engaged in creative
work or public speaking may have an expanded fifth chakra. Psychic or intuitive activities may expand the sixth chakra.

Sequential imbalance associated with a negative issue may be
temporary. It allows for change and growth, and it gives you an
opportunity to focus on the message of the expressed imbalance.

The presence of a diseased organ or illness may not necessarily
manifest itself in an imbalanced energy field. Other factors may
compensate for any contraction in a field caused by disease. The
health of a specific organ can be evaluated using a program directed
at the local area.

Only relative findings are significant in biomechanical determination of chakra energy fields. There is no standardized evaluation
that applies to everyone. Evaluation has to be based on the gestalt
of the entire person. Again, interpreting the meaning of chakra imbalances requires practice in developing your intuitive senses.

An excellent way to practice your intuitive sensing, even without
using the L-rods (as described below), is to mentally focus and hold

your attention on a single chakra at a time while silently asking, "What is important to know about this chakra to facilitate healing?" Open your mind to receive information, then take what you get and work with it. In this way, you can collect a great deal of information simply by focusing your attention.

⊕ EXERCISE: HOW TO EVALUATE YOUR PARTNER'S
ENERGY CENTERS (CHAKRAS)

1. Establish your partner's baseline energy field, as described earlier.

2. Consult the chakra diagram (fig. 2) so that you can clearly picture in your mind where each of these energy centers is located relative to the pelvis, navel, chest, throat, and head.

3. Assess each chakra separately. You may wish to jot your findings on a piece of paper upon which you've drawn a rough sketch of the chakra positions.

You'll want to note two factors: (1) Is the energy field of the chakra you're assessing more expansive or less expansive (contracted) than the baseline energy field? and (2) Is the energy field of the chakra bilaterally balanced, that is, the same on the right side as on the left side? If it is not balanced, some holoenergetic form may be adversely affecting your partner at that chakra level.

⊕ EXERCISE: HOW TO EVALUATE YOUR OWN
ENERGY CENTERS

1. Stand in front of a mirror; identify and mark your baseline, as I've described earlier in this chapter. Once you have found the baseline, move back to a starting position approximately six feet from the baseline.

2. Bring your L-rods to the basic parallel position. Take a deep breath. While holding your breath and this position, silently ask, "Where is the energy field of my first (second, third, and so on) chakra, relative to the energy of my etheric field, at the present time?"

3. Slowly exhale as you release your question and your mental control of the rods. Begin walking slowly toward the mirror. When the rods open to at least forty-five degrees from the midline, you've reached the interface, or boundary, of your reflected chakra.

   If the rods open before you reach the baseline, that chakra field is considered relatively expanded. If the rods open after you pass through the baseline, that chakra field is considered relatively contracted. For now, simply note these results.

   Did one rod open or turn out more than the other? The opening indicates the relative degree of expansion on that side of that chakra's energy field. This can mean that either this side is expanded or the opposite side is contracted. If you are aware of the overall pattern of the chakras, you can usually determine the nature of the imbalance. You can also intuitively ask which side is expanded or contracted.

   If you find bilateral imbalances between right and left, recall that the left side is considered the receptive, feminine side, while the right is the active, masculine side. A contraction of the left side may suggest you are less receptive to issues related to that energy center.

   When you are facing your own image in the mirror, and the rod in your right hand swings open, it indicates expansion of the right side of your mirror image—this also being the right side of your body. On the other hand, when working with a partner, if your right rod opens it indicates expansion of the left side of your partner's body. The same is true when working with your own mental image before you, as in the exercise "Creating a Double." (In other words, if you are facing another person or your own mental double, the right and left sides would be reversed from what they would be when assessing yourself in a mirror.)

If you are assessing another person's chakras, it is best to start out ten to twelve feet away from them. As you face them, focus on one chakra at a time. Program and move toward them slowly until your L-rods indicate that you've found the interface of the field.

In some cases, the L-rods may open the moment you focus your attention on a particular field. If this happens it indicates that the chakra is expanded beyond the point where you're standing. You may then have to increase the distance between yourself and your partner until you find the outer limit of the chakra's energy field. In rare cases, you may find that there is not enough room in the area you're standing in to get far enough away, since the chakra is so greatly expanded. In such situations, you may want to regard each foot as representing one yard. Your intention to alter the scale in this way is all you'll need to do to effect the change.

Remember to keep the rods parallel to the floor rather than pointing them directly at the chakras being evaluated. It is the programming of the subconscious mind that does the targeting. You target by holding the program in your mind; the program can be a command, an image, or a question concerning the chakra you want to read.

Interpreting Information About Your Energy Centers

You've now assessed the energy levels of each of the seven chakras, noting whether they are expanded or contracted. You've also determined whether or not they are balanced, and if they are not balanced which side is contracted.

Using this information, turn to the "Chakras and Their Esoteric Functions" chart (fig. 2) in chapter 2. There you will find information that will give you some clues about what expanded or con tracted, balanced or unbalanced energies mean for each chakra. There are five categories described: (1) location—in the body; (2) associated organs; (3) mental/emotional functions; (4) distortions; and (5) color—for helping to increase or balance energy for that chakra.

Go through your list of chakra evaluations and cross-reference them with the chart. As you work with this chart, you will begin your exploration of the conditions you want to change. Allow yourself to freely associate with the new information you discover. As you do so, your understanding of the present circumstances will become increasingly clear to you.

You might want to explore chakra evaluations and the other material in this book with a friend. Practice chakra evaluations with each other. Discuss your findings and share your observations openly. This interaction with another person can be tremendously supportive.

The process I'm describing takes some time, and to reap the greatest benefits it is important to be honest with yourself. Your detective work will pay off in deeper self-understanding and can give you a clearer picture of what it is you want to change in your life.

OTHER APPLICATIONS FOR BIOMECHANICAL TESTING

There are numerous other applications for biomechanical testing in healing work. For example, a physician might determine when a particular condition or illness first began. A health practitioner might intuitively evaluate the potential effectiveness and appropriate dosage of a given remedy or food supplement, or the adequacy of an exercise program. An allergist might evaluate allergic sensitivities. Or a psychologist might determine a person's sensitivities to certain emotions or memories. And you can apply the same intuitive principles to self-healing. Of course, intuitive techniques need to be employed along with rational knowing and information to arrive at the optimal course of action.

How to Evaluate Structured Wine or Water

If it's still available, use the previously structured wine or water from the exercise in chapter 4 called "Structured Wine or Water." Place a glass of structured wine and a glass of unstructured wine at least ten feet apart to avoid overlapping energy fields. Use L-rods to evaluate their energy fields (see instructions, page 163).

You may find no field or only a small field around the container of unstructured wine. If successfully structured, the treated wine or water will show a noticeable field.

How to Determine the Time a Condition Began

Knowing the time a problem began gives you a starting point for exploring the critical incidents related to a present problem. Once again, identify the baseline and position yourself there. The L-rods will be open. While standing at the baseline, bring the L-rods back to the basic parallel position. To determine that you are in resonance with the rods, take a deep breath and release it. Do the rods respond? When you take a deep indwelling breath, your energy field may contract; you should see this reflected by the rods moving slightly inward. As you release your breath, the energy expands and the rods should move outward again. You are now in resonance with your rods.

Now ask, "At what age did the source of this difficulty begin?" If you are asking about a physical condition, request that your partner sense into that condition. If you are doing self-healing, feel it or visualize it in your mind.

Hold that sense or image of the condition you're inquiring about in your mind and begin naming time intervals. It is easiest to start with five-year time intervals beginning with the person's present age. If a person is thirty years old you might ask, "Did the source of this problem begin between the ages of twenty-five and thirty?" If the rods don't move, regard that as a "no" response. If the rods open, this indicates a "yes." If you continue to get "no" responses between birth and five years, ask if the source of the problem occurred (1) during birth, (2) during the intrauterine period, (3) at conception, or (4) prior to conception. A time can be pinpointed by counting off shorter intervals.

You can also learn about yourself by working with your own image in a mirror or by using a photograph of yourself. You can explore these questions with regard to another person with that person present or, if the person is absent, by using a photograph or mental image of her or him. If you are working with a photograph, the right and left sides will be the same as if you were working directly with the person.

Using L-Rods to Test for Various Influences on Energy Patterns

The ability to monitor your etheric energy field allows you to assess virtually any factor that affects your subtle energy system. These effects, which may have previously been below conscious awareness, can now be brought to a conscious level so that you can have a choice about changing them. They can include factors such as foods, thoughts, feelings, relationships, environments, and any treatments received in the past. Present or future decisions can be evaluated in terms of their effect or projected effect on your energy fields.

While standing at the baseline, where the L-rods move outward, forty-five degrees from the baseline, you can bring to mind any question you might have. For example, you can imagine as vividly as possible the taste, appearance, and texture of sugar. Bring the rods to their basic parallel position. Then ask, "Is this sugar beneficial for me at this time?" If the rods open, that indicates a "yes" answer. If they remain closed, assume a "no."

Although virtually any decision-making process can be enhanced using the L-rods, don't rely exclusively on this method of acquiring information. Regard it as a complement to familiar ways of knowing and deciding that have worked successfully for you in the past.

At this point, you will have completed the first step in the holoenergetic healing process, called Recognition. It is time to go on to step two, Resonance. As you gain practice in the techniques of holoenergetic healing, you'll begin to see that each step blends into the other. Rather than being made up of discrete steps, the entire process will begin to flow freely for you. I divide it into four steps now only because most people find that four smaller steps are much easier to learn than one big leap.

⊕ EXERCISE: EXPLORING ENERGY TRANSFERENCE

The following exercise provides excellent practice for transferring or withdrawing energy from another person or for moving it from place to place within your or another person's body. You will need an orange, a sharp knife for cutting the orange, and a pair of L-rods (optional). If you do not have L-rods, go directly to the paragraph below titled "Evaluation Using Your Senses."

1. Biomechanically test the energy field of an orange using L-rods. Begin by standing four to five feet from the orange and setting your intention: "Show me the energy field of this orange."

2. Breathe in and hold your breath while silently repeating your intended program. As you breathe out release the program and slowly walk toward the orange, allowing the rods to swing out at the interface of the energy field of the orange. An unenergized orange may have a barely perceptible field.

Energizing the Orange

1. To energize the orange, begin by rubbing your hands together to build a charge. As you do so, take several deep breaths at the same time as you are imagining energy coming up through your feet from the Earth. Imagine this energy igniting your hands as it flows into them.

2. Then cup your hands around the orange without touching it or the surface on which it is resting. Focus your attention on the

orange to allow yourself to come into resonance with it. Clarify your intention to energize the orange.

3. Still focusing on the orange, breathe in. This enhances your resonant coupling and activates the orange. While holding your breath, set your intention or program, which is to send the orange vitalizing energy. Also imagine the orange becoming a radiant sphere of light.

4. Now forcibly release your breath through your nostrils, as an ex-pulse, to infuse the orange with your energy. At the same time, imagine energy from your hands infusing the orange.

5. Repeat this three times to augment the transfer of energy.

Evaluation with L-Rods

Next, evaluate the energized orange with L-rods. If this exercise is successful, you should notice that the field of the energized orange has expanded to at least double or triple its original field.

Withdrawing Energy

Now, proceed by withdrawing energy from the orange.

1. Cup your hands around the orange without touching it and come into resonance with it by focusing your attention on it. Set your intention to de-energize the orange this time, stripping it of any charge.

2. Draw your breath in through your nose, as an in-pulse, imagining that you are extracting energy from the core of the orange. Toward the end of the in-pulse, abruptly move your hands away from the orange as though you were grabbing the energy from it. This breaks the field and ensures that you do not recharge the orange when releasing your breath again.

Evaluation with L-Rods

Use L-rods to evaluate the energy field of your de-energized orange. The field may be the same as or smaller than the original field.

Evaluation by Appearance, Smell, and Taste

Cut the orange in half. Set aside one half as a control for comparison. Energize the other half of your orange as described above. Wait ten minutes, then compare the difference between the energized and control halves of the orange. Notice any changes in appearance, fragrance, and taste in the energized half.

Evaluation Using Your Senses

If you don't have L-rods, proceed with this exercise using your senses of taste, smell, and vision to determine your efficacy in transferring and withdrawing energy.

1. Take a fresh, ripe orange and cut it in half, setting aside one half for comparison. Energize the other half of the orange as described above in "Energizing An Orange."

2. Cut the energized half into two quarters.

3. Take one energized quarter and withdraw the energy from it, as described above in "Withdrawing Energy."

4. Wait ten minutes; then compare the difference between the energized and de-energized sections and the control half of the orange. Notice any changes in appearance, fragrance, or taste.

Blessing Our Food and Ourselves

As a part of any health program, we can use the energy of love, joy, gratitude, peace, and healing to infuse our food and drink with energy. When we ingest that food, those energies become a part of us. Frequently, I have patients drink water they have energized with love and healing intent as a way of blessing themselves.

7

The Observer Self

The transpersonal Self that transcends personal boundaries, remains as an experiencer, distinct from what is experienced. The transpersonal Self may first come into awareness with the awakening of the inner witness or observer of experience that remains distinct from the contents of consciousness such as thoughts, feelings, sensations, or images.

—FRANCES VAUGHAN

In the Recognition portion of holoenergetic healing, you had the experience of asking yourself questions and receiving answers. There were times in this self-exploration—especially during biomechanical testing—when you disengaged from your usual sensing, feeling, thinking self and shifted your consciousness to a more detached perspective. In doing so, you were drawing upon the resources of your observer self. Perhaps you made these shifts without being aware you were doing so. In the chapters that follow, you will be taking a more deliberate approach, shifting your consciousness using specific methods that I'll describe here.

JUDGMENT AND THE OBSERVER SELF

In our everyday lives, we are constantly called upon to make judgments and evaluations: Is it safe to cross the street now or should I wait for the next light? Will Dorothy deliver the work before the deadline or should we have an alternate plan? Should I have frozen yogurt or ice cream? Certainly, making such choices is useful. But in doing holoenergetic healing, especially after the Recognition phase, it is also important to know how to use your mind consciously in a different way. You want to be able to stand back, to set aside your judgments and evaluations, ask questions, and receive answers from a more expanded state of self-awareness. To do so you'll want to know how to enter an observer state of mind at will. What is this observer state?

Roberto Assagioli, M.D., the founder of psychosynthesis, has stated that

> At the heart of the self there is both an active and a passive element, an agent and a spectator. Self-consciousness involves our being a witness—a pure, objective, loving witness—to what is happening within and without. In this sense the self is not a dynamic in itself but is a point of witness, a spectator, an observer who watches the flow. But there is another part of the inner self—the *will-er* or directing agent—that actively intervenes to orchestrate the various functions and energies of the personality, to make commitments and to instigate action in the external world. So, at the center of the self there is a unity of masculine and feminine, will and love, action and observation.[1]

There is a part of each one of us that makes sense of or interprets information we receive through our physical senses. Psychologists have called this the *sensorium*. In their book *Beyond Biofeedback*, Elmer and Alyce Green point out that when we say, "My finger hurts," it might be more accurate to say, "Agitation of free nerve endings in my finger are being projected into brain areas that, when activated, and when attention is properly focused therein, give a feeling of pain." This is what we mean by "body consciousness" or "sense perception."

---

1. Quoted in an article by Sam Keen, "The Golden Mean of Roberto Assagioli," *Psychology Today,* December 1974, p. 33.

In the process of *interpreting* information from our senses, we give our own meaning to the messages coming into our minds from all our sense organs. We filter all the sensory information through our past experiences and beliefs; what comes out on the other side of these filters is our present perceptions colored by our past. It is the interpreting part of us that accounts for the way each of us sees the world in a different way.

Some years ago, the philosopher and mathematician Alfred North Whitehead said:

> The mind in apprehending also experiences sensations which, properly speaking, are qualities of the mind alone. These sensations are projected by the mind so as to clothe appropriate bodies in external nature. Thus the bodies are perceived as with qualities which in reality do not belong to them, qualities which in fact are purely the offspring of the mind. Thus, nature gets credit which should in truth be reserved for ourselves: the rose for its scent; the nightingale for its song; and the sun for its radiance. The poets are entirely mistaken. They should address their lyrics to themselves, and should turn them into odes of self-congratulation on the excellency of the human mind.[2]

FILTERS AND
SELF-FULFILLING PROPHECIES

The beliefs we hold within us tend to become self-fulfilling prophecies; we find, in the external world, experiences that support our inner beliefs. We select from the vast possibilities of human existence those that support our inner perceptions. Simply put, what we see is what we *once believed we saw,* not *what is.*

Our filters become structures in our consciousness. And it is these filters that provide us with a semblance of continuity in an infinite and ever-changing reality. While we interpret sensory infor-

2. Alfred North Whitehead, *Process and Reality* (New York: Harper & Row, 1929), p. 383.

mation by, in effect, running it through these filters, we also use the filters in another way, called *projection*.

We use the term *projection* to describe how we transfer our own beliefs, feelings, and structured perceptions onto the external world. It is as if we had an invisible movie projector within our minds. From the projection booth of our consciousness we are constantly playing a film made up of all our past structured experiences. The filters we used to interpret our sensory messages have now become a film. The "movie" we've made is projected onto the external world so that the new experiences before us are all intermingled with old experiences from our past. We're rarely aware of our projections, and therefore it is often very difficult to sort out the new information we're receiving from the old film we're projecting.

As part of their biofeedback research, Elmer and Alyce Green found that

> the energy that triggers our sensations is perceived, or interpreted, according to the nature or structure of our perceiving apparatus. What we see and hear (or detect in any way) resemble projections whose apparent character, nature, or identifying features are shaped according to rules laid down in our mind-body structure. For example, if an extremely powerful magnet is moved across the back of the head so that the magnetic lines of force interact with the visual cortex, we see bands of colored light moving across our field of view. In actuality the magnetic field has no color and isn't a band of light, but its interaction with the brain is interpreted (projected) by the perceptual apparatus in the only way it has been trained to perceive. If you agitate visual nerves you get light; if you agitate auditory nerves you get sound. Everything that we consciously perceive has associated with it some kind of electrochemical activity in our brains, but that activity does not necessarily inform us of the true nature of what we are perceiving, especially if the stimulus is from parapsychological (subtle energy) sources (*Beyond Biofeedback*, p. 154).

So in our interactions with the external world, we both filter information coming in and project information from inside us to the external world. In this way, our own "movie" has an effect on the world outside us.

PROJECTION IN THE ENERGETIC WORLD

Energetically, our projections can be viewed as a set of frequencies that, when matched by the object of our projections, can create an enhanced response, actually encouraging into being the qualities projected. So in this way a projection can become self-fulfilling. If the object of your attention doesn't have the qualities that resonate with your projection, your effect on it will be minimal. We say that beauty or love is in the eye of the beholder; if what is beheld has the same qualities that you're projecting onto it, those qualities will be encouraged. That person or object will become radiant with the energy of beauty and love. Conversely, if you project hostility or abuse onto another, and that person has some of those qualities within him or her, those qualities can be activated, and then you or others could become the recipient of that person's hostility or abuse.

The filters structured in consciousness are at work even in cases of seemingly simple perception of sensations. For example, in my workshops I sometimes have people put one hand in a bucket of hot water and the other in ice-cold water. They leave their hands there for a few moments, then take them out and put them both, simultaneously, into tepid water. Then I ask participants to describe what they feel in each hand. They report that the hand that had been in ice water senses the tepid water as warm; the hand that had been in hot water senses the tepid water as cool.

How can the very same bucket of tepid water seem warm to one hand, cool to the other? From the perspective of the sensing hands, that is, the body consciousness, this is a dualistic paradox. But there is another part of us, the observer self, that has a broader, more integrative awareness. It perceives the whole process, not just what the senses seem to be telling us. The observer self is aware of the sensations but is also aware of where the hands were moments before. It takes into account how the previous conditioning affects the present perception. The observer self also has access to the "sixth sense"—intuition.

If you were to do the water experiment for yourself, you probably wouldn't be upset that the water seemed both warm and cool at the same time. You would be aware of how the previous conditioning of putting your hands in hot and cold water was influencing your present perception. Your observer self would tell you, "Sense perception is only part of the picture here. There is more to be considered." When confronted with this seeming paradox, you would instinctively shift your awareness to a higher level to resolve it.

In holoenergetic healing, we want to make the instinctive process we're describing above a conscious choice.

IDENTIFICATION AND DIS-IDENTIFICATION

The deeper we go into the holoenergetic healing process, the more we draw upon our intuitive sense and the more useful it becomes to shift our consciousness at will. We must both be able to identify with that part of us that experiences an illness or other circumstance we want to change and at the same time be able to step outside that part to seek and make new, more expansive choices. To put it another way, it is important to both identify with our thoughts, feelings, and sensations and be able to "dis-identify" from them.

As you enter the Resonance phase of holoenergetic healing, you will be getting in touch with and identifying with your sensations, feelings, beliefs, and imagery, which create the holoenergetic patterns of your mind. As you do so, old remnants of denial or resistance dissolve and you more fully accept what is.

To take the next step beyond the acceptance and understanding you experience in Resonance (identification), you release identification and shift to the observer self (dis-identification). After the Resonance process, the shift to the observer self might be compared to taking in the view from the top of the mountain after a long climb.

The air is fresh and clear, and from here you can look around. You can observe your holoenergetic pattern as if you were looking down at the camp from which you've just come.

Identification and Understanding

To perceive accurately and understand something, you need to identify with it—to merge with it and become it. Buddha taught that in order to understand the object of our perception we have to be one with what we want to understand. Thus, perception or felt awareness evolves into understanding through identification. Through loving identification, I become you, so I understand you. I see and feel what you see and feel—and I understand. I understand why you are as you are and what you really want.

To identify with so as to understand is to have *compassion*. When the force of compassion and understanding becomes a living, healing force in our lives, it becomes wisdom.

Choice and Dis-Identification

To choose to change something, you need to dis-identify, to step outside and become the *observer-participant*—an objective, loving witness who participates and interacts. You release yourself from the identification, but you hold the understanding that you gained through identification.

Dis-identification is like a fulcrum—the stillpoint of the observer-participant that allows your will to act as a lever, to shift (or change) that which you identified with. It's hard to move a rock if you're standing on it. But if you step aside and use a lever with a fulcrum, you can move even heavy stones. The lever is your will, intention, and imagery; but it needs the fulcrum of dis-identified understanding (via the observer-participant) to be most effective.

Just to step off the rock is to disconnect, to separate from, or to deny its existence. When you dis-identify, you step off with understanding and the intent to change.

In *The Unfolding Self,* Molly Brown comments: "As we become more aware, as we learn to observe without judgment . . . we move into that subtle state of being aware of awareness, becoming aware of that which is aware, the self" (p. 26). When we change our point of view in this way, we can get to the core issues or sources; we can know what is beyond the distortions of our senses and feelings. In the observer state we dis-identify ourselves from our perceptual limitations.

In the Resonance, Release, and Reformation phases of healing, the observer self is primarily transpersonal, able to shift awareness and perceive a truth beyond the perspectives of the physical, emotional, and mental self. The observer self not only knows what the hands are experiencing but also knows the past source or context of that experience. When we have a disease or illness, it is easy to focus on the single reality of disease to define us. It's similar to how each hand defines the water temperature: each hand separately "knows" it's right about the temperature; therefore, the other hand must be wrong. This is an either-or way of interpreting experience.

Frequently, when we are ill, there's a part of us that feels contracted and separate and "knows" that it is "right" about its experience. All the "facts" support it. Only at the level of the observer consciousness, when we take into account the source and meaning of the illness and the beliefs that created the illusion of separation, can the paradox of illness be resolved. I say "paradox" because behind all illness lies a positive life force that has become thwarted and distorted in its expression.

THE OBSERVER SELF AS EDITOR OF OUR PROJECTIONS

The observer self knows that the filters we use to interpret our sensory information and "make the movies" we project can be changed. It knows that present perceptions can be changed by altering previous information and experience that we now hold energetically as geometric patterns in our minds. The holoenergetic process alters previous information by energetically unforming and re-forming the pattern—by shifting the attitudinal and belief structures that color experience, which in turn alters perception.

Beliefs and attitudes directly select perception. Whether the glass is half full or half empty is a choice, an attitudinal choice, since both are true. In holoenergetic healing, we learn not only how to shift from the attitude that the glass is half empty to the attitude that it is half full but also how to fill the glass and perhaps tap into the ocean from which all water comes.

The observer state allows us to see the thoughts, feelings, seeming paradoxes, separation, and illness or disease from a perspective that can then be incorporated, integrated, and resolved. Healing occurs as we incorporate and integrate our illusions of separateness and move toward wholeness. In this movement toward wholeness, our observer self is not only a helper but a model, allowing us to sense our full potential, the whole that is greater than the sum of the parts.

WAYS OF SHIFTING TO OBSERVER CONSCIOUSNESS

In different parts of this book I have described several ways to shift to an observer level of consciousness:

- The Transpersonal Alignment Process (p. 70).
- Breathing techniques such as the balancing breath (p. 105).
- Going to your "Safe Space" (p. 263) and calling upon your higher Self.
- Getting in touch with your intuitive guidance, as in the "Inner Guide" exercise (see Resource 1).
- Using the resonance of the unconditional love (p. 223) and forgiveness states (p. 206).
- Going through the holoenergetic healing process (see chapter 12).

- From a meditative state, focusing attention on the thymus area or heart chakra, also known as the "witness area."

Become acquainted with each of these methods. You'll find that some work better than others for you, and that there are times when some methods are more appropriate than others. Wherever you find instructions for these methods for shifting consciousness, you'll also find comments about their application. Throughout your work in holoenergetic healing, bear in mind that the shift to the observer self is a step toward wholeness, which is the essence of healing.

My Self

I am here for you always. I am beyond attachment. I am beyond sadness. I am beyond fear. I exist in and as radiant love.

Come to me in your sadness and I will hold you in the arms of your mother.

Come to me in your fear and I will care for you, guide you and protect you. Come to me when your lover leaves you and I will be your lover. Come to me when you are torn by guilt. And I shall lift the veil of falsehood and make you whole.

Come to me when you fear you have failed. And I will show you the true magnificence of your success.

I am your golden guide, the shining priestess of your temple,

the living light of your soul. I am surrounded by

the holiest beings in the universe. They are your helpers.

You alone can meet me here. It is through you that others know me, hear my wisdom, feel my infinite love, are comforted and healed.

Your work is to free yourself so that I may embody your life. I give you all that I am. All of my mystical power awaits your command.

All of my love longs to flow through your heart. All of my knowledge I bequeath to you. Speak it! Now!

I am with you always. Bring me forth Oh my self!

—Anonymous

8

Resonance

A human being is a part of the whole, called by us "Universe"; a part limited in time and space. He experiences himself, his thoughts and feelings as something separated from the rest—a kind of optical delusion of consciousness. This delusion is a kind of prison for us, restricting us to our personal desires and to affection for a few persons nearest us. Our task must be to free ourselves from this prison by widening our circle of compassion to embrace all living creatures and the whole of nature in its beauty. Nobody is able to achieve this completely but the striving for such achievement is, in itself, a part of the liberation and a foundation for inner security.

—ALBERT EINSTEIN

In ancient intuitive societies, when a shaman was called upon to find buffalo for the tribe to hunt, he visualized the herd in his mind. He imagined it, then moved with it and identified with it, literally becoming the herd in his mind's eye. When the shaman came out of trance, he was able to tell the hunters exactly where to find their quarry. The hunters followed the shaman's advice and were successful in the hunt.

There were shamans for the hunt and shamans for healing. And whether locating game for the hunters or helping to heal a disease, they shared a common ability: the ability to be at one with their subject. This process is the crux of what we call Resonance in holoenergetic healing.

Resonance is important, because in the resonant state resistance to change is minimal. This maximizes our ability to successfully move toward the healthy state we want.

Resonance is the energetic chemistry between people. Charisma, passion, and compassion between two or more people are expressions of the enhanced response of Resonance.

In chapter 3, I spoke of resonant coupling, which occurs when one structure vibrates at the natural frequency of another. The effects of resonant coupling are twofold:

1. There is enhanced responsiveness, with one structure's energy field reinforcing the other's, thus intensifying the interaction. You may recall that I compared this with what happens when one person pushes another at just the right time on a swing. It is also what happens when a soprano sings a note at the natural frequency of a crystal goblet: The goblet begins to vibrate more and more forcefully. As the vibrations of the singer's voice reinforce the goblet's vibration beyond its structural capacity, the glass shatters. Troops marching across a bridge "break step" to avoid resonant coupling.

2. The sending and receiving frequencies of the energy fields are linked, essentially becoming one. One part cannot move without the other responding. The grape embedded in a bowl of jelly moves every time you push on the jelly, and the jelly moves every time you push on the grape.

Taken together, these two key factors of resonant coupling strongly suggest that very little motion is wasted. Every motion is communicated and has an effect. This means that maximum change can occur at an energetic level, with a minimum expenditure of energy, and with minimal resistance to change.

UNITY, LOVE, AND THE NOW

We can, of course, resonate with other energy fields in a variety of ways. In the example I gave at the beginning of chapter 2 of the drunk on the train, Terry Dobson at first resonated with the drunk's anger and frustration. In the end, the drunk resonated with the old man's love. In holoenergetic healing, we make the choice to resonate with love. In this state of loving resonance we encounter the least resistance to change, and we engender change with maximum efficiency.

History is replete with prophets, poets, healers, and even politicians who have reflected on the power of loving resonance. In such moments we live in the *now*. There is no sense of separation between ourselves and the other or ourselves and our actions of that moment. Walt Whitman spoke of the ecstatic moment when "the singer becomes the song." Similarly, William Butler Yeats spoke of the oneness that occurs when "the dancer becomes the dance." Christ asked us to love our enemy, to become one with our enemy, to be aware of our relatedness—to come into resonance and then act with compassionate love out of that aware relatedness. Abraham Lincoln said that the best way to defeat an enemy is to make him your friend. When you come to know and love your enemy, you will no longer have an enemy.

Loving resonance allows us to address directly the problem of resistance. Many of us are our own worst enemies; we resist change even when we have intellectually chosen it and know it to be healing and beneficial. We ourselves generate and maintain unhealthy states. When we want to change an unhealthy aspect of ourselves, we can choose to attack it, destroy it, and cut it out. Or we can recognize its positive intent by befriending it, blending into loving resonance with it, and then transforming the unhealthy energy patterns we are maintaining into healthy ones. That's acceptance with the intention to understand and change; it's the opposite of resistance. As we use it here, acceptance means fully acknowledging the truth, letting ourselves see what is so, rather than disowning and

179

denying it. Acceptance does not mean acquiescence or resignation, giving in, or giving up. It means coming into resonance with what is so in the moment. It is Recognition occurring at the energetic level of Resonance.

When we come into resonance we enter a state of "at-one-ness" or unity. This unity, occurring in the now, is often called "the point of power." Being in the now, we momentarily transcend space and time; there is no past, no future, only here and now. At the moment when we match frequencies with another event, thing, or person, we become energetically one with it in the present. Once linking in resonance, we can influence, through choice, the possible future, and even the past, of that event or thing. Thus, we can find and change those energy patterns in ourselves that we desire to change.

As we begin working with Resonance, it is important to remember that all matter, as well as every thought, every belief, every event, and every feeling, has a natural frequency or set of frequencies at which it vibrates. When we come into resonance with these other vibrations, it is not always necessary to resonate at exactly the same frequency. Rather, to be in harmony with that frequency is enough.

Harmonies always exist in some ratio to the natural frequency— one-half to one, one-quarter to one, two to one, and so on. We each have an internal sense of proportion that is universal, creating the potential for a sense of harmony between ourselves and the universe in which we live. We all share sacred energy patterns and harmonics that are the basis for what we perceive as beauty, love, health, truth, and unity. Through our internal sense of proportion and order, we can identify and recognize dissonance and resonance.

THE PRINCIPLES OF RESONANCE IN MODERN MEDICINE

Let's look at how modern medicine makes use of the phenomenon of Resonance in the technique of Magnetic Resonant Imaging, or

MRI. Then let's see how these same principles can apply to our healing work.

MRI is a new technique for imaging organs, tumors, and blood flow in the body. To understand MRI we need to first understand some physics.

In the simplest atom, the element hydrogen, there is a positively charged particle called a proton in the center that constitutes the nucleus, and an electron that revolves around it. The proton spins on its axis and, as it spins, it wobbles. Its wobble is characteristic of hydrogen; each element has its own characteristic wobble. Normally, the axes of the hydrogen atoms in our body are randomized, but in the presence of a strong magnetic field they all align in the field, just as iron filings align themselves with the field of a magnet.

For MRI studies, the patient is wheeled into a large, tubular magnet and the magnet is turned on. Then a radio frequency pulse that is resonant with the hydrogen proton is transmitted into the patient. Because it is resonant with the hydrogen proton, the energy pulse is absorbed by the proton. When it absorbs the energy, the proton "flips" out of alignment. Without the presence of a magnetic field, the hydrogen proton does not respond to this resonant pulse.

MRI does not alter any of the protons of the other elements that constitute the body. Only the hydrogen proton flips out, because only it can resonate with the pulse. When the pulse stops, the proton drops back into alignment; as it does, it releases energy. That released energy is picked up by a sensor, fed through a computer, and printed out as an image.

The MRI process can image tumors or the blood flow of coronary arteries. Because the energy "fingerprint" or "signature" of cancer cells is different from that of normal cells, this technique has provided a breakthrough in the identification of some forms of cancer.

How is MRI related to healing? While the energies that cause change in MRI are generated by a magnetic field and a radio frequency resonating with the hydrogen proton, the energies that cause change in holoenergetic healing are generated by our love and intention. A loving field, analogous to the magnetic field in MRI, can be created by our hands, our feelings, thoughts, or even our presence, especially when we are in a heightened transpersonal state. Our intention to heal, with its attendant thoughts, feelings, and images, focused by our attention and directed by our breath, can be resonantly pulsed into our body-mind, much like the radio frequency that targets the hydrogen proton in MRI. Without the magnetic field in MRI, the hydrogen proton doesn't respond to the resonant pulse—it doesn't "flip." Without the loving field in holoenergetic healing, the changes targeted by intention don't readily "flip"; that is, they are less likely to occur. A loving field is the holoenergetic activator of the body-mind, preparing it for the "healing flip," which is the resonant pulsed intention.

THE SHAMAN'S LESSONS REVISITED

Once we have identified what it is we want to change (Recognition), the next step is to target the area by coming into resonance with it energetically. How do we do this? If we are dealing with physical or emotional trauma, or a critical incident that occurred early in childhood, the best way to come into resonance is to reexperience the initiating event. By focusing attention initially on present sensations and emotions associated with the problem, we can go back in our memory and resonate with the problem, reexperiencing it with the intention of understanding its meaning and releasing ourselves from its influence.

If we are dealing with a specific lesion in the body or with a disease that has physical manifestations, we begin by focusing attention on that condition. When we successfully focus attention on something, we come into resonance with it, and in doing so we can begin to access information about it and activate it in preparation for intentional change. How do we focus attention? I do it by asking myself (or the other person) to "go into" that affected or disturbed area with my mind and describe what comes up, especially sensations, images, and feelings. This is similar to what the shaman does when he imagines the buffalo and becomes one with the herd.

Some people are visually oriented, and when they describe their condition they do so in terms of visual imagery. Others are more kinesthetic or auditory and describe their condition in terms of what they feel or hear.

When working with a partner, another way to come into resonance is through induction. Induction occurs when an individual's energy field is stepped up or down in the presence of another energy field. For example, the energy field might be stepped up in the presence of an inspirational person, or a sacred object or place. Dancers, actors, and team athletes who must work in close synchronization with each other use the principle of induction to become closely attuned with each other. They may practice breathing together at the same rates, moving together at the same rhythms, or holding a single note to induce a state of resonance.

While doing healing research in a biofeedback laboratory, I used an electroencephalograph so that I could simultaneously monitor my own and my patients' EEG patterns. During a healing session the patient's EEG pattern became synchronous with mine. Presumably, my energy field induced a similar pattern in the patient's EEG, allowing us to be in a state of brain wave resonance. During periods when our brain waves were matching, it was much easier for both of us to intuitively access pertinent information about the illness and for healing energy to flow between us.

Induction occurs frequently when one person shifts into a transpersonal or elevated state of consciousness in the presence of another. You may also call upon higher guidance to induct yourself into resonance.

In the following paragraphs, I describe how to come into resonance with the situation you want to heal. Prepare yourself by first grounding, aligning, and centering yourself. This preparation gives you greater ability to move in and out of the observer state that we explored in the previous chapter.

Prepare

Start by removing your watch, jewelry, coins, and other metals from your person, since these tend to hold traces of the energy patterns you want to change. Remove your shoes if convenient and loosen any tight clothing.

Find a quiet and peaceful place where you can close your eyes and not be disturbed.

Relax

Use whatever method you desire for achieving a relaxed and open state. You may already be familiar with a meditation or conscious relaxation technique; if you are, use that method now. (If you do not currently have a relaxation technique, turn to resource 1, "The Inner Guide," in the Resources section of this book. There you will find the Relaxation exercise, which will help you with this.

Ground Yourself

In your relaxed state, take several slow, deep, abdominal breaths. As you breathe in, imagine that you are drawing in energy from the center of the Earth, up through the base of your spine to your heart. As you gently exhale your breath, imagine it being released into the center of your chest, into your heart center.

Generally, you want to feel relaxed and calm, yet energized. If you feel overenergized, or slightly "hyper," you can drain off some of this energy: Imagine a cord extending from your solar plexus (or the base of your spine, whichever you prefer) to the center of the Earth. Then draw in a deep breath as if through your solar plexus or the base of your spine and, as you gently exhale, imagine your excess energy flowing out of your body, along your grounding cord to the center of the Earth.

You may choose to repeat the grounding exercise two or more times until you feel thoroughly present and comfortable.

Align Yourself

In your relaxed and grounded state, take several slow, deep breaths. As you breathe in, imagine that you are drawing energy from the

Cosmos, in through the top of your head (your seventh chakra) down through your sixth and fifth chakras to your fourth, or heart, chakra. Now gently exhale into the center of your chest. Each time you draw in your breath, imagine yourself receiving universal energy from the Cosmos, then releasing that energy into your heart center, thus aligning yourself with spirit.

Center Yourself

In your relaxed, grounded, and aligned state, take another deep breath, and, as you do, imagine that you are drawing in energy from two sources simultaneously: from the Cosmos and from the Earth. Imagine these energies coming together at your heart chakra. As these energies merge and fuse in your heart, imagine a burst of brilliant light expanding, flooding your entire body with light as you release your breath.

Now you are relaxed, grounded, aligned, and centered. This alters your state of consciousness, allowing you to maintain an open focus and access information through the intuitive mind.

You are now ready to come into resonance with what you want to change. If at any point along the way, you would like to do so, enter your "safe place" and access your inner guide or higher Self (see p. 259–62 for complete details). You can then quickly and easily receive support and guidance from your intuitive self.

1. COMING INTO RESONANCE WITH WHAT YOU WANT TO CHANGE

Find a comfortable position. You can stand, sit, or lie comfortably on your back for this holoenergetic work. Sitting is generally the most effective position for self-healing. It enables you to relax more readily than if you stood, and it allows you to work better with your hands in the energy field of lower areas of the body. Some people

Healing with Love

prefer standing because they find it affords a greater flow of energy, even though there is increased muscular tension and perhaps difficulty maintaining balance with the eyes closed. Experiment to determine the best position for you. You may find it useful to tape record the following steps.

✪ EXERCISE: THE BALANCING BREATH

This breathing exercise allows you to bring both hemispheres of your brain into balance. In this way, you'll be able to draw freely upon both the intuitive and the reasoning functions of your mind.

(For convenience, I have duplicated this exercise from chapter 4. You may want to go back to that chapter for a detailed explanation.)

1. Assume a comfortable, relaxed position.
2. Gently close your eyes.
3. Exhale, allowing your lungs to empty and relax.
4. As you breathe in, imagine your breath coming in through your left nostril, then up to the center of your forehead.
5. As you exhale, imagine your breath coming out your right nostril.
6. Next, inhale through your right nostril, up to the center of your forehead. Exhale through your left nostril.
7. Breathe in the way described for seven cycles. (Each inhalation followed by an exhalation is one complete cycle.)
8. On your eighth cycle, breathe in through both nostrils simultaneously. Hold that breath for a moment and focus your attention on the center of your forehead.
9. Release your breath as if you were exhaling it through your forehead. This opens up your sixth chakra, or energy center, the center of the intuitive functions of your mind.

As you do this breathing exercise, try to involve as many senses as you can. For example, as you breathe in, notice that the air flowing through your nostrils feels cool. Notice how it feels warmed in your nostrils as you exhale. As you breathe, air moves the tiny hairs that line your nasal passages. Allow yourself to sense these movements.

You might also imagine that you are breathing in light or color, or even a fragrance, such as that of a rose. If you want to balance or increase the energy of a certain chakra, you might now refer to the chakra chart (fig. 2) and imagine yourself breathing in the color that corresponds with that particular chakra.

When the hemispheres of your brain are brought into balance in this way, your consciousness shifts into the transpersonal dimension. In this synchronous state of balance there is a merging, or fusion, accompanied by a release of energy that some people experience as light. In Eastern traditions, this is sometimes referred to as the "Blue Pearl."

You may discover in doing this breathing exercise that sometimes when you achieve the sense of unity and peace associated with this process you also experience this blue light, signaling to you that an energetic fusion of your right and left hemispheres is occurring and that your consciousness has shifted to the transpersonal realm.

If you do not experience this blue light, don't be concerned about it. The most important thing is to allow yourself to experience a sense of relaxation and peace, and perhaps a sense of connectedness or oneness.

In this relaxed and connected state, you may find that it takes considerable energy to maintain a sense of separation. The sense of unity you're experiencing will seem to be a more natural, more normal way to be. It is in this state that we can most easily let go of those habits, or ways of thinking and feeling, that maintain separation and hold in place the energy templates or holoforms that we want to change.

2. MAKING THE DECISION TO HEAL

At this point ask yourself: *Am I really willing to allow healing to occur now?*

Be honest about your answer. If you really feel that you do not want to go on with this healing experience, ask yourself: "Why not?" Then explore why not. If your answer really is "no," do not go further. Remember, healing has its own pace and rhythm, one to be respected. If you are not ready at this time, stop what you are doing with the conviction that there will come a time when you are ready. Consider your honest "no" answer at this time to be part of the healing process, for that is what it truly is.

If you get a positive answer, go on to the next step.

3. FOCUSING ON THE WITNESS AREA

Start all your self-healing by focusing your attention on your witness area/thymus gland, and your heart center. This links your physical, personal, and transpersonal states. The witness area is in the center of your chest, between three and five inches below the level of your shoulders. To activate the body-mind in preparation for change, create a loving field by recalling a time when you were most loved or loving. Building energy in this area brings to conscious awareness experiences related to the issues you want to address for healing. I recommend doing this by assigning one hand as your "energizing hand" and the other as your "sensing hand." Generally you'll be more comfortable using your dominant hand for energizing.

Energizing Hand

Activate your thymus/heart center by positioning your dominant hand three to six inches from your body, fingers extended but relaxed, palm facing the center of your chest. This is your "energizing hand," which you will use in your energy field to build a charge, preparing yourself for change.

Energy can be transferred and transformed through intention. The specific use of the hands and the breath augments our intention. Although not necessary for holoenergetic healing, the physical presence of our hands in the energy field facilitates the transference or transformation, thereby making it easier to effect change.

To energize the area, intend and imagine that your hand is ignited, radiating energy. Slowly move this hand back and forth over the witness (thymus/heart) area, creating an energy flux. This hand movement enhances your ability to perceive sensation in the center of your chest. You may feel a tingling, warmth, coolness, pulsation, or pressure.

Sensing Hand

Scan your witness area by positioning your other hand (the sensing hand) eight to ten inches from your body (see fig. 11), palm toward your heart center. By moving your sensing hand up and down between your shoulder area and your waist, you can find the point of maximum resonance where sensation will be the strongest. Hold your hand in that position to reinforce the field and attune your sensing abilities to any energy shifts that occur there. The sensing hand helps to contain and reinforce the energy field, giving you a "handle" on the energy. You may find it helpful to review the Sensing Subtle Energies exercise at the end of chapter 1.[1]

4. COMING INTO RESONANCE

Breathe in deeply as if through your thymus/heart center and hold your breath. As you slowly release your breath, allow to come to mind the areas of concern that you want to change. If this is a

---

1. For the sake of simplicity, I have separated the energizing and sensing functions between the two hands. However, both hands can send and transmit energy. Experiment with separating the two functions, as I've done here, or combining energizing and sensing functions in both hands. Use whichever system works best for you.

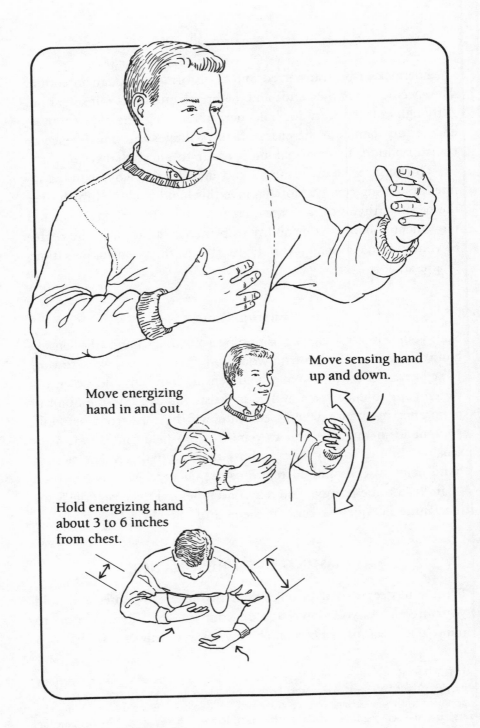

Move sensing hand
up and down.

Move energizing
hand in and out.

Hold energizing hand
about 3 to 6 inches
from chest.

FIGURE 11 Self-Healing

physical symptom, go with your mind to that area of your body. However, if your body-mind directs your attention toward a different area of your body, focus there instead. Follow its wisdom.

When working on a physical sensation such as pain, a symptom, or an illness, feel free to move your hands from the witness area to the affected area. This shifts your focus from the general to the specific. If you can't reach the affected area, continue to hold your hand over the thymus/heart center, thus energizing it while sensing into and focusing attention on the more specifically affected area.

Describe in words whatever comes up, be it a sensation, an image, or a symbol. *What sensations do you feel? What images come to mind? What size, shape, and color are they? Do you hear anything?*

By focusing on sensations and images that enter your consciousness, you come into resonance with the physical symptom or issue you want to change. As you energize this area with your hands, draw a deep breath as if to draw it through the area. Hold your breath while holding the sensation, symptom, or image clearly in mind. As you release your breath back into the same area, go with your mind into the mental or holoenergetic representation of the illness or problem. This focus can take you to the deeper emotions. *What emotions do you feel when immersed in this energy?* Describe these emotions as you go along. Underlying these emotions are associated thoughts. What thoughts arise?

Each step of the way you are resonating with the holoenergetic patterns that no longer serve you. You are coming closer to releasing yourself from the core beliefs that established the now uncomfortable or dysfunctional pattern.

While still inside the holoenergetic form, *recall the earliest time you felt similar emotions.* Allow yourself to relive the experience; let the feelings carry you there. Use a tape recorder or pencil and paper, or a talk with a close friend to describe what happened as best you can. *What beliefs did you have and what decisions did you make at that time about yourself, others, or the world?* In the beginning it may not feel to you that a real decision or choice was involved. But be assured that you did make a choice to interpret and believe something about what happened, even if it was a choice made under duress or a threat to survival, or a choice made with only limited knowledge. When you make contact with that moment of choice, you begin to understand, and you take an important first step toward reconnecting with your own empowerment. If you have difficulty identifying the belief, imagine what belief you might have about yourself that could cause this circumstance to occur or recur.

Now you want to discover and understand the positive intention that underlies the holoenergetic pattern of sensation, feeling, and belief being manifested in your problem. The positive intention behind the difficulty is the life-force energy that the holoenergetic pattern really wants to experience and express.

Draw your breath in, and as you do so, step out of (withdraw your mind from) the form/image with which you had merged. Now see that form in your mind's eye, or sense it. Ask it what it considers its function to be. Feel your appreciation for the service it has tried to render. Ask it what it really wants. What is its positive intention?

If you are working with an emotional issue, allow that issue to come to mind. Usually you will begin to feel physical sensations somewhere in your body. For example, people who are in the midst of the breakup of a romantic relationship frequently feel pressure or tightness in the center of their chests. Other emotional situations might be expressed as a knot in the pit of a person's stomach, or perhaps a tightness or constriction in the throat.

Use your hands to energize the area of your body where you are now focusing your attention. With your sensing hand, note the intensity and quality of the energy level in this area as you begin. Continue monitoring with your sensing hand as you energize with your energizing hand.

As you focus your attention on this area, note if these sensations or feelings correspond with a particular chakra. (In the example above, the chest, throat, and stomach are associated with the fourth, fifth, and third chakras, respectively.) When emotion is the presenting problem, it can be useful to know that it will also have a physical component. As you go into the emotion, you'll discover it is associated with sensations in some area of your body. You can then focus either on the sensation or on the affected chakra to enhance your resonance with the issue.

Even as you begin, you may recognize that a holoenergetic thought or feeling pattern you choose to change is associated with a specific chakra function. If you find this to be true, consider the option of moving your hands to that chakra and starting your work there. Follow the instructions above to discover and understand the positive intention behind the issue.

If you are dealing with emotional or physical trauma, energize the affected area of your body with your hands. As you do so, bring to your attention the event that precipitated the trauma, for example, an auto accident or incident of sexual abuse. Reexperience that event as best you can in your mind; this allows you to resonate with the circumstances around it and become more closely attuned to the feelings, thoughts, and beliefs you had and the decisions and choices you made during that time.

Usually, our first inclination is to avoid recollecting the thoughts and feelings associated with trauma. In holoenergetic healing, however, we focus attention and energy on the sensations associated with the trauma and breathe through them. As we are focusing attention, feelings or memories come up that frequently lead us to their source in past experiences. If tears come up, just allow yourself to feel what you are feeling. Again, follow the instructions above to discover and understand the positive intent behind the issue or difficulty.

9

Release

Blockages are like steam on the bathroom mirror . . .
they keep you from seeing yourself.
Through the blurred image your foggy shape becomes a scary monster,
and you run rather than clean the mirror.
Do you hate yourself for the steamy mirror? Then why do you hate
yourself for your mental fog?
You clean the mirror; you discover yourself.

— LAZARIS

There is an important and often overlooked aspect of healing that I find valuable to look at in holoenergetic healing. It has to do with our resistance to unforming and releasing energy patterns that are maintaining disharmonious states in our body-minds. To let go of or transform these unhealthy forms means that we may need to release much more than just the discomfort with which they are associated. It also means that we may have to face the unknown, or seek new ways of relating to the world and ourselves. A part of us asks, "If I give this up, what will my life be like?" When we ask ourselves this question, we may discover resistance to change.

Why are we reluctant to let go of the present forms? A person receiving disability payments as a result of illness derives financial benefits and may not want to give them up to go back to an unsatisfying job. Benefits of illness may be more subtle, as when an illness allows us to receive the nurturing and love that we believe is not available to us any other way. In *Love, Medicine and Miracles,* Bernie Siegel reflects that physical illness "can be a way of gaining love, or nurturing. It can become a patient's only way of relating to the world, the only control one has over life"(p. 108). Thus it becomes a "treasured wound".

Treasured Wounds

Payoffs for Having Illness
- *Being a victim*—manipulating out of apparent weakness
- *Being a martyr*—suffering in silence to punish another through guilt
- *Attention-getting*—feeling important because of the attention
- *Avoidance*—avoiding responsibility for growth; avoiding boredom

Blockages
- *Fear*—associated with separation, alienation, and loss of love
- *Anger*—frequently associated with perceived loss of power or control
- *Guilt*—associated with anger we feel we have no right to have because we acted contrary to an accepted value
- *Self-pity*—associated with a desire to blame, punish self and others
- *Shame*—once internalized, promotes a sense of worthlessness

---

Illness can occupy our attention, keeping us from being bored or from looking more closely at deeper life issues that are preventing us from realizing our fondest dreams. Illness can also be used to make us the center of attention, allowing us to feel important. These emotional benefits can be elusive, indeed, but they need to be explored and resolved as part of the holoenergetic healing process.

Choices for Response

Martial arts practitioners recognize a variety of ways that we can respond to personal threats, attacks, or abuse. We can

1. *Fight:* we can use physical force or emotional resistance, such as argumentation, verbal counterattack, and so on.

2. *Withdraw:* we can run away from, deny, or avoid facing the issue, thus separating ourselves from the threat.

3. *Negotiate:* we can open a dialogue to work the issue out on a verbal level.

4. *Take No Action:* we can do nothing, carrying on as if the threat did not exist.

5. *Surprise or Divert:* we can use diversion or confusion tactics to mix up our assailant—or, in some cases, ourselves.

6. *Blend:* we can temporarily accept and merge with our attacker's force in order to redirect it and eventually transform it. (Terry Dobson, a teacher of the martial arts from whose work this list was adapted, shows us how this process works in the Blending exercise below.)

For example, one of my patients told me that he received attention as a child only when he was sick or injured. Over time, he learned to manipulate others through playing a victim role, enticing others to take care of him. He realized that his illness—chronic sinusitis—was really an irritation with his own sense of childhood powerlessness and shame, continued in the present. His illness also restricted an activity that he greatly enjoyed, backpacking in the Sierras in the spring, when pollen counts were particularly high. When he became aware of his pattern, he discovered that its deeper positive intent was for him to experience love and affection. He then chose to holoenergetically release both his secondary gain and his illness by blending with and transforming the image of the pattern into its higher purpose.

Though few of us ever make conscious decisions about it, we may discover that we use our illness as an opportunity to avoid responsibility for our growth, or as an excuse to blame or punish ourselves or others, and then feel sorry for ourselves. The silent suffering of the martyr is often used to control others through inducing guilt.

In addition to these secondary gains or payoffs of illness, frequently the circumstances we want to change involve more direct blocks to healing, such as shame, fear, anger, guilt, doubt, and self-pity. These blocks, too, need to be engaged in the overall healing process.

As we move forward, having identified what we want to change and having come into resonance with it, it can be helpful to remind ourselves that regardless of the physical manifestation, we can make new choices that either shift our relationship to that disease or change the symptoms themselves. New choices can be made, regardless of the choices we've made in the past. In the words of Abraham Maslow,

Life is a continual series of choices for the individual in which a main determinant of choice is the person as he already is (including his goals for himself, his courage or fear, his feeling of responsibility, his ego-strength or "will power"). We can no longer think of the person as "fully determined" where this phrase implies "determined only by forces external to the person." The person, insofar as he is a real person, is his own main determinant. Every person is, in part, "his own project" and makes himself.[1]

⊛ EXERCISE: BLENDING

Try the following experiment to get a sense of how blending can work:

1. Insert the index finger of your right hand into the fist of your left hand. (If you're left-handed, reverse this.)

2. Hold the finger very tightly so you can't pull away.

3. Resisting with your clenched left hand as hard as you can, try to pull the finger away. You will probably find it very difficult to withdraw your finger.

4. Now, very quickly, thrust the squeezed finger in the direction it's being held and then immediately pull it away. This should be easy to do.

Try the same exercise with a friend to get a sense of what it's like to have someone hold you against your will and then to release yourself through your own blending efforts.

This release is not a trick. Try it repeatedly with yourself so that you get a good sense of how it works.

It can be valuable to understand this blending principle, since it follows the same practice of Recognition, Resonance, and Release with which we work in holoenergetic healing: Release comes not by fighting, withdrawing, denying, or resisting but by fully Recognizing and Resonating with the energy holding us.

---

1. Abraham H. Maslow, *Toward a Psychology of Being* (New York: Van Nostrand Reinhold, 1968), 181.

Through the processes of Recognition and Resonance, we have begun to accept ourselves as we are, telling ourselves the truth about the present illness and how it functions in our lives. The most complete form of this acceptance is love. Loving yourself as you are is the best way to blend and come into resonance with yourself.

Remember that accepting yourself as you are doesn't mean resigning yourself to the present circumstances. It means accepting the truth of what is, and then being willing to take action to transform it. Some people think acceptance means no change. In holoenergetic healing, acceptance means recognition, resonance, and responsibility, honoring ourselves by identifying what is true for us now so that we can change.

How do you tell yourself the truth? As I have previously noted, in addition to thinking things out rationally, there is another way of knowing. Your intuitive senses can awaken in you the experience of direct, inner knowing. One of the best ways of developing this inner knowing is through a meditative practice. Find a method of relaxation that works for you, allowing you to quiet your mind. As your mind becomes quiet your awareness expands, and you see that thoughts, feelings, and sensations are contained within your awareness, like clouds in the sky.

Usually you are unaware of your body unless it hurts. Yet your body-mind holographically expresses important truths about yourself.

✪ EXERCISE: BECOMING AWARE OF YOURSELF

Take about twenty minutes just to sit quietly and comfortably with your eyes closed. Tell your body to become as relaxed as it's ever been, and feel it relaxing more and more.

Breathe in and out slowly and evenly through both nostrils. Focus your attention on the space between the nostrils. As you do so, your mind begins to be quiet. If your mind wanders, bring it gently but firmly back to the space between your nostrils.

After three or four minutes, shift your attention from your breathing to any physical sensation present in your body. Without trying to change anything, just notice if there are areas of your body you're not aware of at all. Are there parts that call for your attention, through tension or some other sensation? Sense any feelings or thoughts that are associated with these sensations or lack of sensation. Discover what comes to your awareness that was not there before. When you feel ready, take a deep breath and open your eyes.

Another method you may find helpful in developing your intuitive capability is to work with your inner guide (page 260–62). If you choose not to work either alone or with your inner guide, you may find it helpful to explore with an open, supportive, trustworthy friend who will allow you to let the truth flow freely without judging it.

Some years ago, a psychiatrist came to me with back pain that had been getting progressively worse. At the time he saw me he was having difficulty sitting. In college, years before, he had injured himself playing football, but despite the injury and pain he had continued to play.

Nearly a decade later, he continued to work long hours, disregarding physical signs that he needed to rest. During our healing work together he began to communicate with his body through a holoenergetic pattern, asking it to reveal the truth to him. His body-mind told him it was angry that he didn't listen to it. It wanted rest and peace, and it wanted love. It told him that pain was the only language he seemed able to hear. He was astonished and deeply moved by this communication. He had discovered the positive intent that had been behind his pain.

During our holoenergetic session he realized he was holding a belief that he didn't deserve to be loved. All his life he had sought approval and had tried to prove himself worthy of love through hard work both in his profession and in sports. Yet neither of these had targeted the source. Only when he was able to recall the critical football injury—and honestly see its relationship to his belief that he was not worthy of love—was he able to let go of the holoenergetic form that maintained his pattern of attempting to prove his worthiness. Once he discovered and holoenergetically released the belief that he was unworthy, the pain immediately subsided and he could bend over freely. He began living a very different kind of life. He began to love and nurture himself, and he opened more fully to the love of others.

POSITIVE INTENTION

In this example we find a valuable lesson. All life energy has positive intention. Behind all behavior, action, reaction, and response we can find positive intention, although the means for expressing or achieving that intention may have been unskillful and misguided. A positive intention is the desired *inner experience that you really want,* something you can *feel or see yourself as* or hear within you. It is an image, thought, or feeling that is conducive to your well-being and that reflects your life force. Understand that there is a difference between what you want to accomplish by your words, actions, reactions, goals, achievements, and beliefs and the positive intent behind it all—which is what is really wanted, such as freedom, love, peace, empowerment, happiness, or understanding. Behind it all is the desire to love and be loved, to know and be known, and to be free to choose what brings you peace, joy, bliss, and love. Once aware of what you really want, you will find it much easier to give up any resistance to change and attachment to the familiar form.

While you are in resonance with the holoenergetic pattern or image you want to change, you can shift into your observer state and ask that pattern or image what it really wants. In the observer state you can discover the positive intention behind the symptoms or behaviors that are to be transformed. This positive intention is an expression of what your higher Self wants for you. It can then be used to transform the undesired pattern during the Reformation process. To work with it, give the positive intention a holoenergetic representation as an image, perhaps a symbol or a presence, or a person who best embodies its qualities.

In holoenergetic healing, we first recognize and come into resonance with what we want to change; then we *unform* it. To unform an energy pattern we make a conscious choice to release the old form and *transform* it. Using the breathing methods we've described previously, we expel our breath forcefully, as if to unform it, sending the belief, thought, or image we want to change out through the affected area of our body. The release is holoenergetically completed by intentionally withdrawing the released energy with our hands, creating a space or void in which to generate a new, more consciously chosen form.

Another way to transform a holoenergetic pattern is to allow the image of the original pattern to become absorbed into the image of its positive intent. A most effective way is to use tracing, a technique developed to deepen the holoenergetic process (see Resource 2, "Tracing," at the back of this book).

After transforming a holoenergetic pattern, we allow the body-mind to return to its natural harmony, either spontaneously or through introducing the harmonious energy pattern or image of the newly discovered positive intent that promotes wellness and wholeness.

Following this holoenergetic release, it is valuable to choose to forgive. At the moment of release we let go of the old form and sense the natural harmony that comes from letting go; we stop blaming ourselves and others for the difficulties we have experienced with our illness. Through the process of forgiveness, which I describe at the end of this chapter, we are able to release the energies that bind and blind us.

This description of the release process provides the foundation for the instructions that follow. Once again, read this material carefully before actually putting it into practice.

🟢 EXERCISE: RELEASE STARTS WITH AN INTENTION

1. Ask yourself, "Am I willing to release this pattern, belief, or image today and replace it with what I really want?" All beliefs and images are illusions. Why not select more beneficial illusions? You can let go of those that are no longer serving you and choose new, more expansive ones that will benefit you. For example, a man in my workshop discovered that he had chosen a belief that he was not good enough to be loved. This was a choice he had made with the myopic knowledge of a child growing up in a dysfunctional family. Recognizing this choice, and realizing that he could choose again, he made a new choice, based on the more complete knowledge and understanding he had in the present. He chose the new belief that he was lovable and loving. (You can holoenergetically replace the image of the undesired pattern or illness with an image of what you really want, and your body-mind will respond.)

2. Once you have determined your willingness to release this pattern, belief, or image, draw your breath in through the affected area, the selected chakra, or your thymus area. Hold that breath while bringing to mind all that you have honestly chosen to release.

   Holding your breath builds a charge and gets the attention of your subconscious mind. This also brings your body into closer resonance with the Earth so that you are in communication with and mobilizing more of your body's energetic resources.

3. Do this focused breathing while you are energizing the witness area, a specific chakra, or an area of your body that you have targeted during the Resonance phase, using your hands, your thoughts, and your feelings. (See fig. 11.)

4. Forcefully ex-pulse your breath through the area you have energized, with the intention of releasing the disharmonious pattern, image, or illness. Pulse out your breath with force and with the intention of unforming the old thought form. See that energy

form transform. While you are ex-pulsing your breath through this area, further affect the energy field by suddenly withdrawing your hand or hands from the field, this time with the intention of extracting the released energy. Imagine literally pulling out the energy and releasing it, to be transformed.

5. Rest for a moment, allowing yourself to experience the sense of being released from the disharmonious energy form.

6. Go back to the area again and energize it with your hands and your focused attention. What do you feel now? What changes have occurred in your inner experience?

7. With your next breath draw energy up through the bottoms of your feet from the center of the Earth. Hold the breath for a moment, then release it forcefully, imagining that it is going out through the newly cleared area, freeing it completely from any remnants of the old pattern. Repeat this clearing breath one more time.

At this point, you have created a void or formlessness where there was once a specific form. You have released thought patterns that were maintaining a state of illness or lack of ease. The void now becomes a source of growth and transformation.

You now have a choice about how to transform the energetic area that you've released; you can fill it or allow it to be filled with spiritual energy or with a form, image, belief, or positive intention of your own choosing that is more harmonious and supportive of the way you want your life to be.

FORGIVENESS: THE FINAL RELEASE

Once the holoenergetic Release is completed, a final level of release becomes accessible: forgiveness. Although the forgiveness process that follows is optional, forgiveness is a powerful healing tool in itself.

Many people who have completed the Release phase in this way have subsequently experienced profound changes in their lives.

One dramatic example of the power of forgiveness occurred immediately following a workshop I taught in the Southeast. After she had finished the forgiveness process as part of a workshop demonstration, the woman I had worked with received a message from the front desk of her hotel saying there was a phone call for her. Calling the number given her, she discovered it was her former boyfriend, whom she had just forgiven; they had not communicated with each other in more than a year!

As I describe it here, forgiveness is an inner process rather than the act of going up to a person with whom you've had a disagreement and telling him or her all is forgiven. Forgiveness in this case means letting go of an energy form you were holding in your mind. As soon as we let go of that energy form (forgive), we release ourselves; energy we were using to hold on to the anger, disappointment, or hurt becomes available to us for actions that are more positive and healthful for ourselves and others. In this way, forgiving is *for-giving* love to ourselves.

In the light of compassionate understanding, we may choose to forgive *why* something happened and not *what* happened. Most importantly, we must forgive ourselves. For example, children, in the egocentric stage of development, may feel they are to blame for everything that happens to them. When a father dies or leaves home, a child may feel it's because of something she or he has done. Children may feel they are to blame for any physical, emotional, or sexual abuse inflicted upon them. They need to forgive themselves and release these childhood misperceptions.

Frequently, we release both ourselves and others through forgiveness. The anger or hurt we experience and hold on to are constant reminders of our past distress. When we forgive a person for what she or he did or didn't do, our forgiveness is an act of self-love. We release the old form and create the void in which a new form can live.

As often as not, the person you forgive need never be told that you've forgiven them; yet time and again clients, friends, and workshop participants—similar to the one above—have told me that the person forgiven seemed to know. It's not unusual for the person who was the object of the forgiveness process to make contact with the person forgiving them shortly thereafter, initiating a significant shift in their relationship.

I hasten to add that it does not matter whether the person you are forgiving is near at hand, separated by great distance, or even deceased. The most important part of the forgiveness process is that it encourages your own healing by completing your release from energy forms that contribute to illness.

The following are steps for the forgiveness process:

✵ EXERCISE: FORGIVING

1. Relax in a comfortable position, preferably in a place where you will not be disturbed for ten or fifteen minutes.

2. Decide who it is you are choosing to forgive. It can be more than one person. Ask yourself if you are honestly willing to release and forgive this person, or these people.

3. Close your eyes and take deep, slow abdominal breaths, relaxing more with each breath.

4. Focus your attention on your solar plexus.

5. Place one hand three to six inches from your body over the solar plexus and use the other hand to sense the buildup of the field. Energize this area, just as you did when resonating and releasing the energy field associated with your illness.

6. Draw in a deep breath, as if drawing it through your solar plexus. Hold that breath for a moment, and as you release your breath, back through the solar plexus, bring into your mind's eye the images of those you want to forgive, surrounding each image with a circle or oval of violet light.

   By creating a circle, your conscious mind gives your subconscious mind the message to limit the energy to that circle, creating a sense of containment around those you want to forgive. This allows you to fully address your emotions without concern that you will bring harm to or be harmed by those you are forgiving.

7. Silently communicate to the images of these beings, whatever it is that they did or did not do that caused your discomfort. It is important to express to their image what you have been holding back, including your feelings of hurt, anger, grief, sadness, and whatever else you are blaming them for. A part of you (your holoenergetic pattern) may want to punish, hit, or curse them. The more you can experience and express those patterns and feelings (without acting them out in real life) and then transform them into their positive intent, the more complete the forgiveness and healing will be.

   Through your feelings and your imagination, you are accessing the resonance of critical incidents. By recognizing and feeling your feelings, you can holoenergetically transform them. Once you release the blocked, contracting feelings, energy begins to flow spontaneously into the area where the old injury was being held, transforming and replacing it with new patterns.

8. Realize that, in a sense, you have kept the people you have not forgiven imprisoned within you. You have been standing guard, reminding them and you of the disharmony that exists between you. As the jailer you have bound yourself together with them through your own thoughts and feelings of blame and punishment. Forgiveness is a choice to release, to let go, freeing the energy that binds you.

9. Look at your willingness to forgive these people now. See yourself standing outside the jail door, about to release them into the light. Forgiveness is an act of self-love. To forgive is not necessarily to forget, or to love those you've chosen to forgive, but simply to release them. This will free up your energy for your own growth and evolution. Insert the key of forgiveness, swing the jail door wide open, and prepare to release these beings into the light.

10. Focus your attention on your solar plexus area and take a deep breath while holding in your mind's eye the images of those you have chosen to forgive.

11. Ex-pulse your breath suddenly and forcefully through the solar plexus area, and completely release and unform the images, swirling the energy around the room and releasing it into the light, returning it to its highest potential. Using your hands, unform the etheric field by withdrawing the unwanted energy from the area at the same time. Repeat this transformative breath two more times.

12. Then, using your hands, imagine covering your solar plexus with golden light.

13. Shift your attention to the center of your chest and move your hands over your heart center. From now on, when you communicate with those you have forgiven, whether verbally or nonverbally, stop for a moment, focus on the center of your chest, and communicate with them from your heart.

14. Now bring into your mind's eye an image of yourself as either a child, an adolescent, an adult, or perhaps all three. Silently communicate to yourself what you are choosing to forgive yourself for. Take in a deep breath, imagining that you are drawing your breath in through your heart chakra. Put your arms out in front of you, embracing your self-image. As you slowly release your breath from the center of your chest, feel the forgiveness you have for yourself. Hold yourself close. Silently tell yourself all is forgiven, and welcome yourself home.

The following is the transcript of a demonstration of the forgiveness process I conducted at a conference in Seattle. In this dialogue "LL" refers to me and "CL" refers to the client.

LL: Are you willing to release this person, and are you willing to forgive?

CL: Yes.

LL: Fine. Close your eyes. Start taking deep breaths and relax more with each breath.

(To the audience:) When I hold my hand over the heart center in front of CL and my other hand behind her back, I will be creating an energy field and coming into resonance with her.

(To CL:) Do you notice anything as I focus my hands on you?

CL: Yes, at my back.

LL: *(To the other workshop participants:)* As I focus on the thymus gland and heart center, there is a transfer of energy. It takes a while for the body to absorb this energy, but once it does, I start to feel a tingling in my sensing hand. Some people feel warmth; some people feel coolness; others feel pressure or pulsation.

(To CL:) Take a deep breath, hold for a moment, and as you slowly release your breath, bring before you, in your mind, the people you want to forgive. Bring their image into clear focus. Surround each image with a violet circle. Indicate to each one what it is you're choosing to forgive him or her for—what it is that he or she did or didn't do.

Allow yourself to feel the anger, sadness, fear, shame, and guilt before you move on to forgive these people. In a sense you've kept these beings in jail. Now you have chosen to release them. By blaming and punishing, and binding them, you limited your freedom along with theirs, so releasing them releases you, too.

Now see yourself standing outside the jail door. Insert the key of forgiveness. Swing the jail door open and let them come out into the light as you prepare to release them. You don't have to forget the lessons you've learned, you don't have to love them, just release them with your intention, imagery, and breath. This will free up your energy for your own growth and evolution.

CL: *(Nods her head in readiness.)*

LL: Focus your attention on your solar plexus area and take a deep breath while holding the images of these beings in your mind's eye. Bring to mind your intention to forgive and release. *(LL takes in a deep breath as well.)* When I say "Release!" just expel your breath out through your solar plexus. Now totally release those images, swirling the energy around the room and releasing it up into the light.

CL: *(Pulses her breath out.)*

LL: *(Pulses his breath in.)* Take another breath and release. *(Repeats the synchronized pulse breath.)*

Now shift the focus of your attention to the center of your chest. In the future when you communicate with these beings, verbally or nonverbally, just stop for a moment, focus on your heart, and communicate with them from there.

Next bring forward in your mind's eye your own image, this time not enclosed in a violet circle, and silently communicate what it is you're choosing to forgive yourself for. When you have finished your communication, take in a deep breath through your heart center and embrace the image of yourself. As you release your breath through your heart center, allow yourself to feel the forgiveness.

CL: *(Nods her head.)*

LL: All is forgiven. Welcome yourself home by merging with your embraced image.

Once the holoenergetic Release is completed, you are ready for the next step, the process of Reformation.

10

Reformation

To return to the source is to find the meaning, but to pursue appearances is to miss the source.

—SENGTSAN (THE THIRD ZEN PATRIARCH)

I look back now on certain things that at the time seemed to me to be real disasters, but the results turned out to be the structuring of a really great aspect of my life and career.

—JOSEPH CAMPBELL

There is an old story about a traveler who finds himself on the wrong road in a part of the country that is entirely new to him. He sees a farmer plowing a field and pulls his car off to the shoulder. Trudging across the field, the traveler catches up with the farmer, who stops his tractor and looks down at him.

"I'm lost," the traveler says. "I need some help."

"Do you know where you are?" the farmer asks.

"Yes," the traveler says, "I saw the name of the town a half mile or so back down the road."

"And do you know where you want to go?" the farmer asks.

The traveler nods, telling the farmer his destination.

"Then you're not lost," the farmer says. "You just need directions."

In the last two phases of holoenergetic healing, there can be a short period of time when we feel like this traveler. We know where we are—we're feeling pain, discomfort, fear, agitation, or confusion. And we know where we want to be—free of anxiety, healed, and at peace. But we feel lost. In this, the Reformation phase, we find direction and purpose, and we rediscover the strength of our own inner guidance, which was there all along.

MAKING THE CHOICE TO CHANGE

After you have released the energy pattern you want to change, you have created a void. Once the void is created, you can allow your body-mind and your etheric field to return to its natural state of harmony and balance. Or you may want to create a new energy pattern that promotes wellness and wholeness while defining a new purpose or goal in your life.

Bring your hands back into the field around the area of your body or chakra where you have been focusing your work. You'll want to focus your mind on the new image, the positive intention, and create a new belief or purpose that you want to bring into this area. Breathe in deeply through the top of your head, energizing that new image or belief. Then release your breath slowly into the area, filling it with the vibrant new energy form you want to create there or with loving light—a universal form of balance and healing.

You might, for example, want to fill the void you've created with a healthy new image. This could be valuable when dealing with a physical lesion. You might get a picture of a healthy organ, tissue, or cell from an anatomy book in a library and visualize that picture of vibrant health and wholeness filling the affected area.[1]

If you do not have a picture of a healthy organ, or do not wish to use a picture to replace the energy form you've released, you can

---

1. For more information, see Lennert Nilsson, *The Body Victorious,* and Richard G. Kessel and Randy H. Kardon, *Tissues and Organs.*

use a symbol to create a healthy form in the area. For example, you might fill the area with a vibrant symbol of the result you want; this could be a star, a sunburst, a deep blue, serene lake, a purple flame, a tree, a flower, or our planet floating tranquilly in space. You can fill the area with the sense of tingling and warmth that you may associate with feeling healed and healthy. Filling the area with a symbol, feeling, or image of health evokes the natural, balanced energy frequencies of the healthy organ.

When Reforming for primarily emotional issues, you can fill the area with the positive intention behind the issue or illness, with a new belief—"I am a lovable and worthy person," "I am learning to flow joyfully in the moment"—or with light and love. Light and love function as universal harmonics, linking to the structure and reminding it of the natural frequency of its healthy state. Loving energy of a higher frequency can also prevent the released form or pattern from reverting to its old form.

You can also fill the void you've created with your sense of purpose, your vision, or your dream. Keep in mind that the energy that was once bound up in maintaining the disease or disharmony has just been released. That energy is now available to you for goals or purposes that are in alignment with your full potential or higher Self.

IDENTIFYING PURPOSE

Each of us is born with a unique combination of qualities and abilities that define who we are. When we are able to know, accept, and express our own qualities and abilities, we begin living a creative and fulfilling life. These qualities and abilities are reflections of spiritual energy in our lives. Becoming aware of them helps us to align with our purpose. Many spiritual traditions hold that there is one universal purpose in life—to know and be ourselves and yet to be at one with all there is. Each of us expresses this universal purpose in his or her own way.[2]

One way to become aware of your individual purpose is to explore moments of success in your life:

1. Think about successes in your life. Allow yourself to get in touch with the feelings you had then. These may have been experiences when you were at your best, or perhaps moments that were particularly pleasurable for you, moments of ecstasy. Were there moments when you felt deeply fulfilled by whatever you were doing? Moments when you were in the "flow" and felt at one with whatever you were doing?
2. Make a list of the qualities and abilities in you that brought these experiences forth or allowed them to happen.
3. Think about what individual qualities and abilities you have for relating to other people, things, and information.

Recognize that the qualities and abilities that brought these experiences about are already within you. They represent the spiritual force moving through you. As you get to know these qualities and accept them as yours, you are learning your purpose. To know your purpose is to unfold your ability to create success in your life. Deeply fulfilling success comes from your choice to unfold your uniqueness and "follow your bliss."

An important part of discovering your purpose is being conscious of the specific qualities, abilities, and values that make up your uniqueness, and of how you create success in your life. There are many people who are successful without being conscious of how they create success. When they become conscious of their individual qualities and strengths, they begin to discover their purpose.

Another way to become aware of your unique purpose is to get in touch with peak experiences in your life. In helping people to get

---

2. Some of the information in this section is from Mark Thurston, *Discovering Your Soul's Purpose* (Virginia Beach, VA: A.R.E. Press, 1984).

in touch with their peak experiences, Abraham Maslow asked them to "think of the most wonderful experience or experiences of your life; happiest moments, ecstatic moments, moments of rapture, perhaps from being in love, or from listening to music or suddenly 'being hit' by a book or a painting, or from some great creative moment" (*Toward a Psychology of Being,* p. 67).

Peak experiences come to us in both ordinary and extraordinary ways, but the effect is the same. Unexpectedly and effortlessly, familiar ways of thinking and feeling fade away. We open to another part of ourself; we have a feeling of "coming home," a feeling of wholeness and unity.

Take a moment to think about peak experiences in your life. They may have come when you were out in nature, while in a concert hall, while engaged in an athletic event, during meditation, or simply while having a conversation with a close friend. The most important characteristic of the peak experience is the feeling of being more yourself, at the same time that there is a feeling of merging with the activity you are involved in at that moment.

Though your peak experiences may have occurred in an ordinary setting, you perceived what was going on in an exceptional way. Or you may have been in a nonordinary state of consciousness, during meditation or a dream.

Many times, peak experiences occur effortlessly and spontaneously, and you have the sense that you've done nothing to bring them about. During these experiences, often people think to themselves, "This is the real me. I want to feel like this more often."

After you've taken a few moments to get in touch with your peak experience(s), write down a few words and phrases that characterize your experience. From these words, formulate a phrase that expresses the essence of that experience. Examples of these might be

"Pure being, complete in the moment, at one with everything."

"Unconditionally loving and loved."

"Connected, spontaneous, free."

These phrases help you to sense intuitively your higher purpose, to know the source of your bliss and what brings you joy. Your peak experiences give you glimpses of the spiritual force that flows through you from your higher Self.

THREE LEVELS OF CHANGE

In holoenergetic healing, change occurs through awareness, love, and conscious choice. Change is first generated on the emotional, mental, intuitional, and spiritual levels, and then on the physical level. There are three ways to release and reform energetically. These are (1) translation, (2) transformation, and (3) transcendence, the "Three T's" of change. Each is associated with a change in conscious awareness.

Translation

When a skilled linguist translates a thought or feeling from one language to another, the form changes but the substance (source) changes little, if at all. Thus, a love poem would convey approximately the same sentiments in English as it would in French, Chinese, or Russian. Similarly, in holoenergetic healing a translation of energy changes the source little, if at all, while it does change the "language" in which the holoenergetic pattern is expressed.

When a man goes out for a long run to work out his anger toward his boss, he is translating his angry feelings into action. However, the source issues that produced his anger haven't changed. What has changed is that the man has translated that same source from the language of thoughts and feelings to the language of physical movement.

Translation occurs on an emotional level when you shift an emotion to a location where it can be dissipated, such as when you translate anger into action, or when you shift one emotion or feeling to another. Contracted feelings such as pity can be translated into empathy. Stubbornness can be translated into persistence. Judgmental attitudes can be translated into discernments. Negative beliefs, such as "I am not worthy of love," can be translated into affirmations, such as "I deserve love."

The key idea to keep in mind with translational change is that the source doesn't change; that is, the underlying holoenergetic pattern that triggered the circumstance you now wish to change remains intact and continues to affect you. It will continue to function as a disharmonious energy pattern, reproducing and attracting the unwanted thoughts, feelings, or actions until you access the source and transform it.

Translation can work very well on a symptomatic level and is an important part of the healing process. Imagery and visualization can be valuable in dissipating symptoms, and can even result in a cure. In practice a symptom is translated, or converted, into a symbol or image. Then we change the image, and frequently the symptom changes as well.

For example, herpes can be treated symptomatically on a translational level. The lesion, often experienced as a burning sensation, can be visualized symbolically as a red-hot burning ember. Imagining cold water poured over the hot ember symbolically extinguishes it. When, on the physical level, the redness, pain, and swelling disappear, translational change has occurred.

In acupuncture, and with some body therapies, the practitioner may shift energy flow from one area of the body to another in order to bring about balance or shift the energy to a place where it is more useful.

Changing the perception that the glass is half empty to the perception that the glass is half full is an example of translational change, since the amount of water (the level of conscious awareness) in the glass remains the same.

Usually, translation precedes transformation. When you translate a symptom to an image or symbol, then address the critical incident, choices, and core beliefs, and uncover the positive intent, you've begun the transformational process. By releasing and reforming, blending and evolving the image holoenergetically, you complete the holoenergetic transformation.

Transformation

Transformation is a movement to a level of consciousness wherein we are aware not only of the discomfort of the present circumstances we want to change but also of the source, or underlying holoenergetic pattern, that generates and maintains those circumstances. By reaching to the source of an illness, emotion, or belief, we expand our awareness. When an enhanced and enduring awareness of the source of the illness is coupled with consciously evoked energy changes, holoenergetic healing occurs. This holoenergetic healing process is more than a translation, in that it involves both insightful psychological understanding and the changing of unwanted patterns of energy in the form of feelings and thoughts, choices and decisions, beliefs and attitudes associated with illness.

With translational change, awareness expands and contracts continuously within any given level of consciousness. One moment you might be aware of only the page you are reading; at the next you become aware of the room around you. When you are sleepy you are less aware; when you are alert you are more aware. Holoenergetic change takes place when your awareness is expanded in a lasting way through the shift to a higher level of consciousness. As Ralph Metzner says in *Opening to the Light*, transformation implies that "the structure and functioning of our psyche become different" (p. 2).

Each level of consciousness has its own pattern of vibration, structure, and function. The vibrational qualities at higher levels of consciousness expand and reshape the content of your awareness, changing your perceptions, thoughts, feelings, choices, and beliefs.

Transformation is a movement toward a new level of consciousness wherein there is a greater willingness and ability to see the truth about oneself. The energetic patterns that produce illness are like anchors that hold one to a given structure or pattern of consciousness. When those patterns are released, we are freed to rise to a higher level of consciousness and thus to a greater awareness of the source of the illness. At higher vibrational levels we are able to gain access to consciousness that lies at the source and dictates the form taken by an energy pattern.

Transformation and healing can occur on physical, emotional, mental, or spiritual levels, and the results can be expressed at any and all of these levels.

At a physical level, transformation is frequently but not always reflected as a change in behavior and appearance. For example, the Bible recounts that Saul, after his transformative experience, changed from an enemy to a defender of the faith. Similarly, criminals have been known to become exemplary citizens. Others, after transformative experiences, find themselves confirmed in their spiritual practices and life paths, with no obvious outward changes. As the Zen masters have said, after spiritual transformation one may go back to chopping wood and carrying water. As Metzner notes in *Opening to the Light,* "*Bodily appearance* may or may not be altered when consciousness and self are transformed.... In illness and healing recovery, physical form and appearance may change drastically. Anyone who has undergone the 'remission' of a malignant tumor, spontaneously or as a result of psychic healing, has brought about a kind of alchemical transformation of the physical elements of the body"(p. 3).

At the emotional level, transformational change brings lasting awareness and integration of expansive and contractive feelings, as well as an awareness of their source. We can translate feelings of stress to feelings of relaxation through certain breathing exercises; but we transform those feelings when we take breathing techniques a step further and use them to get in touch with the source of our stress, which leads to a lasting reduction of our subsequent experience of stress.

At the mental level, the enhanced awareness we achieve when we undergo a transformational change allows us to assume responsibility for the source, release or evolve the unwanted energy form it produces, and then make a new choice for change. It is as if we were able to restructure in our psyche the life experiences that support our disharmonious beliefs so that we can make entirely new choices, free of the forms that previously dictated the ways we lived our lives. We gain the ability to hear the body's whispers instead of waiting for the shout of illness or trauma.

At the spiritual level, the enhanced awareness associated with the transformational process is often expressed as a greater sense of self and a recognition of transpersonal values such as joy and gratitude. The more aware you are, the more correlations you make, and the more things you can relate to one another and to yourself. The more expanded your awareness, the greater self-knowledge and understanding you will have. With greater understanding there is more forgiveness and compassion, less judgment and blame. When you live your understanding and compassion, it becomes wisdom.

Love facilitates your ability to relate, link, and connect. When you relate to what is so, love brings you to the truth. Love allows you to relate your illness to its source and the greater sense of your self as a cocreator of your reality. Your love can also transform every emotion and every thought by relating it to its source. Your love is the most powerful of transforming energies.

We can transform and grow through love and joy or through pain and suffering. Certainly, pain and suffering have helped many to become more aware of the source of their difficulty. But let's remember that we can also become aware through love and joy. With love and joy comes forgiveness and an ability to stop judging and blaming ourselves and others so that we can let go of our defenses and see the truth of what is. The love and joy of transformation become guiding principles, giving us the directions we need to make the choice for growth.

When we transform a situation in our lives, we gain access to energy that we've been using to maintain our separation from ourselves and others. When we maintain an illusion of separation, it is as if we were using our energy to hold shut the door behind which is a vast amount of energy. When we let go of the illusion of separation, through transformation and transcendence, the door suddenly bursts open. We now have available to us all the radiant energy that was behind that door plus all the energy we were using to hold the door shut.

To use again our analogy of the half-full glass, through transformation that glass becomes filled, sometimes to overflowing as our conscious awareness expands. This is not only a perceptual shift; it also represents the transformative release of abundant energy, energy to heal, to grow, to create with.

Transcendence

With transcendence we experience a shift in consciousness in which we become attuned to a form's essence. By initially resonating with the form, then attuning to its essence, we make a quantum leap, expanding beyond the duality of the form. Now all possible forms that this energy takes can be known to us and can be released or used as we choose.

Many survivors of near-death experiences report moments of transcendence. In both transformation and transcendence there is always a death of the old form. In transformation a new, more evolved form is generated, which is capable of releasing or absorbing more energy; in transcendence consciousness leaps beyond the world of form. We are liberated from form, free to choose and free to be.

Transformation is a natural part of our evolution, and we are all capable of transcendence. By consciously choosing to grow toward wholeness we can experience healing in its fullest sense. This heightened awareness of self and the whole is what distinguishes healing from cure, which is the resolution of pathology.

With transcendence, our glass is not only filled, but we tap into the ocean that is the source of all.

Analogy of the Three T's

Translation is like switching from one AM radio station to another AM station with fewer commercials and with programs that are more useful and enjoyable to you. You can now find relaxing and healing influences more of the time.

Transformation is like becoming the manager and program director of the radio station, boosting the wattage, expanding the output to include FM and TV, and changing the programming. You not only report the news—you become a news maker. You can now make the news and the music that encourage healing and growth.

Transcendence is like opening to ways of communicating beyond the electromagnetic spectrum of radio and television, allowing you to know and create instantly. You have taken a quantum leap into the ocean of universal consciousness.

REFORMATION: THE METHOD

Bring your hands back into the field around the area you are focusing on. In your mind, bring into the area your new, healthy image, positive intention, belief, or purpose. Breathe in deeply from your transpersonal space through the top of your head, energizing the new image or belief. Release your breath slowly into the area, filling it with the vibrant form or loving light.

Fill the area you have cleared with a healthy image, if you know what that healthy image is. This is especially valuable if you are healing a physical lesion. For example, you can look at a picture of a healthy organ, tissue, or cell and visualize that image filling the area.

You can also use a symbol that represents the healthy image or positive intent; filling the area with this symbol evokes the natural frequency of the healthy organ.

When an emotional issue is involved, you can fill the area with a new belief, with positive intention, or with light and love. Light and love function as harmonics linking to and reminding the structure of the natural frequency of the healthy state. Loving energy of a higher frequency can also prevent the old, released pattern from reconfiguring.

You can also fill the void with your sense of purpose, your positive intention, your vision, or your dream. The energy that was bound up in maintaining the old form has now been released, and you can redirect it. You can align now with your spiritual essence and allow that essence to fill the void.

Following Reformation, unconditional love seals the change.

✦ EXERCISE: UNCONDITIONAL LOVE PROCESS

This process allows your own loving energy to complete and seal the healing. You may find it most effective to record this process into a tape recorder, playing it back following the forgiveness process.

1. For a moment, become your own best friend. Take yourself to the most blissful, peaceful place or space that you know of. Allow yourself to begin to feel in the center of your chest a sense of complete and total unconditional love for yourself—a love for every cell, every atom, every organ in your body and every part of your being. This is a love without comparison, without judgment, beyond all time and space, even beyond understanding.

2. Allow your next breath to expand to fill your entire chest with loving light. Allow it to move up into your shoulders and down your arms, to your fingertips. Allow it to move up into your neck and fill your head. Imagine this loving light filling your entire head so much that it begins to flow out the top of your head like a fountain of love, cascading down over your body, lovingly caressing it.

3. While focusing your attention on the top of your head, your crown center, allow yourself to feel the exquisite love that your

higher Self has for you. This is a love that is always there, so you need not learn or earn it. Just allow yourself to receive it. Sense a radiant ball of light six to eight inches above your head. Allow it to slowly descend through the top of your head, down to the center of your chest. Feel yourself radiating and glowing with the love your higher Self has for you. Allow its loving light to suffuse your entire body and being. Allow it in.

4. Now ask your higher Self to:

> Heal what needs to be healed.
> Do what needs to be done
> Bring me into wholeness
> So that we become one.

5. Focus again on the center of your chest, feeling that sense of complete and total unconditional love that you have for yourself and that your higher Self has for you. Take a deep breath, hold it a moment, and then release it, sending a burst of light from the center of your chest to every cell and atom in your body, every part of your being, so that they scintillate and sparkle like stars in the night sky.

PART THREE

11

Putting It All Together

We have to see all becomings as developments of the movement in our true self and this self as one inhabiting all bodies and not our body only. We have to be consciously, in our relations with this world, what we really are—this one self becoming everything that we observe. All the movement, all energies, all forms, all happenings we must see as those of our one and real self in many existences, as the play of the Will and Knowledge and Delight of the Lord in His world-existence.

—SRI AUROBINDO

Joan attended one of my workshops on holoenergetic healing and shortly thereafter made the decision to apply the techniques she'd learned to address the source of her recurring fever blisters (herpes of the lip). Prior to her self-healing work, Joan had herpes outbreaks about three times a year.

Joan's last herpes outbreak occurred while a male companion was visiting. She was making plans for the holidays and hoped he would share Christmas with her and her family. Instead, he told her that he had already made plans to spend the holidays with another friend. She was deeply disappointed and hurt.

"I felt myself pulling away from him and I experienced a searing heat in my heart, feeling my whole chest was aflame," she said. The morning after her discussion with her friend, she developed the fever blister on her lip.

At this point Joan felt ready and willing for a healing to take place. She used the self-healing method described in the previous chapters, finding it most helpful to work with a friend who agreed to be her witness and record her responses. The following is Joan's story about how she used the holoenergetic healing process to heal herself.

Joan began by Relaxing, Grounding, Aligning, and Centering herself. Then she asked the five questions that began the Recognition phase of her healing:

Question One: What do I want to change?
"My herpes attacks."

Question Two: What is prompting me to change at this time?
"It hurts. It's sore. It looks awful. I don't want to suffer any more. I want to understand what it is telling me so that I won't be susceptible to the virus. I want to be completely healed of it."

Question Three: How do I see myself as contributing to the present circumstances?
"I don't know. I get a fever blister about three times a year and I don't know why. It's unconscious."

Question Four: What does having this [fever blister] keep me from doing, being, or having? What does it allow me to do, be, or have? What might I be gaining from this?
"I'm not free to move my lips, to kiss whenever I want to. I'm concerned about getting a blister every so often when I'm stressed. I feel that there is a message the blister is trying to convey and knowing what it is would be empowering.

"I don't know what I'm gaining from having this blister."(A note to the reader: You will notice that Joan's answers to these questions are incomplete. This lack of clarity is not unusual in the rational Recognition phase of holoenergetic healing. As you'll see, the questions nevertheless plant the seeds for the intuitive Recognition that follows.)

Question Five: What result or outcome do I want to create? "I want to heal the source of this fever blister and never have another."

While sitting comfortably on her living room couch, Joan began the holoenergetic phase of her healing by gently moving her hands in her energy field over the area of her thymus gland and heart center. After breathing in deeply, Joan slowly released her breath and allowed her attention and her mind's eye to go to the herpetic lesion of her lip. She shifted her hands to an area three to six inches from her lips.

To come into resonance with the symptom, Joan focused her awareness on the fever blister, identifying with it. She described the affected area as if through the eyes of the symptom itself. She asked her fever blister, "If you could talk to me, what would you say?"

Speaking as the lesion, she replied: "I am blistered and feel like I'm on fire. I'm red and swollen and am very obvious to everyone, right up front on Joan's face. I hurt when she moves her lips. I tingle and burn."

Thoughts that came up for Joan included, "I hurt. I can't move my lips or I'll hurt myself more. Don't talk. Don't kiss. I should hide my face and not let anyone see how ugly I am. I could infect someone if he kissed me so I have an excuse not to kiss, to keep my distance."

She paused for a moment, then said: "I'm angry at myself for not saying what I really wanted, which was that I did not want to share him. I'm angry for not saying what I really felt. And I'm angry at him."

Joan went back to the earliest time she could recall feeling these same emotions. She remembered a time in her infancy when she was nursing at her mother's breast.

"My mother is nursing me and my brother Robert is watching. He doesn't want me to be here. I am taking his place. The message I am getting from him is that I'm taking something away from him. I feel like I shouldn't want all the milk. I shouldn't want all my mother's breast and attention and love. But I'm just a baby and I need all this. I need it for my life. I will not take everything I want so my brother will love me. I will ask for less so my brother will love me."

This was the critical incident for Joan. At this point in her infancy she had formed an unconscious belief that she was selfish for wanting all that she wanted. Unconsciously, she thought, "If I have what I want, someone else will suffer. I shouldn't ask for everything. I don't deserve everything." Joan made an unconscious decision, a critical choice, that she would never ask for everything she wanted because if she got it someone else would be deprived.

Joan had the insight that when her male companion declined her invitation to spend the holidays with her, she resonated with her old belief that she was selfish. She felt she was doing something wrong for wanting all that she wanted—which was to have her companion spend Christmas with her.

"I believed," Joan said, "that I was selfish for asking for all my companion's attention. If I got what I wanted his friend wouldn't get what she wanted. I'd get burned for my selfish request. I don't deserve to have all the attention, all the milk. I'm convinced that at this point my immune system allowed the herpes virus to establish itself again on my lip, my vulnerable point of entry."

Joan asked herself how she would replace this belief and disease. She responded: "I believe I deserve all that I want. It is healthy and right for me to want full nourishment and total attention from the one I love and who loves me. Having what I want does not deprive someone of the fulfillment of his or her needs."

Joan became clear about her core belief. She acknowledged that she was willing to release this pattern. "I am willing to give up the belief that I am selfish for wanting all that I want. I want to give up the belief that if I get what I want, someone else will suffer."

She continued: "I drew my breath in as if right through my fever blister and, holding it, I clarified my intention to release, totally and completely, this belief that I do not deserve all that I want. Then I released my breath forcefully out through the painful blister, feeling as though I'd completely transformed this old belief. As I pulsed out I abruptly pulled my hands from the area of my lips, breaking the field. I repeated this several times, imagining the root of the whole symptom being pushed out and transformed."

In the void that was created, Joan created a new image of herself. She brought her hands back into the affected area and focused her new belief and intention into the area.

"At this point I saw myself in complete health, free to talk and kiss and express my needs. I believed I deserve all that I want. I also saw my lips completely healthy. As I looked at the painful area of my lip I felt very different than I had a few moments ago. The energy that held the herpes virus was completely gone. It was finished. As I breathed in through the top of my head I could feel this new belief being strengthened within me. Then I imagined a loving, healing light filling the area of my lip."

"With my next breath I imagined healing light and love filling me. I saw myself completely healthy, free to talk and kiss and express my needs."

At the time of this writing, Joan has not had a recurrence of herpes attacks in more than three years.

While Joan's is the story of healing a long-term condition, holoenergetic healing can be just as useful in acute situations. The following experience is an example:

While visiting Hill of the Hawk at Big Sur, I had occasion to do healing work with a woman, Jennifer, who stepped on and got stung by a bee.

Jennifer sat down. I had her take a breath and slowly release it into the pain, then focus on the energy form of the pain—its shape, size, and color—and describe it. As she did this, I created a healing field with my hands over the painful area.

I asked her: "What is the pain wanting to tell you? What is the meaning behind it?" I shared with her my intuitive sense that it had to do with watching her step. She instantly confirmed that it was about stepping forward with awareness. She seemed to know exactly what this meant in her life, though I did not ask her to recount it in any detail.

I asked Jennifer to give that meaning or positive intention a presence or form, perhaps that of a person who embodied or personified its qualities, or an archetypal energy or symbol. I then asked her to hold that presence or form in her mind along with the original shape, color, and form that represented her pain.

I said to her: "Tell the pain that its message has been received and thank it for helping you become aware of what you needed to know. Inform it that its work is done and it is now time to return, through the light, back to the unmanifest realm. Trust that it knows what that means.

"Now breathe in through the site of the bee sting, through the form of the pain, and hold your breath while continuing to focus on its form. Still holding your breath, silently tell it that it is time to go back into the light. Then forcefully release your breath into the image of the pain, blowing it out through the sting site with the intention of unforming it and releasing it into the light."

As she released her breath, I extracted the expelled energy using my hands with intention while in-pulsing my breath. I then said: "Bring forward the image of the positive meaning. Hold it clearly in mind while you take a deep breath. Slowly release your breath into the area being healed, filling it with the new image. With your next breath, flood the area with a beautiful, cooling, ice-blue light . . . and know it is done."

When we were done, the pain was gone. There was what looked like a red pin prick in the center of a small, white area, but the swelling, which had occurred almost immediately after the sting, was gone, along with the pain. I told her to put ice on it as an additional precaution.

Several hours later I saw her again. She was delighted to report that her foot was just fine—no pain at all.

12

Holoenergetic Healing, Step by Step

Seeking after wholeness is the heart of the Warrior's quest. And yet what you are striving to become is what you already are in essence; it is your personal myth, that which you are to make conscious, bring into form, express in a creative way. The sun symbolizes the path and illuminates the goal, which is the human heart.

—RALPH BLUM

STEP 1: RECOGNITION (RATIONAL KNOWING)

The first step in holoenergetic healing is to call forth information about your present circumstances, mostly by asking questions and listening quietly for answers.

Relax and Ground Yourself

1. Find a comfortable position. Sit, stand, or lie down, experimenting with which position is most comfortable for you.

2. Relax yourself. Use whatever relaxation exercise you want (see page 258).

3. Ground yourself. Breathe slowly and gently. As you breathe in, imagine drawing in energy from the center of the Earth through the base of your spine to your heart.

4. Align yourself. Breathe slowly and gently. As you breathe in, imagine drawing in energy from the Cosmos. Imagine it coming in through the top of your head, down to the center of your chest. Now gently exhale into your heart center.

5. Center yourself. Breathe slowly and gently. Then take a deep breath and imagine drawing in energy from the Earth and the Cosmos simultaneously, through the base of your spine and the top of your head, fusing at your heart.

Take a few moments simply to enjoy this relaxed, centered state.

Five Key Questions

Ask yourself the five key questions that follow. You may want to record your answers with a tape recorder, write them down, or have a friend act as a witness to jot them down for you.

1. What do I want to change?

2. What is prompting me to change at this time?

3. How do I see myself as contributing to the present circumstances?

4. What does having this (illness or situation) keep me from doing, being, or having? What does it allow me to do, be, or have?

5. Where do I want to go from here? What result or outcome do I really want to create?

Typical Patterns of Illness

An important part of the Recognition phase of holoenergetic healing is the identification of patterns of illness. Look for these and other patterns, aided by the list below:

1. Difficulty receiving love
2. Difficulty receiving pleasure
3. Difficulty expressing and releasing anger
4. Difficulty forgiving
5. Difficulty trusting

STEP 1: RECOGNITION (INTUITIVE KNOWING)

Using the L-rods, evaluate your etheric energy field and your chakras. (Refer back to fig. 2 if you wish.) This is an optional step.

Balancing Breath

To facilitate a shift to the transpersonal healing state, you may choose to use the Balancing Breath exercise described on page 105.

STEP 2: RESONANCE

Ask yourself, "Am I really willing to allow healing to occur now?" If you are not ready at this time, respect that choice. If you are ready, proceed with the following steps (see fig. 12). (Most people who find they are not willing to go on at this point begin asking themselves why. Repeating the first part of Step 1 at a later time can help you explore your willingness to allow healing to occur.)

1. Focus Your Attention

Focus your attention on the witness area/thymus gland, and your heart center, approximately three to five inches below the level of your shoulders, in the center of your chest. Shift to your observer state and call upon your inner guide or higher Self to help you locate the underlying source of the difficulty.

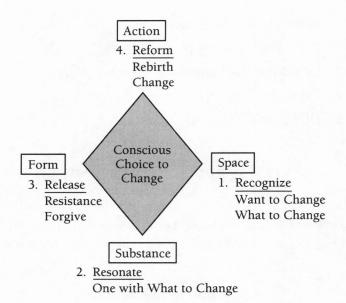

Recognize - in Form   Ways to Come into Resonance
Resonate - with Form
Responsibility - for Form   Address Cause/Source
Release - Unform   Acknowledge/Assume Responsibility
Reform - Reform   Accept/Love Self

FIGURE 12 Conscious Choice to Change

2. Position Your Hands

For simplicity, call your dominant hand your energizing hand, the other your sensing hand.

Instructions for the Energizing Hand

Energize your thymus/heart center by positioning the energizing hand three to six inches from your body, fingers extended, palm facing your heart. Imagine that your hand is radiating energy. Moving this hand back and forth creates an energy flux that can enhance your ability to perceive sensations such as tingling, warmth, pulsation, or pressure in the center of your chest.

Instructions for the Sensing Hand

Scan your field by positioning your second hand eight to ten inches from your body, palm toward your heart center. Move this hand up and down between your shoulder area and your waist to find the point of maximum resonance, where your sensation of energy in this hand is the strongest. Hold your hand in that position to reinforce the field and attune to energy shifts that may occur.

3. Come into Resonance

Take a deep breath and hold. As you slowly exhale, allow the issues or areas of concern to come to mind.

- If it is a physical symptom that comes to mind, sense where in your body you feel it and move your attention to that area.

- If an emotional issue is involved, focus your attention on the area of your body where you feel it as a physical sensation (knot in the stomach, constriction of the throat, headache, etc.).

- You may choose instead to focus attention on the chakra(s) associated with any discomfort you experience. Your selection of a given chakra can be based upon biomechanical evaluation, from Step 1, or upon the table of organs associated with the chakras (pp. 154–55) or your intuitive sense.

- When dealing with emotional or physical trauma, bring forth the precipitating event, reexperiencing it in order to resonate with the circumstances associated with it as well as your feelings, thoughts, beliefs, and choices at that time.

- When working on a physical sensation, symptom, or illness, once you sense where you feel it, you can shift your hands from the thymus/heart center to the affected area, thereby taking yourself from a general to a more specific focus. If you can't reach the area with your hands, continue to hold them over the thymus/heart area.

4. Describe Sensations

- Describe what comes up, be it a sensation, an image, or a symbol. You may want to use a tape recorder as you consider the following:

Where do you sense it in your body?

What do you feel, see, or hear?

What images come to mind?

What size, shape, and color are the images or sensations?

Is there a sound or voice involved?

- Take a deep breath and go into it. Become immersed in it. Merge with it and become it. Describe how you feel inside it.

- While still inside this holoenergetic pattern, go back to the earliest time you can recall feeling similar emotions. Relive the experience as best you can.

- What did you come to believe about yourself, others, and the world as a result of this experience?

5. Discover the Positive Intent

You now know what you've got. It is time to discover and understand the positive intent that underlies this holoenergetic pattern of sensation, feeling, and belief, physically manifest as your problem or issue. (Remember that the positive intent behind the difficulty is the positive life-force energy of what the holoenergetic pattern within you really wants to experience.)

To discover the positive intention, draw in your breath; as you do so, withdraw your mind from the holoenergetic pattern with which you just merged. Shift to your observer self so that you sense or see the pattern as being outside you. Knowing that behind this pattern is a positive life force intention, lovingly ask the pattern what it really wants to sense and experience. Give this underlying life force intention a manifestation as a shape, image, or symbol. Perhaps there is a person or presence, real or imagined, living or dead, who represents for you this life force intent.

Once you have discovered the positive intent behind the energy pattern you want to change, you can go on to release and unform the original disharmonious pattern, or have it become absorbed and directly transformed into the manifestation of its positive intent.

STEP 3: RELEASE

The release phase is a five-part process:

1. Ask yourself, "Am I willing to release this belief, pattern, or image today, and replace it with what I really want?"

2. Once you have determined your willingness to release this pattern, belief, or image, draw your breath in through the affected area, the selected chakra, or your thymus area. Hold that breath while bringing to mind all that you have honestly chosen to release.

3. Forcefully ex-pulse your breath through the area you have energized, with the intention of releasing the disharmonious pattern. Pulse out your breath with force and with the intention of unforming the original thought form. See that energy pattern dissolve. While ex-pulsing in this way, further affect the energy field by suddenly withdrawing your hands with the intention of extracting the energy. Imagine literally pulling out the energy pattern from your body and releasing it to the formless realm.

4. Allow yourself to experience the sense of being released from the original pattern.

5. Take a deep breath, drawing energy up through the soles of your feet, from the center of the Earth. Hold your breath for a moment. Release it forcefully, imagining it going out through the newly cleared area of your body, now freeing the area completely from any influences of the past energy pattern. Repeat this clearing breath one more time.

At this point you have created a void. You can now choose how to fill that area, as described in Step 4.

STEP 4: REFORMATION

Bring your hands back into the field around the area you are focusing on. In your mind, bring into the area your new, healthy image, or the image of your life force intention, your new belief, or purpose. Breathe in deeply from your transpersonal space through the top of your head, energizing the new image or belief. Release your breath slowly into the area, filling it with the vibrant form or loving light.

Fill the area you have cleared with a healthy image, if you know what that healthy image is. This is especially valuable if you are healing a physical lesion. For example, you can look at a picture of a healthy organ, tissue, or cell and visualize that image filling the area. See Richard Kessel and Randy Kardon's *Tissues & Organs* and Lennert Nilsson's *The Body Victorious* in the Bibliography for pictures of healthy structures.

Using a symbol that represents the healthy image or positive intent evokes the natural frequency of the healthy organ.

When an emotional issue is involved, you can fill the area with a new belief, positive intention, or light and love. Light and love also function as harmonics linking to and reminding the structure of the natural frequency of the healthy state. Loving energy of a higher frequency can also prevent the old, released pattern from reconfiguring.

You can also fill the void with your sense of purpose, your positive intention, your vision, or your dream, as you defined for yourself in Step 1. The energy that was bound up in maintaining the disharmonious form has now been released, and you can redirect it. You can align now with your spiritual essence and allow that essence to fill the void.

For help in accessing and transforming the holoenergetic patterns, see Resource 2.

Forgiveness Process

Forgiveness completes your own healing, releasing you from energy forms that otherwise contribute to illness. As an option, you can introduce the forgiveness process as a part of Release or Reformation.

1. Relax in a place where you will not be disturbed for about fifteen minutes.

2. Decide whom you want to forgive and ask yourself if you are honestly willing to do so now.

3. With eyes closed, take deep, slow, diaphragmatic breaths, relaxing more and more deeply with each breath.

4. Focus attention on your solar plexus.

5. Place one hand three to six inches from your body, over your solar plexus, and use the other hand to sense the buildup of the field. Energize the area by moving your hand gently over the area.

6. Draw in a deep breath, as if drawing it through your solar plexus. Hold your breath a moment, and release it slowly through your solar plexus. Bring to mind the images of those beings you want to forgive, framing them with a circle or oval of violet light.

7. Silently communicate to these images whatever it is they did or did not do that caused you discomfort. Express to each image whatever you are holding back, be it feelings of hurt, anger, sadness, or the desire to blame and punish.

8. Look at your willingness to forgive now. Know that beneath the hurt and blame are expansive feelings—feelings of freedom, peace, love, joy, and empowerment—that are trying to come out. In your mind, you have been the jailer of your images of these beings, holding imprisoned within you the feelings of hurt or blame that you now have. See yourself standing outside this jail door, inserting the key of forgiveness, unlocking it and swinging it wide open, preparing to release all your images of these beings and the feelings within you that they represent.

9. While focusing your attention on your solar plexus, take a deep breath and hold in your mind the images you choose to release.

10. Ex-pulse suddenly and forcefully through your solar plexus area, using your hands to draw the disharmonious energy from this area. With your ex-pulse, completely release and dissipate the images, swirling the energy and releasing it into the light. Repeat two or more times.

11. Using your hands, imagine covering your solar plexus with golden light.

12. Shift your attention and your hands to your heart center. In the future, when you communicate with those you have forgiven, whether verbally or nonverbally, focus your attention on your heart center and communicate with them from there.

13. Bring to your mind an image of yourself, perhaps as a child, an adolescent, an adult, or all three. Silently and with feeling, express to your image or images all that you now intend to forgive yourself for. When the communication is complete, take a deep breath, imagining that you are drawing it in through your heart center. As you slowly release your breath from your heart center into the images, feel the forgiveness you have for yourself. You may want to lovingly embrace your image of yourself. Silently tell yourself all is forgiven, and welcome home your image of yourself.

Complete the Holoenergetic Healing Process with Unconditional Love

For a moment, become your own best friend. Take yourself to the most blissful, peaceful place or space that you know of. Allow yourself to begin to feel in the center of your chest a sense of complete unconditional love for yourself—a love for every cell, every atom, every organ in your body and every part of your being. This is a love without comparison, without judgment, beyond all time and space, even beyond understanding.

Inhale gently and fully, allowing your chest to expand, filling yourself with loving light. Allow the light to move up into your shoulders and down your arms, to your fingertips.

Allow the light to move up into your neck and fill your head. Imagine this loving light filling your entire head so that it begins to flow out the top of your head like a fountain of love, cascading down over your body, lovingly caressing it.

Now, while focusing your attention on the top of your head, your crown center, allow yourself to feel the exquisite love that your higher Self has for you. This is a love that is always there, so you need not learn or earn it. Just allow yourself to receive it. Sense a radiant ball of light six to eight inches above your head. Allow it to slowly descend through the top of your head, down to the center of your chest. Feel yourself radiating and glowing with the love your higher Self has for you. Allow its loving light to suffuse your entire body and being. Allow it in.

Now ask your higher Self to:

> Heal what needs to be healed.
> Do what needs to be done
> Bring me into wholeness
> So that we become one.

Focus again on the center of your chest, feeling that sense of complete unconditional love that you have for yourself and that your higher Self has for you. Take a deep breath, hold it a moment, and then release it, sending a burst of light from the center of your chest to every cell and atom in your body, every part of your being, so that they scintillate and sparkle like stars in the night sky.

Holoenergetic Healing Checklist

- Remove your watch, jewelry, coins, and other metals.
- Relax.
- Ground, align, and center.

(Continues)

243

- Take your personal holoenergetic history.
- Evaluate your energy centers (optional).
- Do the Balancing Breath exercise (optional).
- Ask: "Am I really willing to allow healing to occur now?" You may want to call upon higher guidance for deeper insight.
- Focus on the witness area/thymus gland and heart center.
- Position your hands.
- Take a deep breath and hold it for a moment. Release your breath through the thymus/heart center; allow your inner experience of the issue to surface as sensation, feeling, or image. Intuitively sense its location, size, shape, and perhaps color.
- Shift your hands over this area (optional).
- Resonate with the issue or area. Reexperience any events and feelings that come up.
- Go back to the earliest time you recall having had similar feelings.
- Identify the critical beliefs and positive intention behind the issue. Give the positive intention a symbolic manifestation.
- Ask yourself if you are willing to release and transform this pattern.
- Release the form by pulsing through the local area or thymus/heart center and breaking the field with your hands.
- Return your hands to the area.
- Bring in the new, healthy image, positive intention, or loving light, and energize the area with it.
- Energize with your hands and breath from transpersonal space.

HEALING OTHERS

When healing others, you can follow the process described above. When working with another person, however, a few areas require clarification.

As the healer, you ground, align, and center yourself as described. Have your partner relax in whatever way is best for him or her. I have found it most effective to stand with my patients, although if this is difficult for your circumstances you can sit and your partner can sit or lie down.

I suggest you explain the process, particularly the breathing techniques and the use of biomechanical testing, before proceeding, so you won't have to explain it during the healing process.

While taking the holoenergetic history, and whenever questions arise in the healing process, give the person the option of describing his or her own thoughts, feelings, and emotions silently or aloud.

The evaluation of another's energy centers (chakras) is helpful when it is not clear to you or your partner what area to begin to focus attention on in the holoenergetic process. You may or may not choose to do this step.

When you work with others, your loving presence enhances the resonance between you. You come into resonance with the other person's energy field, opening yourself to the heart center and transpersonal levels of that person. Talking to your partner and making physical contact by placing your hand on his or her shoulder can deepen this resonant link.

While you work with your partner, your hands generate and maintain the coherent healing field over the area he or she chooses to focus on (see fig. 13). Place one hand in front and one hand behind your partner's heart/thymus area and establish a transpersonal connection, utilizing aspects of the Transpersonal Alignment Process (see p. 70). Regard the hand behind your partner as your sensing hand, and use it to determine when you come into resonance. This may feel like a pulsing, a pressure, heat, or a tingling sensation.[1]

When you and your partner are ready to release the energy pattern being focused on, take in a breath at the same time that your partner does and hold it as your partner is holding his or her breath. When your partner ex-pulses, simultaneously take in a sharp breath, or in-pulse, of your own to facilitate the process of dissipation. As you in-pulse, quickly withdraw your hands with the intention of extracting the unformed energy in your partner's field.

This completes the transformation. The one being healed ultimately knows what is best for his or her healing. As a healer, you facilitate this process for your partner, allowing him or her to explore and choose the direction he or she feels will most effectively facilitate healing.

Finally, remember that the forgiveness process and the unconditional love process are modules that, when used in conjunction with the holoenergetic healing techniques, create a synergy for healing.

---

1. As you work, keep in mind that your purpose is to help your partner access and transform each holoenergetic pattern involved. For help on this, turn to resource 2, "Tracing," at the back of the book.

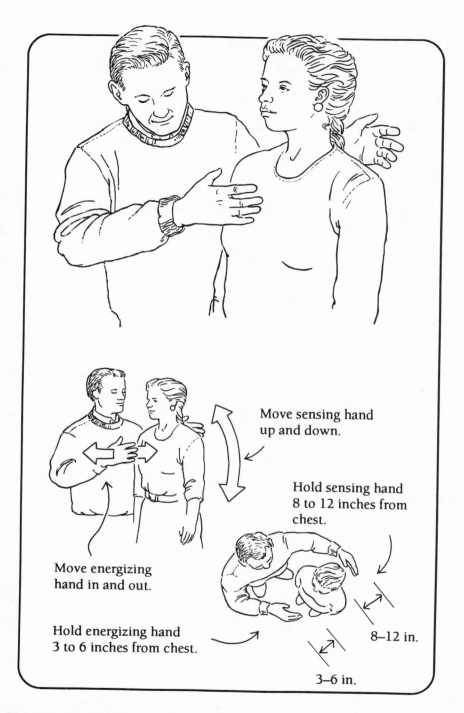

Move sensing hand
up and down.

Hold sensing hand
8 to 12 inches from
chest.

Move energizing
hand in and out.

Hold energizing hand
3 to 6 inches from chest.

8–12 in.

3–6 in.

FIGURE 13 Working with Others

Humanity[2]

Standing together on the threshold of time
Between a past that is gone and a future unknown;
Veil after veil drawing aside, Door after door opening wide;
Ageless wisdom, clear to eyes that can see,
Bearing its fruit, setting us free;
Up from the labyrinth, transcending the mind,
Traveling down the corridors of time;
Joy and pain, penetrating deep,
Loving surrender, unquestioning, complete;
Leaving behind human pride and fear,
Knowing at last that peace draws near;
Gazing into the Creator's face,
A wondrous meeting beyond time and space;
Thus enter the mansion of Father-Mother and Son,
Blessed awakening, we know we are one.

2. This poem was written by Betsy McGregor, M.D., a pediatrician, after a healing session with me.

13

Implications for the Future

Only the similar can know the similar, only the similar can act upon the similar. We can know only what we are: Nothing can be taught to the mind which is not already concealed as potential knowledge in the unfolding soul of the creature. So, also, all perfection of which the outer man is capable, is only a realizing of the eternal perfection of the Spirit within him. We know the Divine and become the Divine, because we are That already in our secret nature. All teaching is revealing, all becoming is an unfolding. Self-attainment is the secret; self-knowledge and an increasing consciousness are the means and the process.

—SRI AUROBINDO

HEALING INTO WHOLENESS

In recent years we have given much attention to physical health. Our attention has been focused predominantly on the body, on the material part of our being. In the West we have only begun to address the states of consciousness that provide the foundation for wellness and healing. As we continue to build on this foundation, we can fulfill the desire for emotional, mental, and spiritual healing, along with physical healing. We're becoming aware that behind every physical illness is an emotional element, with its mental and spiritual concomitants, and that the body is a multidimensional extension of the mind.

Today, advances in science are revealing that we exist in and are part of an infinite ocean of energy. Mind and matter are not separate; it appears that they are different aspects of a single, unifying order. In light of this, now is the time to expand from a body/matter-based orientation to a new reality based on energy, consciousness, and wholeness.

We can heal ourselves by becoming more conscious of our physical, emotional, mental, and spiritual states, and we can help one another heal. The energy-based healing model that we've been exploring describes one way we can do this. Not only can we heal our separate selves through psychoneuroimmunological processes, currently being explored by medical science, but we can also interact with each other and with our environment in ways that facilitate healing. Research described in chapter 1 about our ability to energetically affect cancer cells and bacteria, as well as other research on healing, supports the thesis that we do have the capacity to influence one another energetically. And the most potent of these healing energies is love. As I said in the beginning of the book, healing occurs naturally, and love heals.

Love stimulates healing by relating us to the natural order and harmony inherent in our cells, in our selves, and in universal consciousness. Healing through love is a process of becoming whole. Healing is making whole again what was once whole but has become separate. In this way, love and healing are similar, since love also brings together and dissolves the illusion of separation.

Just as healing bridges the gap from illness to health, from disharmony to harmony, so love bridges the space between fragmentation and wholeness, between separation/individuation and unity.

Like the space between musical notes, love creates the melody through its silent presence. Love says, "Wherever two or more meet in my name, I shall be present." As the energy of "between," love brings duality into harmonic unity. Love is the energy and awareness of "between" that allows us to move beyond.

One of the important implications of the principles I've described in this book is that there are windows of unity, processes that can restore us to our birthright, that is, to the consciousness of unity. Our awareness of the unifying nature of consciousness brings us to wholeness—and this is healing.

Windows of unity can occur through the balancing of polar opposites and complements, through synthesis, through correlations such as analogies, metaphors, and unifying concepts, and through resonance, coherence, and fusion. What we often consider to be polar opposites are in fact complements; they help define each other and together they form a unifying continuum.

As we move toward new unifying visions for healing, it is important to remember the value of individuation, from which our illusions of separation may grow. Individuation is essential in the evolution of both our sense of self and our planetary consciousness. The fear we often associate with the illusion of separation (feelings of abandonment and loneliness) is the result of forgetting or denying our unifying Source. In *On Yoga II: Tome One*, Sri Aurobindo reflects on the qualities of this unifying consciousness when shifting from separation back to the awareness of source:

> One begins to feel others too as part of oneself, or varied repetitions of oneself, the same self modified by nature in other bodies. Or, at the least, as living in the larger universal self which is henceforth one's own greater reality. All things in fact begin to change their nature and appearance; one's whole experience of the world is radically different from that of those who are shut up in their personal selves. One begins to know things by a different kind of experience, more direct, not depending on the external mind and the senses. It is not that the possibility of error disappears, for that cannot be so long as mind of any kind is one's instrument for transcribing knowledge; but there is a new, vast, and deep way of experiencing, seeing, knowing, contacting things; and the confines of knowledge can be rolled back to an almost immeasurable degree.[1]

1. Sri Aurobindo, *On Yoga II: Tome One* (Pondicherry, India: Sri Aurobindo Ashram, 1971), p. 327.

HEALING AND THE HEALTH PROFESSIONS

The healing power of love is a relatively new concept for most people in our society. And yet it is one of the oldest forms of human interaction, allowing us to express giving, nurturing, and caring in ways that bring us back to health. We are now becoming much more interested in learning about healing—of both ourselves and others. Over the past two decades we have seen physicians and patients working together to bring about greater awareness of the healing abilities we each have within us. Initially, the general public will have to lead the way. For healing practices to become a part of mainstream medicine, the consumer, for a variety of reasons, will need to require the health professions to acknowledge new healing modalities and begin incorporating them in practice.

Because healing work is so cost effective, insurance companies, and eventually the government, will support consumers to make healing modalities available to people before they get involved in expensive, elective surgery or undertake various types of medical treatment that could have harmful side effects. If a delay in treatment would not cause any harm to the person, she or he would be offered the option of healing work.

I envision a time, in the not-so-distant future, when healing work becomes an integral part of medicine, dentistry, nursing, psychology, and chiropractic. All health professions will have access to these techniques and methods, which can be taught in the respective schools.

Learning to heal can rehumanize the practice of medicine. Initially, healing may seem to represent a threat to some health professionals, because people trained all their life in other ways may have a genuine skepticism, may question their own healing capabilities, or may just lack confidence. What happens if they start to learn how to heal and find they are having trouble doing this work? Where does that leave them? And what about the financial aspects of it? If somebody can come in for thirty minutes and be healed, instead of having more expensive surgery requiring days in the hospital, what would that do to the economics of medicine? Health professionals might consider that they would have to relinquish some of their power to others involved in healing. That may be a misperception of what will happen, but nevertheless it is a fear that some people have. So these elements may initially stand in the way of incorporating healing into the health professions.

Despite these concerns, transformational methods should be made available to health professionals everywhere, so that they can learn how to do healing work with patients and clients. Many will find holoenergetic healing both clinically effective and cost effective. I believe that healing work will become a module that can be incorporated into every health practice. It is better to develop a cooperative modular concept that can be integrated in this way than it is to set up separate entities that in some way threaten the current practices and status of the health professions.

Conscious healing is clearly a wave of the future—riding the ocean of love, relating us to All-That-Is!

Resources

RESOURCE 1

THE INNER GUIDE

*Intuition, as a mode of knowing that takes as its object the
domain of spirit, can function as an inner guide to the
recognition of everpresent truth.*

— FRANCES VAUGHAN

Many processes in holoenergetic healing take place on an energetic
level, a level that we access through our intuitive senses. In working
with this material, I have found it helpful to have an "inner guide."
(Some people prefer to call them "inner advisers or counselors" or
"spirit guides.") Inner guides, like characters in books, exist within
that area of human consciousness we call the "inner world." Although it is invisible except through the mind's eye, we know that
this world is real. It is in this inner world that we find the source of
our greatest strengths as well as the patterns of illness that we want
to change. Having an inner guide to assist us in becoming more
familiar with this territory is like having a close friend to show us
around when we visit a new town or a country where we've never
been before.

In the holoenergetic healing process, you will be working in this
inner territory to identify patterns of illness, as well as patterns of
strength, in order to effect change in your life. From time to time,
you may have questions or want personal support and assistance. At
these times, it can be helpful to turn to your guide, asking those
questions that you might want to ask me if I were there in person
as you are reading this book. You might also have questions to ask
your guide about the specific nature of your own inner world; in
this respect, a guide can be particularly helpful in the Recognition
phase of the healing process, where you identify sources of illness
that you want to change.

There are many different opinions about the nature of inner
guides. Are they real figures who exist separate from us at a nonor-

dinary level of consciousness, or have we created them in our minds, just as a novelist creates a character for a book? C. G. Jung, whose pioneering work on human consciousness is known and respected the world over, throughout his career used inner guides to explore the inner world. His own guide, Philemon, taught Jung that "the psyche is real" and that many of the figures who appeared there existed quite independently of him.

In the following pages, you will find detailed instructions for contacting your own inner guide. Although having an inner guide is not necessary for understanding the principles of holoenergetic healing that I present here, most people who do have guides find them helpful and supportive.

The exercise for getting an inner guide is in three parts: the first is Relaxation, which helps induce a receptive state of mind; the second is Your Safe Space; and the third is the exercise Meeting Your Guide, in which you employ your active imagination to meet your guide.

Since having an inner guide is not necessary for reading this book and learning how to use the holoenergetic healing process, you have the option of meeting a guide now, waiting until later when you actually start applying the healing tools we describe here, or foregoing the inner guide exercise all together.

✹ EXERCISE: RELAXATION

Choose a time of day and a place where you will not be disturbed for twenty minutes. Give yourself permission to put your undivided attention into doing this exercise and getting a guide. Choose a place to sit where you will be comfortable and alert.

1. Sit with your back straight, feet flat on the floor, hands lying gently on the tops of your thighs. Let your shoulders feel loose and relaxed.

2. Relax your toes and let the soles of your feet make contact with the floor. Loosen tight-fitting clothing.

3. Inhale, filling your lungs and allowing your abdomen to expand as you breathe. Hold the breath for a moment. Now slowly exhale through your nose, releasing air gently through both nostrils. Be aware of your feet—toes, soles, heels, ankles—relaxing.

4. Inhale, filling your lungs. Hold for a moment. Now slowly exhale, releasing your breath through your nose. Be aware of your calf and thigh muscles relaxing.

5. Inhale, filling your lungs. Hold for a moment. Now slowly exhale, releasing your breath through your nose. Be aware of your buttocks and lower back relaxing.

6. Inhale, filling your lungs. Hold for a moment. Now slowly exhale, releasing your breath through your nose. Be aware of your abdomen relaxing.

7. Inhale, filling your lungs. Hold for a moment. Now slowly exhale, releasing your breath through your nose. Be aware of your chest, shoulders, and arms relaxing. Allow your neck muscles to relax.

8. Open your mouth wide. Yawn, or pretend you are yawning. Feel the areas around your eyes relax. Feel your forehead becoming smooth. Feel the muscles around your nose and mouth relax.

9. If thoughts or feelings come into your mind, urging you to think or act at this time, let them just float by like fluffy clouds in the blue sky.

10. Just let yourself be in this relaxed state of mind for a few moments before you go on. Breathe normally, enjoying this relaxed state.

⊕ EXERCISE: YOUR SAFE SPACE

While deeply relaxed, breathe slowly and comfortably. Take yourself in your imagination to the most blissful, peaceful place in nature you know of. For example, it may be

- A meadow
- A clearing in the forest
- A beach
- A place overlooking a beautiful vista

Allow yourself to feel the expansiveness, peace, and safety you have from just being in this place. Use all your senses to enrich your experience of your safe space. Sense into it in any way that allows you to vividly recall it again.

✷ EXERCISE: MEETING YOUR GUIDE

1. While in your safe space, imagine that in a few moments you'll find yourself alongside a stream.

2. Now imagine that as you follow the stream you are approaching a structure. It may be a rustic cabin, a house, a temple. Stop for a moment and look at it. Notice some of its details so that you could describe it to yourself again: what it's made of, what the entrance looks like, what the immediate surroundings are, such as gardens or natural vegetation.

3. Go up to the entrance and knock, or in some other way announce your presence. You may hear a voice in your mind, or you may get a signal or sense to enter.

4. Step inside, feeling you are welcome, safe, and cared for in this place. Look around and notice the interior so that you could describe it to yourself again. Notice the walls, whether the interior is bright or dark, how the place is furnished.

5. Somewhere in this structure you'll be meeting your guide. The meeting may occur where you are right now or in some other place in the structure. Your guide is expecting you and is waiting for you. You will know exactly where to be for this meeting. Go there now and find a comfortable place to sit.

6. Notice that you are facing a special door with no doorknob. It is a sliding door that will open from the bottom up, like a rolltop desk. Your guide will enter through this door. The door slides up a foot or two and stops. You see your inner guide's feet. Take your time to clarify what you see: the kind and color of shoes, socks, sandals, or bare feet. The door slides open to the guide's waistline. Notice the clothes the guide is wearing, if any. You may also see her or his hands, what size and shape they are. Notice any jewelry—rings, wristwatch, belt and buckle, necklace, or other personal item. The door slides up to the guide's shoulders. Note what your guide is wearing—style, colors, any jewelry or other personal items. What is your guide's posture? Now the door opens fully and you see your guide's face. Look at the facial expression, the shape and color of the eyes, the shape of the mouth and nose, the color and texture of your guide's hair and skin. What do you feel when you look into your guide's eyes?

7. Greet your guide. In your mind, you may say, "Hello, my name is _____. What may I call you?" Your guide tells you his or her name, then steps forward to greet you. You may have a sense of your guide hugging you like a dear friend, or shaking your hand, or greeting you with a nod or smile.

8. You now sit down with your guide and begin conversing. Talk about any subject that comes to mind.

9. When you feel like ending this meeting, simply tell your guide that you want to do so. Thank him or her for coming. Tell your guide in your own way you are glad you met and will contact him or her in the future. Say good-bye to each other in whatever way seems appropriate.

10. Now imagine leaving the way you came. Step outside and return to your safe space.

11. When you are ready, take a deep breath, open your eyes, and stretch, feeling fully awake and alert.

After meeting your guide, give some thought to the meeting. How do you feel about your guide? Do you feel comfortable with her or him? Does it seem to you that your guide can be helpful to you in the future?

In the days ahead, think about your guide frequently, just as you might do after meeting an especially interesting new friend. In the process, the guide will become more familiar to you. Imagine that you are sharing your thoughts, feelings, and any questions you might have with your guide.

As you read on in the book, you may find it helpful to share what you are reading with your guide, just as you might share your thoughts and feelings about something you're reading with a friend. If you have questions you want clarified, ask your guide to meet you in your safe space to dialogue.

If you do not get an inner guide on your first try, don't be concerned. Simply try again at a time when you feel more relaxed and receptive.

Throughout this book, you'll find suggestions for ways to consult your guide or go into your safe space. In the meantime, experiment with conversing with your inner guide on any subject you want.

If you are not certain you want to keep your guide, take time to give it some thought; if you decide this is not the guide for you, imagine him or her standing in front of you. Thank the guide for offering assistance and tell the guide you will not be needing his or her help. Let the guide know you will be working with a different guide. Then do the exercise again, with the intention of meeting a new guide.

Treat your guide as you would another person in your life. His or her advice and knowledge are not infallible. Keep in mind that the final choice about accepting or rejecting any advice is your own.

Use of a Safe Space Instead of the Guide

Some people do not get guides after doing this exercise. Instead, they come to a place such as a beautiful park, a meadow, or a room in a house that is a creative work space for them. As they come to this place they feel safe and at peace. They get clear insights and feel in touch with sources of knowledge that they do not seem to have in everyday life.

⊕ **EXERCISE: MEETING YOUR HIGHER SELF IN YOUR SAFE SPACE**

Allow yourself to relax, close your eyes, and imagine yourself in the most blissful, peaceful place or space you know.

Using your intuition, sense what it would be like to be all that you are, unbounded, fully aware, totally free, beyond your thoughts, feelings, and physical sensations. Your higher Self, like a flower in full bloom, is you at your fullest potential.

Invite your higher Self to be with you now. Allow yourself to feel its infinite love for you.

Ask your higher Self if it has a message for you at this time. This message could come as an inner dialogue; or perhaps in the form of an image, a person, or a symbol, a gift, a sound, color, or sensation.

If in need of healing, ask your higher Self to help you to heal completely and fully in accord with your highest good.

Thank your higher Self when you sense the communication to be complete.

When you are ready, take a deep breath, open your eyes, feeling fully awake and alert.

RESOURCE 2
TRACING

A wave on the ocean has a beginning and an end, a birth and a death. But the Heart Sutra *tells us that the wave is empty. The wave is full of water, but it is empty of a separate self. A wave is a form which has been made possible thanks to the existence of wind and water. If a wave only sees its form, with its beginning and end, it will be afraid of birth and death. But if the wave sees that it is water, identifies itself with the water, then it will be emancipated from birth and death. Each wave is born and is going to die, but the water is free from birth and death.*

—THICH NHAT HANH

Tracing represents an intuitive deepening of the holoenergetic process allowing you to discover the source of an illness or trauma and transform it at its core.

Preparation

Allow yourself to relax and take several deep breaths. Gently close your eyes, turn within, and go to the most blissful, peaceful place or space you know or can imagine. In this serene safe space bring forth your higher Self or inner guide to help you with this issue.

Step 1: Recognition

Identify the issue or feeling you want to change; hold it in mind and begin to sense into it. Take a deep breath and as you release your breath, notice where in your body your attention is drawn.

Where do you sense this issue in your body?

Describe what comes up, be it a sensation, image, or symbol.

What size, shape, and color are the images or sensations?

Give this intuitive information and energy a tangible form in which to manifest itself.

Step 2: Resonance

Identify with the form by focusing on it while drawing your breath in and holding it for a moment. As you release your breath, go with your mind into the form. Become immersed in it.

What does it feel like being inside? Describe any sensations, feelings, and images that you experience.

Is there tightness, aloneness, darkness, heaviness, pain, or perhaps, lightness, peace or freedom?

What emotions do you feel?

Do you feel scared, angry, sad, hurt, numb, or joyful?

Follow the feeling by recalling the earliest time you felt similar emotions. Allow yourself to relive the experience, feeling the feelings and emotions as best you can.

What did you come to believe about yourself, others, and the world as a result of this experience?

What did you choose to believe about yourself and about life?

To discover the life force intent behind these feelings, ask yourself what you really wanted to feel underneath these emotions and beliefs.

What were you really wanting to feel, to see yourself as, or to hear about yourself? Give this underlying life force intent a representation as a shape, image, or symbol. Perhaps there is a person or presence, real or imagined, living or dead, who represents for you this life force intent. It may be a mythical being or a grandparent, a flower, the sky, or the ocean.

You can ask your higher Self or inner guide to help bring forth this new form. This new form may be your higher Self.

Step 3: Release

Now that you have recognized and understood the sensations, deep feelings, choices, beliefs, and positive life force intent underlying this issue, you are ready to transform the form.

Draw your breath in and withdraw your mind from the original form in which it has been immersed. When you come out, bring with you the symbol or image of its positive life force intent.

As you release your breath, sense or visualize both the image of the original form and the new life force image before you.

Mentally ask the original image what it considers its function to be. Find out how it sees itself having served you and met your needs all these years.

Silently thank the original image for intending to function in your behalf no matter how disharmonious that may have been, and introduce it to the symbol of the positive life force beside it.

Let the original image know that all the energy it has been expending for you will be used by the new life force image in the most effective way to accomplish what it has wanted for you.

Inform the original image that its work is now done and that it is time to return to the unmanifest realm, releasing its energy to become absorbed and transformed into its positive intentions—the new life force image or presence.

Draw your breath in as if through the original form and affected area of the body (or chakra). Forcefully expel your breath through the affected area and the original form with the intention of totally unforming and releasing the pattern. See or sense it change or transform, perhaps fading like light into infinity. Repeat this breath release two more times.

Step 4: Reformation

Focus again on the affected area and notice what it looks and feels like now. Imagining or sensing the new image before you, ask it to provide you with some way to recognize and remember its life force vitality. Let it know that you want to awaken to its gentle whispers instead of waiting for the cries of illness.

Integrate the new image in your daily life by requesting a sign through which it can communicate with you. Perhaps it is a sequence of numbers such as 33; or a rose; or a star; or an unusual color, sound, or feeling. Agree on some signal in the physical world through which it can whisper to you to awaken you to your Self.

Ask the new image what you need to know now. If healing is required, call upon your higher Self or inner guide to be with you from now on to help you heal what needs to be healed.

Now focus on the new image or presence before you. As you take in your next breath, imagine drawing the image into the affected area completely, filling the area with its energy. Feel the energy radiating throughout your entire body, your whole being.

Imagine your body sheathed in golden light.

Know that healing has occurred.

Optional Processes

You may end tracing here or go on to the forgiveness and/or unconditional love processes.

RESOURCE 3

CRYSTALLINE STRUCTURES AS TRANSFORMERS OF ENERGY

We can build and direct energy with our hands. We can also supplement the energy of our hands through the use of quartz crystals.

I have worked with crystals for transferring and transforming energy and have found them, in some instances, to be useful adjuncts to healing work.

In recent years the use of crystals in healing has been controversial. Within the context of holoenergetic healing, crystals are interesting in that they possess properties that are compatible with the transfer and transformation of energy. While they are not necessary for healing, they can be a useful tool.

In this book we've discussed how energy is often converted from one form to another. At a physical level, vibrational pressure is converted to charge, or charge is converted to vibration, primarily through the crystalline structures that we find in the body, such as bone, cell membranes, hair, and DNA. These structures are piezoelectric, which means they convert pressure to electrical charge and vice versa. This attribute allows these structures to readily convey information and transfer energy.

Like bone and other structures of the human body, quartz crystals are piezoelectric. When pressure is applied to a quartz crystal, electrons are released, producing electricity. Their piezoelectric effect makes crystals useful in electronic equipment such as quartz watches, radios, and phonograph cartridges.

Some quartz crystals can amplify energy by focusing it. If you put a clear, round crystal on a piece of cloth in the sun, it would focus the sun's rays just as a lens does, eventually generating enough heat to burn the cloth.

Crystals are also bioenergy transducers. They can transform and transfer the energy of living systems. Quartz can step down subtle energies into the electromagnetic spectrum, the primary level at which the physical body operates. (If you want to explore this in more depth, see appendix A, "The Scientific Basis for Healing with Subtle Energies," by Glen Rein, Ph.D.)

In healing work, quartz crystals can help us focus and amplify our intent. They are very sensitive to our thoughts and intentions, which makes it possible for us to program a crystal to seek out a certain energy resonance, allowing us to come into alignment with it. When we come into resonance with what we want to change, we can more readily release the dissonant energy pattern.

Influence of a Crystal on an Etheric Energy Field

If you have a quartz crystal, you can observe its effect on your partner's etheric energy field.

First, evaluate your partner's etheric energy field with the L-rods, as described in chapter 6, "Recognition—Intuitive Knowing." Note the baseline.

Now, have your partner hold a natural quartz crystal, pointed end up, at the center of his or her chest. While your partner is holding it in this way, test the field again. The presence of the crystal over the heart center should noticeably expand the energy field.

Repeat the procedure with the crystal pointed down.

To determine the effect of a crystal on your own energy field, place it in a pocket. Then test for your etheric energy field. To have an influence, the crystal does not need to be at your heart center, only in your field. However, its location can make a difference. Experiment with the ways a quartz crystal can expand your energy field by placing it in different areas and different positions within the range of your etheric energy field.

You can use the L-rods with a mirror to explore the influence of jewelry such as pendants, watches, or rings by wearing them or placing them in pockets and evaluating your energy field.

RESOURCE 4

THE RELATIONSHIP OF CONSCIOUSNESS TO LOVE—AN OPERATIONAL COSMOLOGY

Everything depends on what we see, how we look at existence in our soul's view of things. Being and Becoming, One and Many are both true and are both the same thing.

—SRI AUROBINDO

We want to develop here a common language for the understanding of holoenergetic healing and love. This cosmology embraces the paradox of knowing oneself as a separate individual while being aware of one's relatedness with All-That-Is, through love.

Infinite love is the synergistic awareness of unity. Infinitely expanding love is the awareness and energy of relatedness of something to everything and to nothing. How can that be? A state of everything/nothing (E/N) is the total potential state of absolute rest and absolute motion from which all else derives and unfolds. This conceptual state has also been called the ground of being, the void, the fundamental field, the enfolded order, and zero-point energy. This is the domain of All-That-Is.

When something vibrates, it moves back and forth regularly. Each time it changes directions it comes to a momentary stop; at this instant of rest its momentum is zero. Heisenberg's principle of uncertainty, one of the pillars of quantum physics, states that when the momentum of a particle is known its position can not be defined. In other words, when the momentum of a particle is zero it could theoretically be anywhere.

Itzhak Bentov speculates that as the frequency of a vibration increases and the movement between rest periods becomes shorter, at some point the rest periods overlap the movement. The energy in this state is so high that it is beyond vibration. This also applies to "angular momentum" or "spin" where the stronger the field is the faster the spin, until the beginning and the end become one.

Bentov suggested that in this state movement is so fast that it is everywhere at once. If it is everywhere, it is everything. It is fullness. Since it is everywhere and everything, it can't be measured, because it can't be compared with anything else. It is infinite. Therefore, from the human perspective, which only registers motion and rest in a narrow range, it is also nowhere and nothing. It is emptiness, stillness, silence.

When this total potential state of everything/nothing is downstepped into vibration, it becomes "something." It becomes finite.

Sages and mystics throughout the ages have intuited that the first step down was the question "Why?" or "Who am I?," thus creating consciousness, the initial state from which all else derives.

The desire of All-That-Is to know itself, to know "Who am I?," is the first step down into consciousness. It is the urge to move from E/N to "something." It is a individuating, differentiating step, one of devolving, or unfolding, total potential into the energy of motion. A desire to know itself resulted in a separation from E/N to vibrational frequencies. Perhaps what is happening in all differentiation — in separation of charge as well as separation of frequency — is a desire of all in nature to know itself and return back again to the E/N, to oneness/infinity. (See fig. 14.)

Desire maximizes or minimizes difference. It implies movement, either toward or away from the object of desire. Desire gives all movement its value. When the object of your desire is realized, desire disappears, movement stops, and you return again to the place of rest. Desire motivates us to move away from oneness to individuation or toward oneness to unification and wholeness. At the physical level, desire is an urge to move toward or away from separation of charge and frequency. In the realm of consciousness, desire is expressed as the urge to move toward or away from unity.

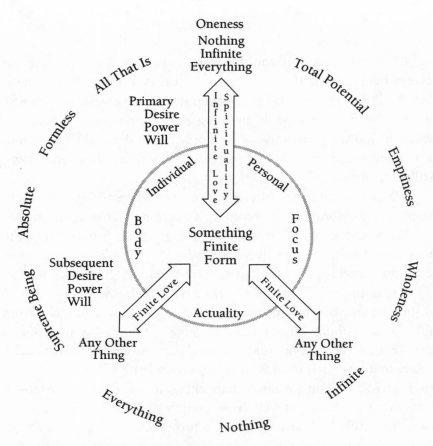

FIGURE 14 Operational Cosmology

The movement itself is *power*. Your potential power is your ability to move, act, or create. Your willingness to act or move and the movement itself allows you to express your power. When you act you exercise your potential power.

Will is persistent focused desire, and it is expressed through doing (willfully) and allowing (willingly). Will often takes form as intention, determination, imagination, and expectation. Aligning with spirit and life force and living your purpose is manifesting your will. This has great implications for healing. The will to live is clearly related to one's sense of purpose. We often hear stories of survivors who have a purpose for wanting to live willing themselves to live. Understanding your desire, will, love, and spirituality enhances the process of self-realization.

272

Glossary of the Operational Cosmology

Primary Desire: The urge to move from "everything/ nothing" or oneness (E/N) to "something" (ST), and from ST to E/N.

Primary Power: The movement itself and the ability to move from oneness to ST and back.

Primary Will: Persistent, focused desire unfolded from oneness.

Primary Awareness: The awareness of primary desire, power, will, and love.

Pure Awareness: Awareness without object. Emptiness, stillness, silence.

Infinite Love: The awareness and energy of the relatedness between oneness and something.

Finite Love: The awareness and energy of relatedness between something and any other thing.

Spirituality: The relationship itself between something or anything and oneness, between the finite and the infinite, between form and the formless.

To evolve in consciousness is to become more aware of what was unconscious and subconscious, that is, to become aware of yourself as being the self. It is the state of recognizing the content of the personal self, existing in the void or ground of being. When the ground of being begins to vibrate, the content of consciousness is created, much like waves on the surface of the cosmic ocean. Thus, self interacting with itself produces frequency waves in consciousness.

Consciousness is the totality of the known in the infinity of the unknown. When something is known it is said to be "real" and is called "truth." To know and be one's self is to be self-realized.

Awareness is the expanding, contracting pupil of the eye of consciousness. Attention is its lens. Together, awareness and attention begin to process the content of consciousness. Unconsciousness is being unaware of the content of consciousness. Awareness is knowing its content. Attention is focusing and holding awareness on the content of consciousness.

The Relationship of Consciousness to Love

All that is is One.

When there is only One, there is no consciousness.

One's desire to know itself creates consciousness. As soon as the One is known, consciousness is created.

The first step down from One is desire: the desire to know itself ("Who am I"?).

At the moment that more than One is created, there is a matrix of relatedness—

A conscious awareness of this relatedness is love.

The energy of this relatedness is love.

Most of what we "know" is outside our level of awareness. A patient "knows" as a consciousness what is transpiring under anesthesia during surgery, but he or she does not have an awareness of it. Hypnosis can later bring to conscious awareness the comments of the surgeon. Positive suggestions made to patients under anesthesia have been shown to reduce the length of the hospital stay and healing time.

Our subconscious mind, usually below our level of awareness, carries out physiological homeostatic processing of the body-mind. It registers, compares, and filters all input through its computerlike programs to determine how to process it.

The Relationship of Love to Power

Power is best veiled until the awareness of love reveals no separation.

Love awakens you to the greatest responsibility—awareness of relatedness.

As you do to others, so you do to yourself.

With this loving awareness, power can be handled responsibly.

Spirituality is the relationship between something and E/N. In this sense, all is spiritual. Love, by connecting us to all, allows us to become aware of our spirituality. It brings heart energy and feeling to our spirituality.

Love discloses the spiritual meaning behind "As you do to others, so you do to yourself." When you love and experience that love reflected back, you become conscious of its effect and the responsibility implied. With your awareness of effect, you can handle power responsibly. It is this loving quality of consciousness, coupled with a transferring breath, that becomes such a powerful force for healing.

In the holoenergetic healing model we describe love as an awareness of relatedness that brings us into unity. Once unity occurs subject and object merge and disappear. Only love remains as everything, nothing, all.

Love is the
>   Awareness of unity
>   Energetic impulse toward unity
>   Action evoked by this awareness and energy

Love is the
>   Energy of *between* that opens to *beyond*

Love is the
>   Space
>   Silence
>   Oneness
>   All

Appendixes

A

The Scientific Basis for Healing with Subtle Energies

Glen Rein, Ph.D.

Quantum Biology Research Laboratory, Palo Alto, California

The basic tenet in energy medicine is the existence of an energy body related to yet distinct from the physical/chemical body. Numerous alternative treatment modalities, including acupuncture, psychotronics, and homeopathy, utilize this bioenergy body to facilitate healing of the physical body. Although this new field of energy medicine has had some remarkable successes in the clinic, the underlying scientific mechanisms responsible for healing with these subtle energies are largely unknown.

Despite increasing evidence that the body emits a broad spectrum of electromagnetic (EM)[1] and acoustic radiation,[2] the orthodox medical establishment continues to ignore the functional role of such endogenous energy. In medical electronics these energies are routinely measured using sophisticated equipment such as thermography, magnetic resonance imaging (MRI), the electroencephalogram (EEG), the electrocardiogram (EKG), the electromyogram (EMG), and ultrasound and are used to monitor and diagnose diseases. However, these energy fields coming from the body are considered by-products (almost waste products) of the biochemical reactions in the body and are not considered by most biomedical researchers to be involved with the basic functioning (or healing) of the body. The concept of an energy body is alien to the medical community.

In addition to EM and acoustic energy, the bioenergy body is more likely composed of other types of energy as well. The quasi-particles[3] and vector/scalar quantum potentials[4] recently discovered in quantum physics are likely candidates as quantum components of the "aura." In addition, the more fundamental level of the superquantum potential has been proposed as a higher dimensional energy.[5] It is proposed here that energies often referred to as spiritual due to their association with the nonphysical world and higher states of consciousness exist at a level even more subtle than the superquantum potential. The terms non-Hertzian, quantum, and subtle will be used to refer to energies associated with the superquantum potential level. Numerous other terms have been introduced by unorthodox scientists to describe the subtle energies they were working with: scalar, longitudinal, motional, time-reversed, radiant, gravitational, orgone, vital, free, cosmic, etc. It is presently unknown whether these energies are identical or distinct from non-Hertzian waves.

The properties of these subtle energies are believed to be different than those of classical EM vector fields (E and B) described by Hertz and Maxwell and the fields associated with quantum potentials (A and 0).[6] The term *subtle energy* has been previously used by others, including Einstein, in referring to energy which has not yet been measured. At present, subtle energy cannot be measured using conventional electronic equipment. Although several investigators such as Beck, Puharich, Kelley, and Davidson have built devices which may detect subtle energies, these devices also detect conventional EM fields and/or quantum potentials.

An alternative approach uses biological systems as "biodetectors" since such systems appear to be sensitive to subtle energies. Although these "new"energies have been incorporated into the mathematical formalism of quantum physics, they are not being considered by the biomedical community. Nonetheless, they are likely to be involved in biological processes since biological systems display quantum mechanical properties. This appendix will briefly review the physical and biological relevance of subtle energies and present new experimental evidence (obtained by the author and other unorthodox scientists) to support the hypothesis that they are a likely component of the bioenergy body and are involved with the body's own intrinsic healing mechanisms.

The crystalline transduction theory and the holoenergetic quantum consciousness theory will be presented as new theories to explain how consciousness utilizes external subtle energy to bring about profound physiological changes resulting in healing. The theories are based on contemporary scientific research from quantum electrodynamics, quantum biology, psychoneuroimmunology, and bioelectromagnetics.

THE ENERGY BODY AND THE NATURAL HEALING PROCESS

Although the conventional biomedical community does not acknowledge the presence of an energy body, the research of frontier western scientists like Burr, Becker, Nordenstrom, Popp, Bentov, Frohlich, and numerous eastern block scientists has strongly indicated the presence of an energy body, or bioplasma, as it is referred to in eastern Europe. The physical nature of this energy body has been variously described as electrical, magnetic (alternating or static), and acoustic. In addition to these physical (i.e., measurable) energies, many esoteric traditions throughout the world refer to the subtle nature of the "aura." This subtle energy has been given different names (e.g., prana, chi). It is the author's opinion that the energy body is composed of a mixture of physical and subtle energies which interact in a complex, nonlinear manner. The new energies generated by such a nonlinear interaction would be quantitatively and qualitatively different from the individual components. The focus of this appendix is the biological role of these subtle energies and how they relate to the more conventional EM body.

In bioelectromagnetics research, the relationship between the EM body and disease has been investigated by studying the ability of exogenous EM fields to cause physiological effects and heal diseased tissues. The possibility that endogenous (naturally occurring) EM fields associated with the energy body might also be involved in the healing process was first demonstrated by Becker when he measured the "current of injury" associated with wounds and bone fractures.[7] Thus, locally generated endogenous EM fields can also mediate the healing process.

The possibility that EM fields generated from the brain might also promote healing in distant parts of the body has not been considered. The new field of psychoneuroimmunology offers a scientific basis for the concept of mind/body interactions by demonstrating a bidirectional link between the brain and the immune system. Additional research in this field has led to the conclusion that altered states of consciousness, especially those associated with stress, can have profound effects at the cellular level.[8] Since different states of consciousness are generated from specific thought patterns and each thought is associated with the activation of specific neuronal networks, the patterned information accompanying a given thought could be communicated to distant parts of the body via the energy body.

Exactly how this patterned information propagates from the brain to distal parts of the body, thereby made manifest as a physiological effect, is unknown. One obvious route is via the peripheral nervous system, which sends messages from the brain to the body. An alternative mechanism was postulated by Nordenstrom[9] who suggested that electrical activity travels throughout the body via blood vessels (rather than nerves). A third theory has been proposed by the author who suggested that EM energy could propagate throughout the body through the extracellular matrix (the space between cells), which is composed of a complex lattice network.[10] This network is composed of several highly structured protein molecules that are piezoelectric by virtue of their helical shape and could therefore carry propagating EM fields. It is unclear to what extent these mechanisms may be involved with the acupuncture meridians and the flow of *chi* through the body.

Although the mechanism of EM propagation to diseased cells in the body is unknown, they can certainly produce a healing effect once there. Numerous studies from the new field of bioelectromagnetics indicate that weak electromagnetic fields with patterned information similar to that occurring naturally in the body can have profound physiological effects on a variety of biological tissues.[11] These effects have been observed at the organismic, cellular, and molecular levels.

In an attempt to explain how cells sense, amplify, and utilize such weak EM fields and to develop a hypothesis that would predict the biological effect associated with the patterned informational content of a given EM field, several theoretical models have been proposed. Theories based on classical Newtonian mechanics have not proved adequate to explain these EM effects.

Frohlich's theory is more successful.[12] It describes resonant interactions between EM fields and harmonic oscillators or dipoles within biological systems. If the oscillations from the EM field and the harmonic oscillators are close enough in frequency, they resonate together and exchange energy. The same principle applies in psychoenergetic healing where resonance can occur between the healer and the disharmonious energy of the person being healed, thereby neutralizing the distorting energy.

The more recent cyclotron resonance theory[13] proposes that electrically charged ions in the body, like calcium and sodium, resonate with the imposing EM fields and move through the cell membrane in a spiral motion. In quantum physics this idea has been extended to consider the spiral motion of energy and the anomalies associated with vortexes. It is interesting to note that many clairvoyants and healers describe the energy from the chakras as being spiral in nature.

Quantum mechanical models have also been introduced that give far more accurate predictions and descriptions of electromagnetic phenomena. In order for these models to be applicable to biological systems, the latter must be nonlinear, must be in a state of nonequilibrium, and must allow an energy flux through them. Recent experimental data[14] indicate that biological systems satisfy all of these criteria. For example, biological systems show nonlinear responses to weak EM fields, i.e., the cellular response is greater than and/or different from the energy which is put into the system. Nonlinear coupling between harmonic oscillators[15] has also been observed. In biological systems, harmonic oscillations between electrically charged regions can occur within one molecule or between molecules. When analyzed mathematically, the nature of this coupling has been shown to be nonlinear.

Energetic interactions within the same molecule are EM in nature and have been described as short-range forces. On the other hand, resonant interactions between distant molecules are referred to as long-range. Several examples have been uncovered of long-range, nonlinear coupling in biological systems. A relevant example of the mechanism of action of weak EM fields is the nonlinear coupling between lipid molecules in the cell membrane.[16] Long-range coupling can occur not only between molecules but also between collections of molecules that form macroscopic structures. Nonlinear coupling between different neuronal networks,[17] for example, may comprise the energy matrix behind thoughts and even consciousness itself.

Although the nature of long-range, nonlinear coupling is unknown, it is proposed here that it is non-Hertzian in nature and occurs at the level of the superquantum potential. These quantum fields have received little interest from the biomedical community. Before describing the role of these fields in biological systems, in healing and in consciousness, their physical properties will be discussed briefly.

NON-HERTZIAN QUANTUM FIELDS

Contemporary quantum physics recognizes that physical reality cannot be adequately explained exclusively in terms of the actions of classical EM vectors interacting with matter. It has been demonstrated that the magnetic vector potential (A) and the electrostatic scalar potential (0) underlie EM field vectors, i.e., EM fields are mathematically derived from these quantum potentials.[18] The macroscopic significance of quantum potentials was first proposed by Aharonov and Bohm.[19] Subsequently, quantum potentials were generated around a solenoid that confines the magnetic fields. Quantum potentials in the absence of any EM fields caused a shift in the wave function of electrons passing through that space.[20] Bohm described the quantum potential as an enfolded, implicate structure underlying the explicate order of the EM field. Although quantum potentials exist in our 4-D reality, the idea of a more fundamental energy underlying this reality has been proposed by Bohm in referring to the superquantum potential which is enfolded within the quantum potential. It is the author's belief that non-Hertzian fields reside at this level.

Classical electromagnetic field theory and classical electrodynamics developed by Maxwell, Faraday, and Hertz[21] describe the interaction of EM energy with matter (i.e., elementary particles such as electrons) in terms of forces acting on matter. The quantum hypothesis first proposed by Planck[22] in 1911 described the EM fields generated from matter (the black body) as being quantized, in discrete energy packets, rather than being a continuous process. In addition to a black body, matter was often modeled as a harmonic oscillator—two elementary charges of opposite sign vibrating together. In modeling the radiation emitted from such an oscillator at absolute zero temperatures, Planck introduced the concept of zero-point fluctuations and zero-point energy (ZPE). By the late 1920s quantum mechanics had been well established by pioneering contributions from Schrödinger, DeBroglie, Dirac and Heisenberg. The nonlinear quantum equations used in the new physics confirmed the existence of the ZPE.[23] Unfortunately, the mathematical description of the ZPE was infinite, incoherent, and chaotic in nature. Several scientists attempted to alleviate the troublesome infinite values by modifying the mathematics.

The concept of higher dimensional universes has been proposed in superstring theory.[24] In the model presented here, ZPE resides in the higher dimensional level of the superquantum potential. Despite the difficulty of the physics community in interpreting the notion of ZPE, it has been used successfully to characterize and predict several macroscopic phenomena in physical chemistry. When ZPE was incorporated into the mathematical descriptions of these physical phenomena, the theoretical predictions came closer to the experimentally determined values. Similar successes were obtained when examining atomic and subatomic phenomenon, especially when ZPE was combined with quantum field theory.

A basic tenet of general relativity, according to Einstein, is that local curvature of space/time (the addition of time to the 3-D universe) is not possible. Space/time has been mathematically modeled as a vacuum in which an equilibrium exists between particles and antiparticles.[25] It has been proposed that the local curvature of space/time is possible and would result in changes in the magnitude of the vacuum. Oscillations in the virtual energy of the vacuum would therefore account for ZPE. According to this model, the vacuum occupies higher dimensions which are believed to be the source of the virtual ZPE.

King has incorporated these ideas in his virtual plasma model to explain how ZPE can manifest and cohere in our 4-D reality.[26] According to this model, the ZPE normally passes through our 3-D space randomly, therefore not affecting us. However, in certain situations, the ZPE flux can be slightly twisted or orthorotated into our 3-D space and generate virtual particles that in turn generate elementary particles. The separation of these virtual particles generates a virtual plasma, which can interact nonlinearly with ZPE. In this way, a small amount of the infinite ZPE can be tapped or made coherent and used to provide enough energy to form macroscopic metastable plasma vortex rings. Thus, the theory predicts that the random, incoherent ZPE can be tapped and used to generate coherent, structured macroscopic phenomena in our 4-D reality. Although King's theory contradicts the third law of thermodynamics, it does offer an explanation for experimentally observed vortex rings and the anomalies associated with several "free energy" devices.

Recently, Puthoff modeled the ground state of the hydrogen atom as being dependent on the amount of ZPE absorbed.[27] By calculating the power absorbed from the ZPE field, he concluded that the ZPE maintained the equilibrium between the hydrogen and the ZPE and prevented the collapse of the ground state. Therefore, the most fundamental state of matter, the ground state, contains ZPE. These results extend the classical interpretation of the role of ZPE in the ground state and imply that stability of the matter itself (in this system at least) is mediated by ZPE. The results also support the original 1916 hypothesis of Nernst[28] who first proposed that ZPE and matter were in a state of equilibrium and that only small amounts of ZPE were necessary to maintain this equilibrium. Nernst also proposed a mechanism for the conversion of ZPE into matter—via "ultra-particles," known today as elementary particles. A similar conclusion was reached by DeBroglie, who proposed that ZPE could interact with such particles and change their mass.[29] Quantum electrodynamics also states that ZPE is the basis for the radiation field emitted by all particles and all quantum states. According to Puthoff[30], these are zero-point fluctuation determined states.

Based on these unusual properties of ZPE unorthodox scientists have proposed a new type of energy field with similar properties. The now popular term *scalar wave* was introduced to refer to this type of energy. While there is disagreement about the origin of this energy, its proposed properties are higher dimensional in nature (residing at the level of the superquantum potential).

According to King, scalar waves propagate in hyperspace guided by vortex rings, but under the proper conditions it can be orthorotated, like ZPE, into our 4-D reality.[31] By confining the propagation of the scalar wave to the higher dimensions, one can avoid breaking the laws of quantum physics.

Contrary to King, Bearden, who coined the term *scalar electromagnetics,* proposes that scalar waves are not from higher dimensions but are generated by the oscillating contraction and relaxation of a stationary electron. A scalar "squeeze" wave would propagate/translate from this source if the overall symmetry of the system was broken. Breaking of symmetry is also associated with local curvature of space/time and the conversion of virtual particles into elementary particles. Since breaking of symmetry is mathematically allowed, conservation laws have had to be revised. The modified laws allow the existence of negative time (time reversal). Bearden has proposed that the revised laws be further modified to include energy, entropy (the tendency of the universe toward disorder), and gravity. This would allow negative energy, antigravity and negentropy (a counterbalancing force that would tend to bring the universe back to an ordered state). Therefore, scalar waves would acquire these properties.[32]

Bearden sees the scalar wave coupled to conventional EM waves resulting in a positive energy/positive time EM wave and a negative energy/ negative time wave superimposed on each other. The positive energy wave interacts with negatively charged electrons, whereas negative energy waves interact with the positively charged protons in the nucleus. Bearden further proposes that under certain experimental conditions, conventional EM vectors and scalar waves can be separated. This notion is supported by the presence of a scalar term in the original quarternion equations Maxwell used to describe electromagnetic fields. Mathematically, crossing two quarternion equations results in the cancellation of the vector components, with the residual scalar term remaining. This is the principle behind the caduceus coil described below. When the scalar terms were removed from the original equations to simplify the mathematics, scalar electromagnetics was also discarded.

The possibility that scalar waves, unlike most EM fields, can interact directly with the nucleus is intriguing and implies that this form of energy can interact with matter at the very fundamental subnuclear level. According to Bearden, excitation of nuclear protons by scalar waves results in the emission of virtual photons. Bearden further postulates that the nucleus contains virtual protons, which in turn interact with the virtual photons. Although this theory falls outside of conventional physics, it is supported by the idea of virtual particles first described by Dirac.[33] According to Bearden, the process of charging and discharging the nucleus with virtual particles allows the nucleus to act like a capacitor, accumulating ZPE. Bearden further proposed that all atomic nuclei in the universe are connected by scalar waves and interchange their virtual particles.[34]

Some of Bearden's ideas are supported by Puharich who also uses the term scalar wave. Puharich[35] has used the help of a clairvoyant to "see" inside the nucleus and proposed that protons are composed of ten magnetic monopoles and ten antimonopoles. These monopoles communicate with each other via scalar waves in a complex manner, thereby accounting for the nuclear forces well known in physics. The interacting monopoles form an information network, which can be considered holographic in nature. Monopoles from different molecules also communicate with each other. Although the hypotheses of Bearden and Puharich fall outside of conventional physics, they are supported by recent studies in quantum electrodynamics that mathematically describe nuclear binding forces in terms of the ZPE.

Although the term scalar wave is now in popular use, it has a different meaning in classical physics. In physics, a scalar refers to a quantity that is described by only one parameter, for example, magnitude, which is the same in all coordinant systems.[36] A scalar field is a region in space described at each point by a scalar function. The atmosphere is often cited as a familiar example of a scalar field, since temperature, a scalar function, varies at different locations. Byrd uses the common battery as a vivid example of a scalar. The potential energy in the battery is a scalar function that does not vary when the battery is in different locations. Byrd further points out that the potential energy in a battery cannot be measured directly—one can only measure its current, the physical manifestation of that energy in our 4-D space/time.[37] To avoid confusion with the use of the word scalar in physics, the scalar wave concept will be referred to as a non-Hertzian quantum field, since non-Hertzian fields do not obey the laws of classical electromagnetic field theory as outlined by Maxwell and Hertz. The concept of non-Maxwellian propagation has been previously suggested by DelGiudice.[38]

EXPERIMENTAL GENERATION OF NON-HERTZIAN FIELDS

Several devices have been built that should generate non-Hertzian fields, although it is likely that they also generate quantum potentials and conventional EM fields. Most of these devices generate non-Hertzian fields by causing the interaction of two EM fields 180 degrees apart in order to cancel their EM vectors. Psychotronic devices utilize a caduceus coil to achieve this cancellation.[39] In nonlinear optics it is achieved using four-wave mixing and phase conjugation. In four-wave mixing experiments, an

EM field is introduced into a vector canceled space, thereby generating a non-Hertzian wave with a greater amplitude than that of the EM field that triggered the reaction.[40] This approach, therefore, is capable of generating high-powered non-Hertzian waves. In phase conjugation experiments, an EM field is reflected off of a nonlinear mirror.[41] This generates a non-Hertzian field that is referred to as a phase conjugate replica of the original EM vector. The replica travels backward in time and retraces the path taken by the EM vector. This technique was used by Raymond Rife in the 1930's when he built the high-powered Rife microscope. The microscope utilized the convergence property of phase-conjugate waves, thereby minimizing distortion normally associated with conventional EM fields, which diverge as they move away from their source.

Another method for generating non-Hertzian waves, which is used in nonlinear plasma physics, is to abruptly pulse a plasma.[42] Plasmas are complex macroscopic structures composed of several types of EM fields including light, circularly polarized Alfven waves, and ion acoustic waves. Plasma theory has described well the complex nonlinear interaction among these plasma waves and their nonlinear propagation via a self-focusing mechanism. Vortex ring structures associated with plasmas have been observed experimentally.[43] The non-Hertzian emissions from plasma tubes are the basis of Priore's cancer-curing machine and Rife's beam ray tube. Finally, some radionic devices may generate non-Hertzian fields by using psychotronic plasma generators.

Non-Hertzian waves cannot be measured using conventional EM detectors, which detect only translational movement of electrons. The possibility of a new kind of energy intrigued Einstein, who used the term *subtle energy* to describe the energy remaining in the absence of all known forces, that is, energy that could not be measured. Nonetheless, the generation of non-Hertzian fields by the devices described above seems to result in the manifestation of anomalous behaviors in the measurement of temperature, inertia, or mass.[44] Such anomalies were observed by Tesla as ball lightning during the experiments with his magnifying coil.[45] More recently, anomalous behaviors have been observed in association with some of the modern free-energy devices.[46]

NON-HERTZIAN QUANTUM FIELDS IN
BIOLOGICAL SYSTEMS

Although the biological community has not incorporated the non-Hertzian/ZPE concepts discussed above, basic quantum mechanical models are being introduced to explain the increasingly apparent nonlinear behavior of biological systems. The results of these observations show that biological systems follow the laws of quantum mechanics. Therefore, biological systems should either contain or be sensitive to non-Hertzian fields. Although this hypothesis has not been proven, because quantum fields cannot be measured, increasing theoretical and experimental evidence supports this conclusion.

Experimental evidence for the role of non-Hertzian quantum fields in biological systems is based on the known significant and universal role of cations and anions in physiological processes. The bioelectromagnetic community already acknowledges that ions are involved in the action of weak EM fields on biological systems,[47] thereby forming a bridge between energy and matter. Ions within the body can exist in the coherent domains within crystalline lattices,[48] for example, liquid crystals in the cell membrane. Ions have also been suggested to mediate the interaction of ZPE with biological systems.[49] Since it has been proposed that coherent oscillations of ions facilitate the orthorotation of ZPE into our 4-D space/time, similar oscillations of ions in biological tissues may mediate orthorotation of ZPE into biological systems.

Earlier in this report the nonlinear interaction between ions (or charged regions) in dipoles was discussed. These interactions can also be coherent. Coherence between calcium ions and proteins on the surface of cell membranes has been used to explain how weak EM fields affect cells.[50] These coherent oscillations may also explain how the body is sensitive to non-Hertzian waves and ZPE. Therefore, in accordance with King's theory,[51] such coherence should result in a more efficient interaction with the ZPE. In certain situations it is believed that ions can travel through the cell membrane in a helical manner.[52] If this helical movement of ions is analogous to vortex rings described in plasmas, then an enhanced ZPE interaction should occur. These helical movements may be the biological equivalent to ion acoustic modes of plasmas.

Lawrence and Adey[53] proposed a comprehensive quantum model based on quantum quasi-particles, called *solitons*. The theory proposes that glycoproteins on the surface of the cell membrane interact cooperatively in response to weak EM fields and communicate this information to the inside of the cell via solitons that propagate through the cell membrane along the backbone of helical proteins. The idea that quantum solitons can carry biological information has also been proposed by others. Most of this research has focused on the DNA molecule because of its helical nature.[54] In addition, other quantum particles have been suggested to have a biological role. Excitons, for example, which survive and propagate best in crystalline lattices, have properties that are dependent on the dielectric constant and the resonant frequency of the lattice.[55]

Collating the above information, the author has proposed that piezoelectric liquid crystals in cell membranes act as transducers of EM radiation and non-Hertzian waves.[56] This Crystalline Transduction Theory proposes the interconversion of these types of energies. It extends the soliton theory of Adey and Lawrence in several ways: (1) it expands the type of energetic input to include all forms of subtle energy; (2) it proposes a bidirectionality for this conversion; (3) it proposes that the transduction from one form of energy to another can occur within liquid crystals in membranes and solid crystals in organs (e.g., the pineal), as well as the highly structured helical proteins in the cell membrane; and (4) it proposes that the energy fields generated by these crystal lattices more closely resemble naturally occurring (endogenous) energy fields associated with self-healing than do the various types of exogenous (unnatural/external) energy that have been used in energy medicine. The Crystalline Transduction Theory also proposes a two-stage transduction process whereby spiritual energy is converted into the more dense non-Hertzian energy, which in turn is converted into the more dense EM energy through crystal lattices in the brain and body. The EM fields so generated trigger the resultant biological effects. Recent experimental evidence by the author (presented later) indicates that non-Hertzian fields may also have direct effects at the cellular level. Therefore, it is also possible that non-Hertzian fields from the environment (astrophysical or geological), those from various psychotronic and radionic devices, or those associated with psychoenergetic healers could directly initiate a physiological response without having to be converted into EM fields. A third and likely possibility is that the EM fields act as a carrier wave for non-Hertzian energy. This type of information modulation of the EM field would impart additional abilities to heal the body. Since it is experimentally difficult, if not impossible, to obtain non-Hertzian fields in the absence of EM fields, the relative roles of EM and non-Hertzian fields in the healing process are currently unknown. Nonetheless, a natural corollary to the Crystalline Transduction Theory is the presence of an endogenous subtle energy body, distinct from the EM body. It is further proposed that non-Hertzian fields are at least one of the major components of this subtle energy body.

Although the biological function of solitons as information carriers has been proposed, until a recent paper by DelGiudice,[57] the fate of the soliton after carrying its quanta (packet) of biological information was not addressed. DelGiudice used quantum field theory to explain the unusually electric properties of biomolecules immersed in water by considering the biomolecules and the water molecules as two distinct oscillating dipole systems. Each dipole, which formed a collective state, was modeled as a ground state, characterized by zero-frequency oscillations (i.e., ZPE). EM forces between dipole systems were shown to be generated from solitons released from the biomolecules. Solitons, generated from chemical energy in the system, propagate along the backbone of the biomolecule (as previously proposed for the DNA molecule).

In addition to facilitating the propagation of solitons, DNA may also act as an energy transducer analogous to the piezoelectric proteins in cell membranes (as discussed above). Merkl has presented evidence to support this novel function of DNA using crystallized preparations of DNA and RNA, which he refers to as *life crystals*.[58] According to Merkl, life crystals transduce subtle energy (referred to as scroll waves) into biologically usable energy.

In a second paper, DelGiudice considered the interaction of exogenous EM fields with interacting dipoles. Using quantum field theory, he proposed that the energy of the EM field is stored in the interacting dipole network and is emitted from it as a new kind of long-range EM field.[59] Unlike conventional short-range forces, the long-range fields are believed to propagate in a novel manner—via a self-focusing, coherent, superconductive mechanism. DelGiudice postulates that long-range fields propagate inside filaments, where symmetry would be broken, resulting in a "non-Maxwellian" propagation. Recently, superconductivity has been measured in biological systems.[60] DelGiudice's filaments in the aqueous internal environment of the cell may be similar to vortex rings in the gaseous environment of a plasma.

DelGiudice also proposed that breaking of symmetry is associated with propagation of solitons in biomolecules.[61] After the solitons discharge their energy into the water, symmetry would be restored, thereby resulting in increased organization of the system. Thus, the theory proposes that biological self-organization is associated with the generation of solitons. Other quantum mechanical models of self-organization in biological systems utilize phase transitions[62] and plasma anomalies.[63] Taken in conjunction with Adey's proposal associating solitons with exogenous EM signals,[64] these theories suggest that quantum mechanical particles may link chemical and EM events within biological systems.

Breaking of symmetry has also been suggested by Bearden as a prerequisite for propagation of scalar waves.[65] Although the exact nature of these long-range fields is unknown, DelGiudice concludes that (1) they are associated with quantum potentials, (2) their photons acquire a nonzero mass, (3) they propagate without losing energy (first described by Tesla) and (4) they are associated with several anomalous phenomena. If non-Maxwellian propagation of solitons in water is truly associated with breaking of symmetry, this may be the first example of biological systems functioning at the level of the superquantum potential. At least the results indicate biological systems function at the quantum potential level.[66] Furthermore, the study suggests that biological systems are capable of converting conventional EM fields into the new type of coherent (long-range) fields, supporting the transduction mechanism proposed by the author in the Crystalline Transduction Theory.

DelGiudice's findings indicate a key role for water in biological systems. The physiological role of water surrounding biomolecules and at the surface of the cell membrane has received some attention from the scientific community. Using proton Nuclear Magnetic Resonance (NMR), this "interfacial" water has been shown to be more structured and organized than bulk water, where decreased hydrogen bonding between individual water dipoles results in a more random orientation.[67] A functional role for structured water is indicated by experiments where the hydrogen bonds are intentionally broken, causing a shift in the orientation or the "order parameter" of biomolecules (e.g., glycoproteins in the cell membrane).[68]

Structured water in biological systems is characterized by altered electrical properties (e.g., dielectric constant and conductivity) and is readily and reversibly converted to random bulk water.[69] Thus, structured water and bulk water are in equilibrium. Although the nature of the transition energy between these two forms is unknown, protons can travel between the two water phases via hydrogen bonds.

Structured water has also been proposed to mediate the biological effects of EM fields. The ability of biological tissues to absorb microwaves is proportional to the amount of structured water.[70] It is believed that the energy of the EM field is transferred to the tissue after it is first absorbed by the structured water. One theory proposes that a phase transition in the water results in decreased hydrogen bonding and a corresponding shift in the orientation and/or conformation of molecules in the cell membrane.[71] This could change the susceptibility of the cell membrane to exogenous EM fields. Since the binding of ions to the cell membrane is a critical step in the action of weak EM fields on cell membranes, a second theory suggests that a change in the water shell around these ions is critical.[72] These theories are supported by observed shifts in the NMR spectra of water after exposure to diseased tissues.[73]

Although water is composed of hydrogen and oxygen ions, the hydrogen ion has been the focus of attention in terms of understanding the interaction of non-Hertzian fields with animate and inanimate matter. Puthoff considered the ground state of the hydrogen atom as a ZPE determined state and used quantum electrodynamics to calculate the amount of ZPE absorbed and emitted by hydrogen.[74] Puharich also uses the hydrogen molecule in predicting the subnuclear origin of scalar energy. As previously discussed, Puharich has proposed that scalar waves originate in the monopoles and antimonopoles located within protons.[75] Similarly, Bearden believes that protons and neutrons in the nucleus, and not electrons, absorb scalar energy when it interacts with matter.[76]

Bearden has also extended his hypothesis to include biological systems.[77] He proposes that each cell in the body is composed of subatomic biopotentials. The biopotentials, which are located in the atomic nuclei, are composed of disordered, unstructured charge patterns of scalar energy that form virtual substructures. Bearden further proposes that exogenous scalar waves are absorbed by cells thereby charging and organizing their biopotentials. EM fields, on the other hand, will only change the magnitude of the biopotential. Cells which are in open exchange with their extracellular environment also discharge scalar energy from their biopotentials by releasing structured/scalar photons, as well as conventional photons. The scalar photons released from diseased cells, which have a characteristic information pattern associated with the particular disease, can communicate the diseased energy pattern to all cells in the body. Bearden also proposes that all disease could be cured if we could isolate the diseased energy pattern, apply it to a phase conjugate mirror, and generate a time-reversed scalar wave to neutralize the disease pattern. A parallel approach would be to generate the scalar information pattern from an antibody isolated from the diseased patient's blood. A scalar wave with this information would charge the immune system, resulting in a permanent *scalar immunization*.[78]

EXPERIMENTAL EVIDENCE FROM BIOLOGICAL SYSTEMS

Although there are several theories suggesting a role for non-Hertzian energy in biological systems, there is relatively little direct experimental evidence. One line of research focuses on the biological role of coherent light or scalar photons in Bearden's terminology. Gurwitsch originally showed that energy from rapidly dividing cells in the onion root could stimulate the growth (i.e., mitogenic) of nondividing cells, even if the two cell populations were physically separated.[79] This mitogenic radiation was further studied by Kaznacheyev who showed diseased cells could transmit their diseased energy to healthy cells when the two sets of petri dishes were separated by a quartz barrier.[80] Using different filters as barriers, Kaznacheyev showed that ultraviolet light was the carrier of the diseased energy. A functional role for biophotons is also supported by Popp's research. Popp discovered that biophotons are stored and released from within the helical structure of the DNA molecule and observed that biophotons are coherent in nature.[81] This conclusion has been supported by recent studies by other investigators.[82] Popp hypothesizes that the biophotons he measured originate from a holographic virtual EM field that permeates the whole body and is involved with the healing process. Although Popp's biophotons may be coherent and therefore function at the level of the quantum potential, their non-Hertzian nature has yet to be proved.

A second series of experiments that cannot be readily explained in terms of conventional EM fields comes from the work of Reid.[83] This research was based on the original observation that blood collected under different physiological conditions crystallized into distinct patterns. Since the crystals were largely composed of sodium chloride, Reid simplified the system by studying the crystallization of simple salt (sodium chloride) solutions. Certain chemical reactions (e.g., those involving copper) could influence the crystallization pattern of the salt and increase the electrical properties (impedance) of the salt solution even if twelve feet away. The results indicate that the phenomena cannot readily be explained in terms of conventional EM fields. Read proposes that the effect is mediated by quantum fields. The results therefore suggest that chemical reactions, and possibly those occurring within biological tissues, can be connected through non-EM fields and may indicate a biological role for non-Hertzian fields.

As an alternative to using biological tissues as a source for non-Hertzian fields, a different approach would be to generate them artificially (as discussed above). The plasma tube generator of Priore generates an energy field, theoretically non-Hertzian in nature, which has been shown to inhibit the growth of tumors in animals.[84] More recently, free-energy devices and psychotronic devices have been built[85] that may also generate non-Hertzian waves, although their circuitry does not follow conventional engineering principles, and the quantum physics described above cannot readily predict the nature of subtle energy they generate. Although radionics and psychotronics devices have been used successfully "clinically," their ability to effect biological systems has not been studied scientifically.

Several years ago, Puharich used a Mobius strip to trap EM fields, which should theoretically generate a sum-zero vector space. He then coupled the Mobius strip to the mechanical motion of a wrist watch, thereby generating a scalar shielding device which was claimed to generate a non-Hertzian field between 7 and 8 Hz.[86] This claim has since been disputed. Nonetheless, numerous anecdotal case reports from people wearing the shielding device suggested a significant biological effect. A more scientific approach was taken by Byrd who observed a decrease in overall amplitude and a shift toward lower frequencies in EEG recordings from individuals wearing the shielding device. Morley used electro-diagnostic devices with EM-sensitive patients to determine the effect of the shielding device after exposure to harmful environmental EM fields. Meridian readings for most organs that showed abnormal patterns after EM exposure were normalized.

Despite these encouraging preliminary results, it is still possible that the observed effects were due at least in part to the belief system of the individuals. Some of the reports, however, suggest placebo effects may be minimal, since loss of noticeable beneficial effects correlated with loss of function of the shielding device. In order to eliminate placebo effects and to determine whether the presumed non-Hertzian energy emitted from the shielding device might have direct effects at the cellular level, the author designed a series of in vitro experiments using nerve cells and immune cells grown in tissue culture. Unlike the previous studies, biological effects were determined using two types of shielding devices: with and without the Mobius strip. Removing the Mobius strip (control devices) results in a 7 to 8-Hz EM field without a non-Hertzian field being present. On the other hand, the experimental shielding device, containing a Mobius strip, should predominantly generate a non-Hertzian field with a residual EM field. By comparing the biological effects of these shielding devices (laid directly on top of the petri dishes), a modified biological response was observed, for the first time, due to the addition of a non-Hertzian field in the presence of an EM field. However, since it is unknown to what extent the two fields couple, this approach does not give information about the direct effects of non-Hertzian fields in the absence of an EM carrier.

The PC12 neuronal cell line was chosen for initial studies since the author had previously shown that the functional properties of the neurotransmitters present in these cells resemble those in the normal brain[87] and that norepinephrine (one of these neurotransmitters) release[88] and uptake[89] were altered when the cells were exposed to weak EM fields. Norepinephrine uptake was reassessed, using the same standard biochemical protocol, following a thirty-minute exposure of the cells to the two shielding devices. Results from six independent experiments indicated that experimental shielding devices (with the Mobius strip) showed an additional 19.5 percent inhibition of norepinephrine uptake compared with control devices.[90] The results therefore suggest that non-Hertzian fields (in the presence of EM fields) can have even more profound effects on biological systems than conventional EM fields.

Since the immune system is a key focal point for healing a wide variety of diseases, the same methodology was used to determine whether non-

Hertzian fields could stimulate the growth of lymphocytes (critical white blood cells involved with cellular immunity) in vitro. Using standard biochemical techniques, a pooled preparation of T and B lymphocytes was isolated from the blood of healthy volunteers and grown in tissue culture for two days in the presence of radioactive thymidine.[91] The rate of thymidine incorporation into rapidly dividing DNA is a quantitative measure of the amount of cell division. In the presence of the control shielding device, lymphocyte growth (90 ± 31 cpm/10^5 cells) was stimulated by 34 percent relative to cells grown in the absence of any exogenous field. When grown in the presence of the experimental shielding device, lymphocyte proliferation increased to 159 ± 53 cpm/10^5 cells. Thus, as in the previous experiments with nerve cells, the addition of the non-Hertzian field increased the biological response, in this case by 76 percent.

These initial studies may be the first to demonstrate a direct effect of non-Hertzian fields at the cellular level and indicated that such effects occur in the absence of placebo effects. This delivery system, the shielding device, is somewhat unconventional and the output frequencies and amplitudes could not be altered. In collaboration with T. Gagnon of Dynamic Engineering, the author conducted further studies on the effect of non-Hertzian fields on lymphocyte growth, using a novel delivery system developed by Mr. Gagnon.

The delivery system, referred to as Structured-Electromagnetic Quotient Stimuli (S-EMQS), consists of two concentric coils within a transducer carrying current in opposite (anti-parallel) directions. The input current (three milliamps) consisted of a series of S-EMQS envelopes repeated at five microsecond intervals. Each envelope was composed of three to seven superimposed, computer-generated, square waves varying in frequency from 2 kHz to 6 kHz. Freshly isolated lymphocytes received four fifteen-minute treatments during a twelve-hour period and their growth rate determined as described above after an additional twelve hours. Control cells (no energy treatments) showed low growth rates (358 cpm/10^5 cells). S-EMQS-generated non-Hertzian fields caused a twentyfold stimulation of cell growth (6880 ± 183 cpm/10^5 cells) in the absence of chemical growth factors.[92]

Conventional EM fields are also capable of stimulating lymphocyte growth, although the magnitude of this response is substantially less than twentyfold, typically on the order of onefold or less.[93] It was therefore of interest to determine whether the large effect observed here was due to the non-Hertzian fields or to the specific and complex set of frequencies used in the S-EMQS signal. Therefore, the exact frequency information was put through a conventional coil (impedance matched to the caduceus coil) where the current flow was parallel (i.e., in the same direction). This coil arrangement, which would generate only conventional EM fields, just produced a sevenfold biological stimulation. These results support the previous experiments with the shielding device and indicate that the large biological effect observed here was only partially due to the EM frequency information, and more profoundly due to the way in which the information was delivered, that is, with a non-Hertzian field.

Using a slightly larger current input (nine milliamps), we determined whether it was possible to transfer the subtle frequency information patterns into the lattice structure of water. Water charged with the non-Hertzian fields was then tested for biological activity. Using a modified S-EMQS signal (which turned out to be less effective at stimulating lymphocytes), direct exposure of the cells to the caduceus coil stimulated cell growth by 87 percent (relative to cells receiving no energy), whereas the charged water caused a 61 percent stimulation. Although a detailed scientific study was not done to determine how long the water would hold its charge, Gagnon has observed that water treated with a specially designed S-EMQS chamber retained its charge for several months. In the next series of experiments we demonstrated that the information pattern in the water could be restructured by the subsequent addition of a different non-Hertzian field. A second set of S-EMQS signals, which were designed to inhibit lymphocyte growth, were then superimposed onto the original pattern, which enhanced cell growth. The doubly charged water caused a 58 percent inhibition of lymphocyte growth, thereby canceling the original stimulatory information pattern.[94]

These results indicate that unlike conventional EM fields, which have only a limited capacity to structure and transfer their energy to water,[95] non-Hertzian fields can store their subtle information in the lattice structure of water for relatively long periods of time. The results further indicate that the information can then be liberated from the water and cause the same biological effect as the original non-Hertzian field. This apparent transfer of energy without loss supports Tesla's original claim that energy could be propagated over the planet without loss.[96] The S-EMQS results also support DelGiudice's idea of non-Maxwellian propagation in water without loss of energy.[97]

The data reported here may also explain the anomalous behavior of homeopathic remedies which have the ability to store (for very long periods) the energetic information matrix associated with a chemical or drug. The fact that the stored homeopathic information can have a biological effect opposite from the original chemical or drug supports Bearden's idea that diseased energy of the body can be neutralized by orthorotating it 180 degrees to generate the subtle energy counterpart to the diseased energy. The ability of non-Hertzian fields to neutralize charged water, as demonstrated here, supports this idea. Thus, non-Hertzian quantum fields may be the physical energy behind homeopathy.

QUANTUM FIELDS AND PSYCHOENERGETIC HEALING

Quantum fields may also be the energetic mechanism behind psychoenergetic healing. This hypothesis is based on the observations that some of the phenomena associated with psychoenergetic healing can be explained by the properties of non-Hertzian energy. As discussed above, it is proposed that the subtle energy body and healing energy are composed of EM fields, quantum fields and uncharacterized forms of subtle energy. Healing at a distance is one of the main phenomena that cannot be readily explained by conventional EM fields. On the other hand, the ability of quantum fields to propagate without loss of energy would explain such long-distant healing. The ability of quantum fields to converge, rather than diverge, would help explain how healers can "focus" their energy to one individual or one petri dish amidst an environment of similar targets. The instantaneous nature of some healings could be explained by the independence of quantum fields on time and their ability to travel faster than the speed of light. Based on these observations, it is proposed here that the energetic information transferred from healer to healee is mediated by non-Hertzian quantum fields.

Scientific Experiments with Healers

In an attempt to verify the phenomenon of energetic healing, nearly all scientific studies have been limited to phenomenological observations about the efficacy of healers to influence biological systems. These studies have been hindered by the numerous and complex factors that can affect the results of clinical protocols using humans. Although the placebo effect is the most well known, other factors, such as the emotional state of the subject and the healer and even their chemical intake (drugs and/or food) prior to an experiment, must be considered. In addition to these internal factors, external factors, such as the EM environment, astrological/astronomical variations and subtle energy influences not generated from the healer, may also affect the results. In an attempt to minimize these confounding variables, several investigators have used nonhuman targets for healing energy.[98] These studies have revealed that healers can affect biological systems at the level of the organism (animals), at the cellular level (tissue culture), and at the subcellular level (enzymes within cells). These studies indicate that healers can have direct effects on the body that are not mediated by the mind (belief system) of the person being healed.

Although the results from these studies indicated a wide spectrum of biological responses to healing energy, the question of specificity is still unresolved. Due to the profound effects of the brain/mind to control so many physiological processes, biochemical communication in the brain was chosen as a biological endpoint that might mediate the variety of physiological responses to healing energy. Neuronal transmission between nerve cells in the brain is mediated by a group of chemicals called neurotransmitters. The functional properties of one class of neurotransmitters, norepinephrine and dopamine, which mediate the adrenergic nervous system, were studied in vivo with mice and in vitro with mammalian cultured cells. The animal study[99] involved measuring the amounts of the neurotransmitters themselves and the cellular study[100] involved measuring the activity of an enzyme, monoamine oxidase, which regulates the actual amounts of the neurotransmitters. Since the author had previously studied the effects of EM fields on norepinephrine in cultured nerve cells[101], experiments were conducted to determine whether healing energy and EM energy shared the same biological endpoints. The results indicated that both EM fields and healing energy were able to effect neurotransmitters and both caused quantitatively and qualitatively similar biological responses, e.g., enhanced adrenergic neurotransmitter function. More recent experiments, described above, indicate that non-Hertzian quantum fields generated from the scalar shielding device are also capable of enhancing the same neurotransmitters in cultured nerve cells.[102] These results support the hypothesis that healing energy is composed of quantum fields as well as conventional EM fields.

An alternative approach in studying the healing phenomenon is to study the healers themselves, rather than the healee or the target of the healing energy. These studies have measured the psychological and neurophysiological state of the healers in an attempt to characterize their state of consciousness. The neuropsychological approach has been extensively studied by Cade and Blundell in England using a specifically modified EEG called the Mind Mirror, which displays the relative amounts of beta, alpha, theta, and delta frequencies from each side of the brain.[103] Different states of consciousness were represented by characteristic brain wave patterns. Although there was no universal pattern depicting the "healing state of consciousness," it could be demonstrated that the person being healed could acquire the brain wave pattern of the healer, presumably at the point of energy exchange.

Other studies using conventional EEG reveal that the healing state has different brain wave patterns distinguishing this state from other alternative states of consciousness like sleep or hypnosis.[104] Preliminary results obtained with Laskow using conventional EEG at the Biofeedback Institute in Cotati, California, support these previous findings.

Krippner[105] and Cooperstein[106] have used a psychological approach to characterize the state of consciousness of healers. Using specially designed tests, these investigators have defined several psychological traits associated with different types of healers, e.g., magnetic, spiritual, energetic, etc.

Relatively few studies have attempted to combine the biological and psychological approaches. Bill Sweet and Gladys Myers of the Spindrift group have compared two different healing states of consciousness—goal directed and qualitative.[107] Since qualitative healing, as they characterize it, is the surrender of one's will to the will of God, there is no focused intention as in goal-directed healing. These different states of consciousness produced different biological effects on the growth of yeast and seeds. Sweet and Myers conclude that qualitative healing is more effective, although this interpretation is likely to be dependent on the particular biological endpoint, since we did not reach the same conclusion in our results with tumor cells (discussed below).

In another series of experiments conducted by Beverly Rubik,[108] the relationship between biological responses and different healing states of consciousness was also examined. Using a different biological endpoint, these experiments were designed to determine whether Leonard Laskow could protect bacterial cells in culture from inhibition induced by an antibiotic (ampicillin). Using different focuses of consciousness Laskow could either protect bacteria from the lethal effects of antibiotics or inhibit their growth in the absence of antibiotics depending upon his intention.

Healing Experiments with Laskow

1. Experimental Protocol

Based on these studies, it was of interest to explore the role of the consciousness in the holoenergetic healing process and to correlate different mental content (imagery, intent, and thought) with biological effects in tissue culture. In order to verify the hypothesis that the healing effects are target specific, a new biological endpoint was chosen. The growth of tumor cells in culture was chosen because it could be monitored quantitatively using state-of-the-art biochemical techniques and is highly relevant clinically. The protocol involved measuring DNA synthesis by quantifying the incorporation of radioactive thymidine. The rate of cell proliferation was then determined relative to the total number of cells that were counted in a hemocytometer.

Laskow shifted into a specific state of consciousness and mentally and energetically focused on three petri dishes held in the palm of his hand. Another aliquot of cells from the same stock bottle was being held simultaneously by a nonhealer in an adjacent room. The nonhealer was reading a book to minimize the interaction of his consciousness with the cells. Both sets of petri dishes (n = 6) were brought back to the tissue culture hood where they were labelled (blindly) and scrambled. The author then labelled the cells with radioactive thymidine and processed them after 24 hours growth to measure cell proliferation. Precisely the same protocol was followed in a parallel set of experiments done with distilled water contained in a plastic lid-sealed test tube rather than cells in a petri dish. This water, as well as control water, was then used to make a standard tissue culture medium, which was then added to the cells at the beginning of the 24-hour growth period.

2. Healing States of Consciousness

Laskow explored five different mental intentions, some of which are an integral part of the holoenergetic healing process. He described an overall loving state, which was maintained throughout, that allowed him to be in resonance with the tumor cells. The technique for attaining this nonordinary state is a form of meditation that allows intentional focusing and cohering of energy. Laskow refers to these intentions as different contents of consciousness. He distinguishes the intentions as: (1) returning to the natural order and harmony of the cell's normal rate of growth, (2) circulating the microcosmic orbit, (3) letting God's will flow through these hands, (4) unconditional love, and (5) dematerialization.

Laskow describes the psychoenergetic state of consciousness as follows:

> I shifted to a "transpersonal healing state" of consciousness by using a balancing breath that balanced and cohered both hemispheres of my brain followed by aligning, centering, and energizing techniques. These processes produced, for me, a loving state which allowed my mind to come into resonance with the tumor cells as I focused on them. While in this transpersonal loving state I varied the content of my consciousness to specifically evaluate the differential influence of changes in mental content on tumor cell growth. We evaluated five different intentions while I was holding petri dishes containing tumor cells in my hands for each of the mental intentions.
>
> We were interested in varying what I was intending in my mind for these tumor cells. The first intent was the focused instruction that the tumor cells return to the natural order and harmony of their normal cell line. By normal I meant that the cells should grow at a normal rate, rather than at their present accelerated tumor cell rate. Another intention was to "let God's will flow through these hands," so there wasn't a specific direction given. Unconditional love was giving no direction at all. When I do healing work, I shift into an unconditionally loving transpersonal state. While in that general loving state, I superimposed unconditional loving intent without giving specific direction to the energy.

I used two forms of dematerialization, dematerialize into the light and dematerialize into the void. I wanted to see whether there was a "reluctance" on the part of the cells to go into the unknown. Or is it better to give them direction into the light? Obviously, this has import for people who are doing healing work in terms of giving direction to tumor cells and energy forms that you want to release. Is it easier to release them giving them a direction or releasing them into their potential, but without the light?

3. Experimental Results on Tumor Cells

The results indicated that the different focuses of consciousness could be distinguished in terms of their biological responses. Of the focuses studied, only a few showed a significant effect on inhibiting the growth of the tumor cells. The most effective intention was "return to the natural order and harmony of the normal cell line" (39 percent inhibition). Allowing God's will to manifest appeared to be only half as effective (21 percent inhibition). Under the same experimental conditions, unconditional love neither stimulated nor inhibited cell growth. Its effect was neutral and seemingly accepting of the present condition. These results have important implications for healers. The results suggest that certain healing states and contents of consciousness are more effective than others. As mentioned above, however, we do not know to what extent these effects are target specific. It is possible that other focuses of consciousness would have been effective if other biological endpoints were chosen. For example, treating water with microcosmic orbit (41 percent inhibition) was equally as effective as returning to the natural order, although the two focuses of consciousness were significantly different when treating the tumor cells directly. Alternatively, the content and states of consciousness that were effective in this experiment for Laskow may not have been optimal for another healer treating the same tumor cells. Thus the results may be healer specific. These questions, however, are amenable to study using the protocol followed in this study. Future studies will in fact compare different states of consciousness with different biological endpoints.

4. The Role of Thought, Imagery, and Intent

In the next series of experiments we were interested in further defining the specific contents of consciousness in order to determine the relative role of nonfocused thought, imagery, and intention. These experiments were done by changing these contents in a given state of consciousness and determining the corresponding effect on the growth of the tumor cells. The results indicated that different biological effects could be observed by changing the intent or the imagery associated with the healing process but nonfocused thought had no effect. Thus, while Laskow was in the microcosmic orbit state of consciousness, the mental image of visualizing only three cells remaining in the petri dish after the experiment caused an 18 percent inhibition of cell growth. On the other hand, switching only the mental image to one where many more cells were visualized in the dish resulted in an increased growth of tumor cells (15 percent). The results are remarkable since not only could a different biological response be observed by changing the mental image, but an actual reversal of the biological process of cell growth was achieved.

We were then interested in determining to what extent intention, as focused planned will, might contribute to the healing response. This was achieved by intending and instructing the cells to return to their normal order and rate of growth, while holding no visual image, thus separating intent from imagery. This experiment can be directly compared with the previous one, since the microcosmic orbit state of consciousness was maintained throughout, and the previous experiment involved no consciously focused intent. We found that focused intent for the cells to return to the natural order of their normal growth rate produced the same inhibitory biological response (20 percent inhibition) as did imagery alone.

When we included the intention for the cells to return to the natural order of the normal cell line together with the imagery of reduced growth, the inhibitory effect was doubled to 40 percent. These results suggest that imagery and intent each contributed equally in influencing the psychoenergetic inhibition of tumor cells in culture.

5. Experimental Results with Water

Since previous studies indicated that healers could influence the physical/chemical properties of water[109] and that this energetically charged water could then influence biological systems,[110] we were interested in extending these experiments using the above protocol. Specifically, we wanted to determine whether there were differences in the energetic information patterns associated with different states and contents of consciousness and whether these patterns could be transferred to water. If the energetic patterns could be detected in water by differential biological responses, it would suggest that specific spectral patterns are associated with different states and contents of consciousness. The rationale for such a hypothesis is based on the reported ability of healers to change the spectral patterns of water.[111] Preliminary experiments with Laskow indicated he could nonspecifically alter the Raman spectra of water he charged holoenergetically.[112] In our approach to this question, we studied whether altering the content of consciousness while in a nonordinary state could inhibit tumor cell growth when water was treated psychoenergetically and then used to constitute growth medium.

The results indicated that water was in fact capable of storing and transferring the information associated with different contents of consciousness to the tumor cells. Thus water treated with the natural order and harmony intent resulted in a 28 percent inhibition of cell growth, quite similar to that obtained when the cells were treated directly. Even more surprising, however, was the fact that two other intents that were ineffective when the cells were treated directly were effective when the water was treated. Thus unconditional love caused a 21 percent inhibition of growth, and dematerialization caused a 27 percent inhibition. These results suggest that the efficacy of different focuses of consciousness depends on the target being healed. The data also suggest that water may be a more universal target. It is possible that pure water is more capable of picking up certain types of energy and information than cells. In other situations, with different environmental energy influences present, water may not store or release information. The practical application of this observation is that healers can give their clients water to drink that has been previously charged with their healing energy. This may also be the basis for blessing food and wine.

In summary, of the biological experiments presented in this article indicate that (1) non-Hertzian fields can in fact have marked effects directly on biological systems, independent of the belief system of the individual, (2) water is a key mediator in this response, and (3) the nature of this interaction is quantitatively and qualitatively different from that occurring with conventional EM fields. If EM fields are just derivates of non-Hertzian fields and the latter can interact with matter at the level of the nucleus (rather than the electron shell), non-Hertzian fields have the potential to affect biological systems at a very profound level indeed and should constitute a key role in energy medicine of the future.

6. *Magnetic Field Emission from Laskow's Hands*

The previous results indicate that energetic information patterns associated with specific intentions and images can manifest in our 4-D reality as biologically detectable changes in water. In other studies, different energetic patterns manifested as brain wave spectra during the healing state[113] and as spectrographic changes in water[114] that had been charged psychoenergetically. To further study the correlation between energetic patterns and the different states and contents of consciousness associated with holoenergetic healing, temporal patterns of the magnetic fields emitted from Laskow's hands during healing were measured.

The magnetic fields were measured using a flux-gate magnetometer. Laskow cupped his hand over the probe but did not touch it. Chart recordings were used to display magnetic field patterns. Nonhealers were unable to influence magnetometer readings. Touching or moving the probe gave characteristic, sharp patterns that were readily distinguishable from energetic patterns.

An initial and critical part of the holoenergetic healing process is opening the crown chakra. The magnetic pattern manifesting from opening Laskow's crown chakra was recorded and appeared distinctly different from other patterns obtained in that it had a very sharp onset, an equally sharp dissipation, and only lasted eight seconds. Thus the event was short-lived and caused a shift in the magnetic field pattern only during its duration. This rapid return to the normal baseline was not necessarily characteristic of patterns produced by other states of consciousness.

It is interesting to note that in some tracings the magnetic pattern shifted downward, implying a decrease in the magnetic field strength in the environment around Laskow's hands. This unusual response could be due to the generation of a non-Hertzian field from Laskow's hands, which canceled in part of the background magnetic field causing its diminution.

Since we had observed that not all states or contents of consciousness produced magnetic patterns, it was of interest to compare the patterns from two states which gave different biological responses as measured by an inhibition of tumor cell growth. We therefore compared the magnetic pattern obtained when Laskow was in an unconditional loving state and then in the return to natural order state. The results indicate that indeed these magnetic patterns were different from each other. Compared to the robust effect with the natural order state, the unconditional loving state produced a weak, nonspecific pattern. The important point, however, is that there is a correlation between the magnetic patterns and the biological effects produced by these states of consciousness, since the unconditional love state also produced a small biological response. This may result from the lack of a specific image or intention (critical contents of consciousness demonstrated above) associated with the unconditional love state, which could be thought of as a universal carrier of subtle energetic information. The carrier by itself, without modulation, does not appear to influence the tumor cells, almost as if there was an unconditional acceptance of the situation.

In general these patterns were obtained most consistently when Laskow was allowed to generate the different states and contents of consciousness spontaneously, rather than following a given sequence. One of the most interesting spontaneous magnetic patterns was obtained when Laskow inwardly asked that Spirit flow through him. He asked Spirit to demonstrate its presence to science with a characteristic signature pattern. The tracing obtained gave a uniquely different pattern from the other patterns obtained and was characterized by sharp, frequent peaks in the negative direction.

7. Modulating Laskow's Magnetic Field with Non-Hertzian Energy

Since it is not possible at this point to measure the subtle energy emitted from the body during psychoenergetic healing, it is difficult to test the hypothesis that this energy is non-Hertzian in nature. Since the magnetic field emission pattern seems to be a measurable manifestation of psychoenergetic healing, we postulated that non-Hertzian fields might modulate these magnetic patterns. This is a novel experimental approach that has not been previously tested. We used the scalar shielding device (discussed above) to test our hypothesis. The shielding device was placed in Laskow's energy field during the experimental session. The tracing obtained indicates that prior to addition of the device, the magnetic pattern was consistent, showing numerous sharp, small positive peaks. Upon addition of the shielding device, the magnetic pattern was substantially altered. The new pattern was qualitatively similar in shape but gradually increased in overall magnitude. These results suggest that non-Hertzian quantum fields enhanced the magnetic field emitted from Laskow's hands during holoenergetic healing.

THE NATURE OF HEALING ENERGY

The original data presented here support the hypothesis that non-Hertzian fields mediate aspects of psychoenergetic healing: (1) the ability of water to store the subtle information from a healer or a non-Hertzian field for long periods of time, (2) the transfer of this stored information to biological systems, and (3) the ability of non-Hertzian energy to modulate magnetic emissions from a healer. Taken in conjunction with Puharich's report that the manifestation of non-Hertzian energy emitted from healers can be measured and is independent of distance,[115] the experimental data suggests that other energies in addition to conventional EM fields are involved. Exactly how EM fields, which presumably mediate "magnetic healing," and non-Hertzian fields interact in the healing process is unknown. It is possible, for example, that EM fields may act as carriers for the more subtle information associated with non-Hertzian energy.

Action at a distance is well recognized in quantum physics and may explain healing at a distance. To explain this phenomenon physicists have introduced the idea of nonlocality, as described in Bell's theorem.[116] Nonlocality is one of the key concepts in quantum mechanics and suggests that all matter in the universe is related by nonlocal forces (as well as the traditional local forces such as gravity, nuclear, and EM energy). The nature of these nonlocal forces is unresolved.

Of the numerous theories which have been proposed in quantum physics to explain the type of energy that mediates action at a distance, Bohm's theory of the implicate/explicate order is most relevant.[117] Bohm has proposed that our ordinary 4-D explicate reality is enfolded into a more subtle implicate order. Since it is proposed that the implicate order can actualize into or manifest as the explicate order, the implicate order can be considered a potential, nonmanifest energy. Using quantum field theory, Bohm defined this energy as the quantum potential and mathematically demonstrated the manifestation of conventional EM fields from the underlying quantum potential.[118] Therefore, the quantum potential can be said to put form into (or manifest as) matter via the EM field.

Bohm's theory has recently been expanded by introducing the concept of a superquantum potential behind the quantum potential.[119] Thus, the 4-D quantum potential is a manifestation of the even more subtle superquantum potential. The superquantum potential and the "active information" within it refers to a subtle, higher dimensional order. In this way information can be transferred from the subtle, higher dimensional super quantum level to ordinary matter in 4-D space/time. The quantum field associated with the superquantum potential is likely to be analogous, if not identical to, the non-Hertzian field described above. The domain of the superquantum potential is also likely to be the source of the zero point energy. By further postulating that all matter depends on a common pool of "information," Bohm's theory also explains nonlocal action at a distance and the inter-connectedness of all matter in the universe.

Recently, Bohm has extended the concept of the implicate order into the domain of mind where the ebb and flow of thoughts is analogous to the implicate order.[120] According to Bohm, the superquantum potential supplies the subtle information behind thoughts. Thus active information, at the level of the superquantum potential is postulated to be a bridge between the mind and body.

THE HOLOENERGETIC QUANTUM CONSCIOUSNESS THEORY OF HEALING

The Holoenergetic Quantum Consciousness Theory extends Bohm's theory to include interactions between the minds of the healer and the healee. It proposes that contents of consciousness other than nonfocused thoughts, i.e., intentions and images are critical components necessary for psychoenergetic healing. The holoenergetic theory also incorporates Bearden's concept of the biopotential[121] as the biological correlate of the quantum potential. The Holoenergetic Quantum Consciousness Theory introduces the idea of a holoenergetic field. The holoenergetic field of the healer, after activation, can transfer its subtle information pattern to the healee via non-Hertzian fields. Once the information is received by the healee it activates their holoenergetic field and triggers their intrinsic healing mechanism.

The holoenergetic field is a subtle energetic aspect of the mind that links consciousness and the mind to the body via the biopotential. Therefore, the holoenergetic field, which functions at the level of the superquantum potential, is supplied information from (1) thoughts, images and intentions of the mind; (2) consciousness of the spiritual world; and (3) consciousness of the biologic world. These subtle energetic patterns, which are enfolded in the holoenergetic field of an individual, may be harmonious or disharmonious with the natural order of their being. Recognizing, understanding, releasing, and reforming the disharmonious pattern is an integral part of holoenergetic healing.

After subtle energetic information patterns in the mind are transferred to the biopotential via the holoenergetic field, the information is then transferred to the brain/body via conventional EM fields. Although the mind and the holoenergetic field function at the higher dimensional levels of the superquantum potential, the biopotential and the body function at the ordinary 4-D level. This process, which links mind and body, is the intrinsic healing mechanism of the body. It is triggered by activation of the holoenergetic field.

For example, the holoenergetic field of the healee can be activated by information transferred from the holoenergetic field of the healer. When the healer's field is in turn activated by spirit, healing information is transferred to the healee along with the healer's loving intention via the level of the superquantum potential. Healing can also occur at the level of the quantum potential (via the biopotential) or by direct interaction with the physical/chemical body. Depending on the practitioner and the treatment modality used, healing can occur at one or all of these levels. Self healing can also be induced in a similar manner.

The Holoenergetic Quantum Consciousness Theory is supported by the theoretical and experimental data presented above. The original data presented here suggests that the subtle energetic patterns in the mind associated with different states and contents of consciousness can be measured as magnetometer tracings and altered by non-Hertzian quantum fields. Furthermore, the ability of non-Hertzian fields to cause direct effects at the brain/body level indicates their key role in psychoenergetic healing. Although the exact mechanism of action of non-Hertzian fields is presently unknown, the holoenergetic theory predicts that they activate the holoenergetic field of the healee and facilitate the transfer of subtle information from the healer and higher realms. Healing may thus be enhanced by the understanding and harvesting of these subtle, higher dimensional energies for the betterment of humanity.

1. R. O. Becker and A. A. Marino, *Electromagnetism and Life* (New York: State Univ. Press, 1982).
2. D. T. Barry, "Muscle Sounds from Evoked Twitches in the Hand," *Arch. Phys. Med. Rehabil.* 72 (1991): 573.
3. R. P. Feynman, "Space-time Approach to Quantum Electrodynamics," *Phys. Rev.* 76 (1949): 769.
4. D. Bohm, "A Suggested Interpretation of Quantum Theory in Terms of Hidden Variables," *Phys. Rev.* 85 (1952): 166.
5. D. Bohm, "Toward a New Theory of the Relationship of Mind and Matter," *Frontier Perspectives* 1 (1990): 9.
6. T. E. Bearden, "Comments on the New Tesla Electromagnetics: Discrepancies in Present EM Theory," *Planet. Assoc. Clean Energy Newsletter* 3 (1982): 10.
7. R. O. Becker, "The Basic Biological Data Transmission and Control System Influenced by Electrical Forces," *Ann. N. Y. Acad. Sci.* 238 (1974): 236.
8. R. Ader, ed. *Psychoneuroimmunology* (New York: Academic Press, 1981).
9. B. E. W. Nordenstrom, "Biokinetic Impacts on Structure and Imaging of the Lung: The Concept of Biologically Closed Electric Circuits," *AJR* 145 (1985): 447.
10. G. Rein, "Bioelectromagnetism and Psychic Healing," *Light* 103 (1983): 116.
11. P. E. Tyler, ed. "Biological Effects of Non-Ionizing Radiation," *Ann. N. Y. Acad. Sci.* 247 (1975).
12. H. Frohlich, "Long Range Coherence and Energy Storage in Biological Systems," *Int. J. Quantum Chem.* 2 (1968): 641.
13. A. R. Liboff, "Geomagnetic Cyclotron Resonance in Living Cells," *J. Biol. Phys.* 13 (1985): 99.
14. W. R. Adey and A. F. Lawrence, *Nonlinear Electrodynamics in Biological Systems* (New York: Plenum Press, 1984).

15. J. E. Treherne, W. A. Foster, et al. "Cellular Oscillators," *J. Exper. Biol.* 81 (1979).

16. A. F. Lawrence and W. R. Adey, "Nonlinear Wave Mechanisms in Interactions Between Excitable Tissue and Electromagnetic Fields," *Neurol. Res.* 4 (1982): 115.

17. F. E. Yates, "Physical Causality and Brain Theories," *Am. J. Physiol.* 238 (1980): R277-290.

18. S. Olariu and I. Popescu, "The Quantum Effect of Electromagnetic Fluxes," *Rev. Modern Phys.* 57 (1985): 339.

19. Y. Aharonov and D. Bohm, "Significance of Electromagnetic Potentials in Quantum Theory," *Physics Rev.* 115 (1959): 485.

20. R. Chambers, "Shift of an Electron Interference Pattern by Enclosed Magnetic Flux," *Phys. Rev. Lett.* 5 (1960): 3.

21. J. C. Maxwell, *A Treatise on Electricity and Magnetism,* vol. 1, (New York: Dover Publications, 1954), p. 54.

22. M. Planck, *The Mechanics of Deformable Bodies* (London: MacMillan & Co., 1932).

23. T. H. Boyer, *Phys. Rev. D.* 13 (1976): 2832.

24. H. Everett, *The Many World Interpretation of Quantum Mechanics: A Fundamental Exposition* (Princeton, NJ: Princeton Univ. Press, 1973).

25. S. M. Christensen, *Particles Do Not Exist, Quantum Theory of Gravity* (Oxford: Oxford Univ. Press, 1984).

26. M. King, *Tapping the Zero-Point Energy* (Provo, UT: Paraclette, 1990).

27. H. E. Puthoff, "Gravity as a Zero-Point Fluctuation Force," *Physics Rev,* A39 (1989): 2333.

28. See E. T. Wittaker, *A History of the Theories of Aether and Electricity* (New York: Philosophical Library, 1954).

29. L. DeBroglie, *Nonlinear Wave Mechanics* (New York: Elsevier, 1960).

30. See note 27 above.

31. See note 26 above.

32. T. E. Bearden, *AIDS: Biological Warfare* (Greenville, TX: Tesla, 1988).

33. P. A. M. Dirac,"Quantum Theory of the Electron," *Proc. Royal Soc. London,* A117 (1928): 610.

34. See note 32 above.
35. A. Puharich, "A Unified Field Theory," *14th USPA Conference on Bioenergy,* Dayton, OH, 1988.
36. See note 3 above.
37. E. A. Byrd, personal communication.
38. E. DelGiudice, S. Doglia, et al.,"Magnetic Flux Quantization and Josephson Behavior in Living Systems," *Physica Scripta* 40 (1989): 786.
39. W. B. Smith, *The New Science* (Mississauga, Ontario: Fern-Graphic, 1964).
40. R. L. Abrams and R. C. Lind, "Degenerate Four-wave Mixing in Absorbing Media," *Opt. Lett.* 2 (1978): 94.
41. D. M. Pepper, "Nonlinear Optical Phase Conjugation," *Optical Engineer* 21 (1982): 155.
42. D. R. Wells, "Dynamic Stability of Closed Plasma Configurations," *J. Plasma Phys.* 4 (1970): 654.
43. W. H. Bostick, "Experimental Study of Plasmoids," *Phys. Rev.* 106 (1957): 404.
44. H. Aspden, "The Principles Underlying Regenerative Free Energy Technology," *Proc. 26th Intersoc. Energy Convers. Engineer. Conf.,* Boston, MA, 1991.
45. N. Tesla, "Possibilities of Electro-static Generators," *Scientific American* 150 (1934): 132.
46. See note 44 above.
47. W. R. Adey, "Tissue Interactions with Non-Ionizing Electromagnetic Fields," *Physiol. Rev.* 61 (1981): 435.
48. J. Bednar, *Internat. J. Radiation Biol.* 48 (1985): 147.
49. See note 26 above.
50. See note 16 above.
51. See note 26 above.
52. A. R. Liboff in *Interactions Between EM Fields and Cells,* ed. A. Chiabrera, et al. (New York: Plenum, 1986).
53. See note 16 above.
54. S. W. Englander, N. R. Kallenbach, et al., *Proc. Natl. Acad. Sci.* 77 (1980): 7222.
55. R. S. Know, *Theory of Excitons, Solid State Physics* (New York: Academic Press, 1963).

56. G. Rein, "Psychoenergetic Mechanism for Healing with Subtle Energy," in *Mechanisms of Psychic Perception,* eds. J. Millay and S.-P. Sirag (forthcoming).

57. E. DelGiudice, S. Doglia, et al. "A Quantum Fields Theoretical Approach to Collective Behavior of Biological Systems," *Nucl. Phys.* B251 (1985): 375.

58. G. Merkl, "The Third Application of Scalar Technology—Part 2: The Genesis Factor," *Extraord. Sci.* (July–Sept. 1990): 12.

59. See note 38 above.

60. F. W. Cope, "On the Relativity and Uncertainty of EM Energy Measurement at a Superconductive Boundary," *Physiol. Chem. Physics* 13 (1981): 231.

61. See note 57 above.

62. H. Halken, *Synergetics* (New York: Springer Verlag, 1978).

63. See notes 26 and 42 above.

64. See note 16 above.

65. See note 32 above.

66. See notes 38 and 60. Also M. Conrad, "Quantum Mechanics and Cellular Information Processing," *Biomed. Biochim. Acta.* 49 (1990): 743.

67. G. D. Fullerton, V. A. Ord, et al., "An Evaluation of the Hydration of Lysozyme by NMR," *Biochem. Biophys. Acta.* 869 (1986): 230.

68. S. Das and G. S. Singhal, "Role of Interfacial Structured Water in Membranes," *J. Membrane Biol.* 86 (1985): 221.

69. B. Ecanow, B. Gold, et al., "Structured Water in Biology: A Revolution in the Making," *J. Pharm. Sci.* 65 (1976): iv.

70. A. W. Dawkins, N. R. Nightingale, et al., "The Role of Water in Microwave Absorption by Biological Material," *Phys. Med. Biol.* 24 (1979): 1168.

71. E. S. Ismailov, "Influence of Ultra–high frequency EM Irradiation on Electrophoretic Mobility," *Biofizika* 22 (1977): 493.

72. F. W. Cope, "Pathology of Structured Water and Associated Cations," *Physiol. Chem. Phys.* 9 (1977): 547.

73. W. Drost-Hanson, and J. S. Clegg, eds. *Cell-Associated Water* (New York: Academic Press, 1979).

74. See note 27 above.

75. See note 35 above.

76. See note 32 above.
77. See note 32 above
78. See note 32 above.
79. A. A. Gurwitsch, "Die Mitogenetische Strahlhung des Markhaltigen Nerven," *Pflugers Arch. ges. Physiol.* 231 (1932): 234.
80. V. P. Kaznacheyev, L. P. Mikhailova, et al., "Distant Intercellular Interactions in a System of Two Tissue Cultures," *Psychoenergetic Systems* 1:3 (March 1976).
81. F. A. Popp, et al., eds., *Electromagnetic Bio-Information*, (Baltimore: Urban & Schwarzenberg, 1979), p. 123.
82. R. Edward, M. C. Ibison, J. J. Kenyon, and R. R. Taylor, "Measurements of Human Bioluminescence," *Acupuncture & Electrotherap. Res. Internat. J.* 15 (1990): 85.
83. B. L. Reid, "On the Nature of Growth Based on Experiments Designed to Reveal a Structure for Laboratory Space," *Med. Hypothesis* 29 (1989): 127.
84. M. R. Riviere, A. Priore, et al. "Action de Champs Electromagnetiques Sur les Greffes de la Tumeur TB," *Compt. Rend. Acad. Sci.* 259 (1964): 4895.
85. See note 44 above.
86. H. K. Puharich, "Method and Means from Shielding a Person from the Polluting Effects of ELF Magnetic Waves and Other Environmental Pollution," U. S. Patent #616–183, June, 1984.
87. L. L. Greene and G. Rein, "Synthesis, Storage and Release of Acetylcholine by a Noradrenergic Pheochromocytoma Cell Line," *Nature* 268 (1977): 349.
88. R. Dixey and G. Rein, "Noradrenaline Release Potentiated in a Clonal Nerve Cell Line by Low-Intensity Pulsed Magnetic Fields," *Nature* 296 (1982): 253.
89. G. Rein and K. Korins, et al. "Inhibition of Neurotransmitter Uptake in Neuronal Cells by Pulsed EM Fields," *Proc. 9th Bioelectromag. Soc.* (June 1987).
90. G. Rein, "Biological Interactions with Scalar Energy-Cellular Mechanisms of Action," *Proc. 7th Internat. Assoc. Psychotronics Res.* (1988).
91. G. Rein, "Effect of Non-Hertzian Scalar Waves on the Immune System," *Jour. U. S. Psychotronics Assoc.* 1:2 (Spring 1989): 15.

92. T. A. Gagnon and G. Rein, "The Biological Significance of Water Structured with Non-Hertzian Time Reversed Waves," *Jour. U.S. Psychotronics Assoc.* 4 (Summer 1990): 26.

93. P. Conti, G. E. Gigante, et al. "Reduced Mitogenic Stimulation of Human Lymphocytes by ELF Electromagnetic Fields," *FEBS Letters* 162 (1983): 156.

94. See note 92 above.

95. C. W. Smith and S. Best, *Electromagnetic Man* (London: J. M. Dent & Sons, Ltd., 1989).

96. N. Tesla, "Transmission of Energy Without Wires," *Scientific Amer. Suppl.* 57 (1904): 23760.

97. See note 38 above.

98. D. J. Benor, "Survey of Spiritual Healing Research," *Complimentary Med. Res.* 4 (1990): 9.

99. G. Rein, "An Exosomatic Effect on Neurotransmitter Metabolism in Mice," *Sec. Internat. S. P. R. Conf.,* Cambridge Univ., 1978.

100. G. Rein, "A Psychokinetic Effect on Neurotransmitter Metabolism: Alterations in the Degradative Enzyme MAO," *Research in Parapsychology* (1986): 77.

101. See notes 88 and 89 above.

102. See note 90 above.

103. M. C. Cade and N. Coxhead, *The Awakened Mind* (New York: Delacorte, 1979).

104. C. T. Tart, *Altered States of Consciousness* (New York: John Wiley & Sons, 1969).

105. S. Krippner and A. Villoldo, *The Realms of Healing* (Millbrae, CA: Celestial Arts, 1976).

106. M. A. Cooperstein, "The Myths of Healing: A Descriptive Analysis of Transpersonal Healing Experiences." Ph.D. diss., Saybrook Institute, San Francisco, CA, 1990.

107. B. Sweet, "Spindrift and the Politics of Prayer," *Sprindrift's Occasional Newsletter* 4 (1991): 1.

108. E. A. Rauscher and B. A. Rubik, "Human Volitional Effects on a Model Bacterial System," *Psi Res.* 2 (1983): 38.

109. D. Dean and E. Brame, "Physical Changes in Water by Laying-on of Hands," *Proc. 2nd Internat. Conf. Psychotronic Res.* (1975): 200.

110. G. Rein, "Psychobiological Mechanism for Subtle Energies," *14th U.S. Psychotronics Assoc. Conf.*, Dayton, OH, 1988.
111. S. A. Schwartz, R. J. DeMattei, et al., "Infrared Spectra Alteration in Water Proximate to the Palms of Therapeutic Practitioners," *Subtle Energies* 1 (1991): 43.
112. W. Gough, "Joint U.S.–China Experiment on the Effect of External Qi on Molecular Structure Using Raman Spectroscopy," unpublished report.
113. See notes 103 and 104 above.
114. See note 111 above.
115. A. Puharich, *ELF Magnetic Model of Matter and Mind*, Essentia Res. Assoc., Route 1, Box 545, Dobson, NC, 1987.
116. J. S. Bell, "On the Einstein Podolsky Rosen Paradox," *Physics* 1 (1964): 195.
117. D. Bohm, *Wholeness and the Implicate Order* (London: Routledge & Kegan Paul, 1980).
118. See note 4 above.
119. See note 5 above.
120. See note 5 above.
121. See note 32 above.

B

Human Volitional Effects on a Model Bacterial System*

E. A. Rauscher, Ph.D., and Beverly Rubik, Ph.D.

We have examined, in four extensive studies, the field effects of human volitional intention to accelerate growth in bacteria under toxic effects. Strains ST1 and ST 171 of *Salmonella typhimurium* were exposed, under sterile conditions, to the growth of inhibitors, antibiotics tetracycline and chloramaphenical, which both inhibit protein synthesis. Growth was measured spectrophotometrically. Multiple samples of each test condition were exposed to the volitional intention of a healer for two minutes to see whether the effects of the growth inhibitors could be reduced. All test cases had controls, and comparison was made to extensive previous baseline studies done previously.

Intentional treatment, along with the "laying on of hands" by Olga Worrell, reduced the effect of tetracycline. There was a maximum difference from controls of 121 percent more bacteria surviving in the presence of 1 microgram/ml tetracycline at twenty-three hours. The maximum dif-

---

*This is an abstract of a paper published in *Psi Research*, March 1983, pp. 38–47.

ference observed in the cultures treated with 10 micrograms/ml tetracycline was 28 percent more bacteria at twenty-one hours. Similar results were obtained for 100 micrograms/ml chloramphenical.

A person with no intentional volition was placed in the same relative position in the laboratory, but his presence demonstrated no such effects on bacteria. We conclude that there are demonstrable effects of healer treatments on the growth of bacterial cultures inhibited by various doses of different antibiotics.

Bibliography

Achterberg, Jeanne. *Imagery in Healing*. Boston: Shambhala, 1985.

Badgley, Lawrence E. *Healing Aids Naturally*. San Bruno, CA: Human Energy Press, 1986.

Bailey, Alice. *Esoteric Healing*. Albany, NY: Lucus, 1953.

Becker, Robert. *The Body Electric*. New York: William Morrow, 1985.

Bennett, Hal, and Mike Samuels. *The Well Body Book*. New York: Random House, 1983.

Bennett, Hal, and Susan J. Sparrow. *Follow Your Bliss*. New York: Avon Books, 1990.

Bentov, Itzhak. *Stalking the Wild Pendulum*. Rochester, VT: Destiny Books, 1988.

Bird, Christopher. *The Divining Hand*. Black Mountain, NC: New Age Press, 1979.

Bohm, David. *Wholeness and the Implicate Order*. London: Arkana, 1980.

Bonewitz, Ra. *Cosmic Crystals*. Wellingborough, Great Britain: Turnstone Press, 1983.

Borysenko, Joan. *Minding the Body, Mending the Mind*. Reading, MA: Addison-Wesley, 1987.

Bradshaw, John. *Healing the Shame That Binds You*. Deerfield Beach, FL: Health Communications, 1988.

Brennan, Barbara Ann. *Hands of Light*. New York: Bantam, 1988.

Brown, Molly. *The Unfolding Self*. Los Angeles: Psychosynthesis Press, 1983.

Campbell, Joseph. *The Power of Myth*. New York: Doubleday, 1988.

Chopra, Deepak. *Quantum Healing: Exploring the Frontiers of Mind/Body Medicine*. New York: Bantam, 1989.

Dossey, Larry. *Space, Time & Medicine*. Boulder, CO: Shambhala, 1982.

Ferrucci, Piero. *What We May Be*. Los Angeles: J. P. Tarcher, 1982.

Frankl, Viktor. *Man's Search for Meaning*. New York: Simon & Schuster, 1984.

Gerber, Richard, M.D. *Vibrational Medicine*. Santa Fe, NM: Bear, 1988.

Gittleman, Ann Louise. *Beyond Pritikin*. New York: Bantam, 1988.

Godman, David. *Be As You Are: The Teachings of Sri Ramana Maharshi*. Boston: Arkana, 1985.

Green, Elmer, and Alyce Green. *Beyond Biofeedback*. New York: Dell, 1977.

Jahn, Robert G., and Brenda J. Dunne. *Margins of Reality*. Orlando, FL: Harcourt Brace Jovanovich, 1987.

Joy, Brugh. *Joy's Way*. Los Angeles: J. P. Tarcher, 1978.

Justice, Blaire. *Who Gets Sick?* Los Angeles: J. P. Tarcher, 1988.

Kessel, Richard G., and Randy H. Kardon. *Tissues & Organs: A Test-Atlas of Scanning Electron Microscopy*. San Francisco: W. H. Freeman, 1979.

Keyes, Ken, Jr., and Penny Keyes. *The Power of Unconditional Love*. Coos Bay, OR: Loveline Books, 1990.

Lazaris. *The Sacred Journey: You and Your Higher Self*. Beverly Hills: Concept Synergy, 1987.

LeShan, Lawrence. *The Medium, the Mystic and the Physicist*. New York: Ballantine, 1966.

—. *How to Meditate*. Boston: Little, Brown, 1974.

—. *Cancer as a Turning Point*. New York: E. P. Dutton, 1989.

Meek, George W. *Healers and the Healing Process*. Wheaton, IL: Quest, 1977.

Metzner, Ralph. *Opening to the Light*. Los Angeles: J. P. Tarcher, 1986.

Milewski, John, and Virginia Harford. *The Crystal Sourcebook*. Sedona, AZ: Mystic Crystal Publications, 1987.

Motoyama, Hiroshi. *Theories of the Chakras*. Wheaton, IL: Quest, 1981.

Nielsen, Greg, and Joseph Polansky. *Pendulum Power*. New York: Excaliber Books, 1977.

Nilsson, Lennert. *The Body Victorious*. New York: Delacorte Press, 1987.

Porter, Garrett, and Patricia A. Norris. *Why Me? Harnessing the Healing Power of the Human Spirit*. Walpole, NH: Stillpoint Publishing, 1985.

Rendel, Peter. *Introduction to the Chakras*. New York: Weiser, 1974.

Roman, Sanaya, and Duane Packer. *Opening to Channel*. Tiburon, CA: H. J. Kramer, 1987.

Ross, T. Edward, and Richard D. Wright. *The Divining Mind*. Rochester, VT: Destiny Books, 1990.

Rossi, Ernest L. *The Psychobiology of Mind-Body Healing*. New York: W. W. Norton, 1986.

Rossi, Ernest L., and David Cheek. *Mind-Body Therapy: Methods of Ideodynamic Healing in Hypnosis*. New York: W. W. Norton, 1988.

Rossman, Martin. *Healing Yourself*. New York: Walker, 1987.

Selby, Uma. *The Complete Crystal Guidebook*. San Francisco: U-Read Publications, 1986.

Shealy, C. Norman, and Caroline M. Myss. *The Creation of Health*. Walpole, NH: Stillpoint Publishing, 1988.

Siegel, Bernie S. *Love, Medicine and Miracles*. New York: Harper & Row, 1986.

—. *Peace, Love & Healing*. New York: Harper & Row, 1989.

Simmons, Robert H. *Achieving Humane Organization*. Malibu, CA: Daniel Spencer, 1981.

Simonton, O. Carl, Stephanie Matthews Simonton, and James Creighton. *Getting Well Again*. Los Angeles: J. P. Tarcher, 1978.

Small, Jacquelyn. *Transformers*. Marina del Rey, CA: DeVorss, 1982.

Talbot, Michael. *Beyond the Quantum*. New York: Bantam, 1986.

Tansley, David. *Radionics and the Subtle Anatomy of Man*. Essex, England: Health Science Press, 1972.

—. *The Raiment of Light*. London: Routledge & Kegan Paul, 1984.

Thich Nhat Hanh. *Miracle of Mindfulness*. Boston: Beacon Press, 1976.

—. *The Heart of Understanding*. Berkeley, CA: Parallax Press, 1988.

Vaughan, Frances. *Awakening Intuition*. Garden City, NY: Anchor Books, 1979.

—. *The Inward Arc*. Boston: Shambhala, 1985.

Weil, Andrew. *Natural Health, Natural Medicine*. Boston: Houghton Mifflin, 1990.

Westlake, Aubrey. *The Pattern of Health*. New York: Devin-Adair, 1963.

Wilber, Ken. *The Holographic Paradigm*. Boulder, CO: Shambhala, 1982.

Wolf, Fred Alan. *The Body Quantum*. New York: Macmillan, 1986.

Woolf, V. Vernon. *Holodynamics: How to Develop and Manage Your Personal Power*. Tucson, AZ: Harbinger House, 1990.

Young, Arthur M. *Which Way Out?* San Francisco: Robert Briggs, 1980.

Index

Becker, Robert O., 281
"Bedside manner," 22
Bee sting, 231–32
Beliefs: core, 56, 58, 59, 122, 145,
191–92, 230; healers' effects
independent of, 301, 307; and
perception, 168–70, 174;
Resonance process and, 191–92;
self-fulfilling, 168–70. *See also*
Positive intention
Bell, J. S., 310
Bentov, Itzhak, 99, 270–71
Beyond Biofeedback (Green &
Green), 167, 169
Bible: and AUM sound, 93–94;
physical transformation in, 219
"Biodetectors," 280
Bioelectromagnetics, 281, 282, 290
Bioenergy field, 40, 145, 268–69,
279–80
Biofeedback, 169
Biological systems: non-Hertzian
quantum fields and, 290–310. *See
also* Body; Healing
Biomechanical testing, 112n, 133–65,
269
Biophotons, 295
Bioplasma, 281. *See also* Energy body
Biopotentials, 294–95, 311, 312
Black body, in physics, 284
Blame: holding onto, 129–30; release
from, 10; responsibility vs., 76
Blending: exercise, 198; response of,
196, 198–99
Blessing: drink, 111–12, 165, 307;
food, 111–12, 165, 307; ourselves,
165
Blockages: boundaries and, 9; to
healing, 78, 195, 197
Blood vessels, electrical energy
through, 282
Blue Pearl, 106, 187
Blum, Ralph, 233
Blundell, 302
Body: breathing for increased
awareness of (exercise), 88–89;
energy, 8, 279–84. *See also*
Healing; Physical level

"Body consciousness," 167–74
Body Victorious (Nilsson), 240
Bohm, David, 39, 90, 284, 310–11
Bone cancer, 17
Boundaries, 9, 67
Brain: balancing breath exercise and,
100–107, 110, 186–87, 235, 304;
energy body and, 281–82;
measurement of waves
(electroencephalograph), 81, 100–
101, 103, 183, 279, 302; vs. mind,
44–45; Recognition process and
hemispheres of, 115–16
Breathing, 61, 80–112; balancing,
100–107, 110, 186–87, 235, 304;
in biomechanical testing, 143, 150,
152, 163; chest, 85; controlled, 81,
82, 97–98, 109; diaphragmatic,
84–86; exercises, 85–86, 88–90,
96–97, 99–100, 104–6, 111, 186–
87; four phases of holoenergetic,
90–94; holding, 92, 93, 98, 99;
in-pulse, 87, 88, 246; nine key
functions of, 81–82; observer self
shift through, 174; pulsed, 61, 87–
90, 246; in Reformation process,
87, 98, 212, 219; in Release
process, 87, 88, 98, 202, 203–4,
208, 239; in Resonance process,
82, 99, 101–2, 109, 184–85,
186–87; in tracing process,
266. *See also* Ex-pulse breathing
Brown, Molly, 173
Browning, Elizabeth Barrett, 53
Buddha, 172
Byrd, E. A., 288, 296

Cade, M. C., 302
Campbell, Joseph, 93, 211
Cancer: and anger suppression, 128–
29; bone, 17; cervical, 25–26;
MRI and, 181; research with,
26
Carbon dioxide, breathing and, 86,
87
Causes, of disease, vs. symptoms and
sources, 56–60

Centering: beginning healing with, 228, 234; and healing others, 245; in Resonance process, 185
Cervical dysplasia, 25–26
Chakras, 46–49, 154–55; biomechanical testing of, 153–60; breathing and, 105, 187; and esoteric functions (charts), 50–51, 154–55; etheric field and, 145; evaluating, 152–60, 245; exercises evaluating, 157–59; Intuitive Recognition and, 133, 134, 145, 152–60; magnetic pattern from Laskow's crown, 308; and observer self shift, 175; photons from, 64; in Resonance process, 184–85, 187, 188, 192–93, 237; and spiral energy, 283
Change: in breathing, 82, 84, 89; choice for, 212–13, 236; focusing on, 119; motivation for, 74–75, 119–21; in Reformation process, 212–13, 216–22; in Resonance process, 178, 179, 185–87; techniques for, 60–61; three levels of, 216–22. See also Resistance
Charge, energetic: breathing and, 81, 86, 91, 97, 143; crystals and, 268; in Resonance process, 188–89
Charisma, resonance and, 178
Chi, 80, 281, 282
Chinmoy, Sri, 53
Choice: breathing and, 106; to change, 28, 212–13, 236; critical, 58, 191–92, 230; of future, 59–60, 124–25, 213; growth, 28; to heal, 59–60, 188; past, 58, 121–23, 180, 191–92; in Reformation process, 212–13; in Release process, 196, 197–98; to shift consciousness, 171–73; and source of disease, 58, 59–60
Chopra, Deepak, 53
Christ, 179
Circle, in forgiveness exercise, 206–7
Codependence, 120
Colds, 56–57
Compassion, 172, 178, 220

Concentration camp, Nazi, 122
Consciousness, 249, 250, 271, 273–74; body, 167–74; breathing and, 81, 82, 84, 105, 106; evolution in, 273; of function, 8; goal-directed, 302; Holoenergetic Quantum Consciousness Theory, 281, 311–12; in Laskow experiment, 302–9; levels of, 218–19; love related to, 65, 67, 270–76; and observer intent, 5, 8, 36, 73; observer self shift in, 171–73, 174–75; of purpose, 8; qualitative, 302; reflecting, 82; Reformation process and, 218–19, 221; shifting, 82, 171–73, 174–75; subtle energy utilized by, 281, 282, 302–9, 311–12; of success capacities, 214; unifying, 251; void and, 73–74, 270. See also Feelings; Thoughts
Control: anger and, 128; fear of losing, 57, 128; third chakra and, 48
Cooperstein, M. A., 302
Coronary arteries, MRI and, 181
Cosmology, operational, 270–76
Coupling, resonant, 62, 65, 178, 282–84
Course in Miracles, 115
Creation, desire for, 9
Crisis, changes initiated by, 17
Critical choices/incidents, 58, 58–59, 191–92, 230
Crystalline Transduction Theory, 281, 291–92, 293
Crystals: in biological systems, 290, 291–92, 296; healers using, 24, 32–33, 268–69; life, 292
"Current of injury," 281
Cyclotron resonance theory, 283

Death, in Reformation process, 221
DeBroglie, L., 285, 286
Decision. See Choice
DelGiudice, E., 288, 292–93, 300
Dematerialization intention, in Laskow experiment, 305, 307
Denial, dissolving, 171

Gerber, Richard, 43
God's will, in Laskow experiment, 304, 305
Grad, Bernard, 6, 35–36
Gravity, scalar waves and, 287
Green, Alyce, 80, 167, 169
Green, Elmer, 80, 167, 169
Grief, hormones triggering, 57
Grounding: beginning healing with, 228, 233–34; and healing others, 245; in Resonance process, 184
Ground state, of matter, 286
Guide, inner, 174, 185, 200, 257–63, 265
Guilt, 10, 18–19; healing inhibited by, 78, 195, 197; love difficulties and, 55, 58, 59
Gurwitsch, A. A., 295

Hands: in bacteria experiment, 320; breathing and palm position, 89–90; breathing through, 96; energizing, 188–89, 192, 236, 268; and healing others, 245–46; in Laskow experiment, 308–10; in Resonance process, 188–89, 191, 192, 193, 236; sensing, 188, 189, 192, 236, 237, 245–46
Harmonies, 10, 180
Headaches, 96, 121
Healers, 19–22, 245–46; effects of (experiments), 6, 26, 38, 302–9, 320–21; Holoenergetic Quantum Consciousness Theory and, 281, 311–12
Healing: blockages to, 78, 195, 197; breathing and, 108–12; consciousness levels of, 219; experiments, 300–309; foundational principles of, 4–10; love as force of, 22, 27, 28, 55–56, 61–65, 131, 250; others, 245–46; psychoenergetic, 300–312; "Scientific Basis for Healing with Subtle Energies," 279–319; template for, 74. *See also* Holoenergetic healing
Health, defined, 74

Health professions, 3, 252–53; acupuncture, 217, 282; psychotherapy, 55–56. *See also* Medicine
Hearing, attention to condition through, 183
Heisenberg, Werner, 270, 285
Herpes, 23–24; and anger expression, 127, 128, 129; and forgiveness, 129; and love difficulties, 126; self-healing, 227–331; translation with, 217; and trust testing, 130–31
Hertz, H. R., 280, 284, 288
High blood pressure, 25
Higher dimensional universes, 285, 286
Higher Self: alignment with, 9, 10, 11; love of, 223–24; observer self and, 201; in Resonance process, 183, 185, 265; in safe space, 174, 185, 263
Hippocrates, 22
History, holoenergetic healing, 118–25
Holding phase, of holoenergetic breathing, 92, 93, 98, 99
"Holodynes," 57n
Holoenergetic activation, 132
Holoenergetic healing: breathing and, 61, 80–112; checklist, 243–44; defined, 3; history, 118–25; love and, 53–79; and perception of observer self, 173–74; process of, 73–79, 163; step by step, 233–48. *See also* Recognition; Reformation; Release; Resonance
Holoenergetic Quantum Consciousness Theory, 281, 311–12
Holoforms, 56, 57, 58, 59, 60, 108–9
Holographic functioning, 44, 57
Homeopathy, 55, 56–57, 300
Homeostasis, 98
Hormones, triggering anger, 57
"Humanity" (McGregor), 248n
Hydrocephalus, 45

Index

transpersonal space and, 106;
ultraviolet, 35
Lincoln, Abraham, 179
Local forces, in physics, 310
Love, 53–79; conditional, 68, 126;
consciousness related to, 65, 67,
270–76; difficulty receiving, 55,
126–27, 200–201; expressions of,
68–69; "falling in", 68; finite, 273;
forgiveness as self–, 205, 207, 208;
as guiding principle for healing, 3,
79; as healing force, 22, 27, 28,
55–56, 61–65, 131, 250; healing
process completed with, 223–24,
242–43; infinite, 270, 273; in
Laskow experiment, 303–4, 305,
307; levels of, 66–69; power and,
69–70, 275; in Reformation
process, 220, 240; in Release
process, 199; resonance of, 62, 65–
66, 67, 179–80, 181–82, 188, 199;
in source of disease, 59; three
aspects of, 65–66; and
transformation, 31–35, 55, 220;
unconditional, see Unconditional
love
Love, Medicine and Miracles (Siegel),
53, 195
L-rods, 112n, 136–44; chakra
measurement with, 157–59; and
crystals, 269; etheric energy
measurement with, 149–51;
exercises with, 157–59, 163–65;
holding, 141; making, 138–40;
many uses of, 143–44, 162–65;
programming, 141–43, 151; and
time a condition began, 161–62
Lymphocyte growth, non-Hertzian
fields and, 297–99

McGregor, Betsy, 248
Machine, body compared with, 8
Magnetic Resonant Imaging (MRI),
180–82, 279
Man's Search for Meaning (Frankl),
122
Martial arts, 29, 196

Martyrdom, disease benefit of, 195,
197
Masculine energy, 91
Maslow, Abraham H., 28, 197–98,
215
Masters, W. H., 17
Matter: and antimatter, 287; energy
and, 4, 5, 8, 31–32, 73–74, 284–
85, 286, 290; interconnectedness
of, 311; resonance and, 180;
thoughts and, 27, 31–32; as
trapped light, 64. *See also* Forms
Maxwell, J. C., 280, 284, 287, 288
Medical school, 15–16
Medicine: allopathic, *see* Modern
medicine; energy, 279–84;
homeopathic, 55, 56–57, 300. *See
also* Psychoenergetic healing
Meditation, 175, 199, 304
Memory, energy fields and, 42, 44
Mental energy fields, 43–46
Mental level: transformation at, 219–
20. *See also* Mind
Merkl, G., 292
Metzner, Ralph, 82, 218, 219
Microscope, Rife, 289
Mind: breathing and, 82; conscious,
82, 98; healers' effects independent
of, 301; location of, 44–45;
subconscious, 82, 97–98;
unconscious, 82, 98. *See also*
Consciousness; Thoughts
Mind Mirror, 302
Mirror: biomechanical testing and,
147–48, 162; and crystals, 269; in
Transpersonal Alignment Process,
73, 148
Modern medicine, 3, 15–16; energetic
interchange between physician and
patient in, 16–17, 22; and energy
body, 279–80, 281, 284; healing
with love and, 252–53;
information in, 117;
psychoneuroimmunology in, 26,
45, 250; and purpose, 8; resonance
in, 180–82; and sources of illness,
55, 56–57

334

Monoamine oxidase, 301
Morley, 296
Motoyama, Hiroshi, 64
Muscular tension, 60
Myers, Gladys, 302

Near-death experiences, 221
Negotiation, response of, 196
Nernst, 286
Nervous system: adrenergic, 301;
   autonomic/involuntary, 82, 83, 84,
   92–93, 102, 104, 105; breath and,
   82–84, 92–93; parasympathetic,
   83, 84, 92–93, 102; peripheral,
   282; somatic/voluntary, 82, 84;
   sympathetic, 83, 84, 102, 104
Neuropeptides, 45
Neurotransmitters, 301
Neutrons, 4, 294
Newtonian mechanics, 282
Nilsson, Lennert, 240
Non-Hertzian quantum fields, 39,
   280, 284–312
Nonlocality, in physics, 310, 311
Non-Maxwellian propagation, 288,
   292–93, 299
Nordenstrom, B. E. W., 282
Norepinephrine, 301
Nourishment, breathing for, 81
Now, resonance and, 179–80
Nuclear Magnetic Resonance (NMR),
   293, 294

Observer effect, 16–17, 36–38
Observer intent, 5, 8, 36–38, 73
Observer-participant, 172–73
Observer self, 156, 166–76, 183,
   201–2, 238
Obstetrics, 15, 17–18
On Yoga II: Tome One (Aurobindo),
   251
Opening to the Light (Metzner), 218,
   219
Operational cosmology, 270–76
Orange, energizing (exercises), 163–
   65

Paradox, of illness, 173

Passion, resonance and, 178
Pause phase, of holoenergetic
   breathing, 90–91, 92, 99–100
Peak experiences, purpose and, 214–
   16
Perceptions: of events, 57–59; sense,
   167–74; of "substance", 91;
   translation with, 217
Pert, Candace, 45–46
Phase conjugation experiments, 289
Photographs: biomechanical testing
   with, 162; as energetic "witnesses,"
   33
Photons, 38–39, 64; biophotons, 295
Physical level: crystals and, 268–69;
   emotional level behind, 249; of
   energy body, 281; Reformation
   process at, 219, 222, 240;
   Resonance process at, 191–92,
   237. *See also* Diseases
Physics, 4–7; and light particles, 64;
   of MRI, 181; observer effect in,
   16–17, 36; "Scientific Basis for
   Healing with Subtle Energies,"
   279–319; and subatomic level, 38–
   39, 294–95; uncertainty principle
   in, 270. *See also* Energy
Piezoelectricity, 34, 268, 282, 291
Placebo effect, 6, 26, 297, 298, 301
Planck, M., 284
Plasma physics, 289
Plato, 15
Pleasure, difficulty receiving, 127
Popp, F. A., 295
Positive intention (behind difficulty):
   breathing and, 109; in Recognition
   process, 123–24, 232; in
   Reformation process, 201–2, 212;
   in Release process, 78, 197, 200,
   201–4; in Resonance process, 192,
   193, 201, 238–39; in tracing
   process, 265
Power: anger over loss of, 128; love
   and, 69–70, 275; movement as,
   272; "point of", 180; primary,
   273. *See also* Control
Power of Myth (Campbell), 93

Transpersonal Alignment Process, 70–73; biomechanical testing and, 148, 156; and healing others, 245–47; observer consciousness shift with, 174; resonance and, 24, 75

Transpersonal self, 66–67, 166, 173

Transpersonal space, 106–7; in Laskow experiment, 304; resonance in, 107, 183; in Transpersonal Alignment Process, 71

"Treasured wounds," 195

Trusting, difficulty with, 130–31

Truth: consciousness and, 273–74; in Reformation process, 220; in Release process, 199–200

Trypsin, and structured water, 6

Tumors: in Laskow experiments (tumor cells), 6, 26, 38, 303–7, 308–9; MRI imaging, 181; negative thought form and, 7; plasma tube generator and, 296; remission of, 219

Ulcers, 47–48

Ultrasound, 279

Uncertainty, principle of, 270

Unconditional love, 54, 67, 68, 70; and healing others, 246; healing process completed with, 10–11, 223–24, 242–43; in Laskow experiments, 304, 305, 307, 308–9; and observer consciousness, 174

Understanding: identification and, 171, 172; transformation and, 220

Unfolding Self (Brown), 173

Unforming, 60; breathing and, 88; Release process and, 10, 77–78, 194, 202, 204, 208

Unity: desire and, 271; love and, 179–80, 270, 275–76; Resonance process and, 179–80, 187; windows of, 250–51

Universal energy fields, 7, 31–32

Universal frequency, 67

Universal purpose, 213–14

Unworthiness feelings, 55, 59, 126, 200–201

Upanishads, 69

Vaughan, Frances, 1, 69, 116–17, 166, 257

Vector/scalar quantum potentials, 39, 280, 284, 287, 288–89

Vibration: breathing and, 91; consciousness and, 218–19, 271, 273; crystals and, 268; love and, 61–62, 65, 270. *See also* Frequencies; Resonance

Vibrational Medicine (Gerber), 43

Victimization, 120, 195, 196–97

Vietnam, Marines dowsing in, 135, 142

Virtual particles, 287

Virtual plasma, 285–86

Virtual protons, 287

Viruses, 57; herpes, 23–24

Vision, desire and, 9

Visualization, 60; holoenergetic field and, 311–12; in Laskow experiment, 26, 38, 305–6, 309; resonance through, 183; in Tiller experiment, 37–38; as translation, 217

Void: breathing and, 90–91, 93; consciousness and, 73–74; dematerialization into, 304–5; everything/nothing state, 270; photons and, 38–39; Reformation process with, 212–13, 223, 240; Release process creating, 204, 239. *See also* Zero-point energy

Walsh, Roger, 1

Water: blessing, 165; body, 5–6; bulk, 293–94; dowsing detecting, 135; in Laskow experiment, 306–7, 310; non-Hertzian fields and, 293–94, 299, 300, 310; perception of temperature (experiment), 170–71; structured, 5–6, 35–36, 110–12, 161, 293–94, 299

Waves, standing, 7, 108, 109

Weather, and ions, 87

Werntz, D. A., 102–3

Which Way Out (Young), 8

Whitehead, Alfred North, 168

Whitman, Walt, 53, 179

For further information regarding lectures, seminars, tapes, training programs, and consultations, please write to:

Leonard Laskow, M.D.
20 Sunnyside Avenue, Suite A334
Mill Valley, CA 94941
415-381-5000